365

WINNING

BRIDGE TIPS

DANNY KLEINMAN | MASTER POINT PRESS, TORONTO

Master Point Press
331 Douglas Ave.
Toronto, Ontario, Canada
M5M 1H2
(416) 781-0351
Website: http://www.masterpointpress.com
Email: info@masterpointpress.com

Library and Archives Canada Cataloguing in Publication

Kleinman, Danny
   365 winning bridge tips / Danny Kleinman.

ISBN 1-897106-04-1

   1. Contract bridge. I. Title.

GV1282.3.K53 2005   795.4'15   C2005-905201-5

Editor	Ray Lee
Cover and interior design	Olena S. Sullivan/New Mediatrix
Interior format	Luise Lee
Copy editing	Suzanne Hocking

Printed in Canada by Webcom Ltd.

1 2 3 4 5 6 7   09 08 07 06 05

Can you learn from the errors of others?

Here is a collection of simple problems that gave a variety of players, mostly "intermediate" but including occasional beginners and experts, some trouble. You won't find bidding problems here worthy of the Master Solvers' Club (a monthly *Bridge World* feature) or declarer play problems fit for "Test Your Play" (another *Bridge World* feature) or problems to challenge defensive maven Eddie Kantar. Instead you will find the kinds of "bread and butter" problems that arise several times a session each time you trudge to your local duplicate bridge club or travel to a sectional or regional tournament.

In these problems, you will always be "South" during the auction and for any questions relating to the auction. You will always be South as declarer and either East or West, as indicated, when you are a defender. Distributions are shown as four numbers: 5431 indicates any hand that contains a five-card suit, a four-card suit, a three-card suit and a singleton, but 5-4-3-1 represents a particular hand pattern in the order spades-hearts-diamonds-clubs, with five spades, four hearts, three diamonds and one club.

You can read this book in two ways. You can examine the problems and proceed directly to the analyses and solutions. Alternatively, you can cover the analyses with a sheet of paper or cardboard and try to solve the problems on your own before looking at my solutions.

Happy learning and good luck!

Danny Kleinman

Bridge players sometimes ask, "What is the most important part of the game?"

I've heard it said by an expert, "Bidding is 80% of bridge."

I've also heard from a student, "I think I'm an excellent bidder. All I really need to do is improve my card play."

Who is right?

Neither. The student was mistaken, but the question is inadequately phrased. It's like asking, "What percentage of skill is genetically determined, and what percentage comes from the environment, that is, education and experience?"

The answer to that question varies with the population in question. Among experts, bidding may account for 80% or more of the variation in matchpoint scores, because card-play skill is largely presumed. Among non-experts, competent handling of most declarer play and defensive problems cannot be presumed, so bidding may be expected to dominate less.

In the process of compiling this book, I inadvertently obtained a rough estimate of the relative importance of various aspects of bridge, as measured by the numbers of problems of each kind found difficult and usually mishandled by ordinary duplicate bridge players.

Initially, I estimated that bidding is 60% of bridge and play is 40%. However, there are finer distinctions to be made than simply between bidding and card play. For instance, in which category would you place opening lead problems? I believe that opening lead problems are far more akin to bidding than to play. To my mind, opening lead problems involve, primarily, *listening* to the bidding and drawing appropriate inferences from there. Taking that into account, I estimate the ratio at closer to 65% bidding to 35% play.

Bear in mind that these are rough estimates only. I culled the 365 deals of this book from a larger sample of 500 problems collected from actual play over a period of about a year. Five hundred problems may be too small a sample, and the players who faced these problems may not be representative of duplicate bridge players in general.

365

WINNING
BRIDGE TIPS

We'll start off with one of the very easiest kinds of problem.

Matchpoints, Both vul.

> **NORTH** (dummy)
> ◇ Q 3

WEST (you)
◇ J 6

You're defending against 3NT. Two rounds of diamonds have been played, with everybody following. Now, with several cards remaining in the other suits, including at least one possible entry to dummy, declarer leads the ◇8, the thirteenth diamond. Which diamond should you play?

   Play the jack, which can only gain and can't lose. Then your six will be high. If you play low, you unwisely give declarer a chance to let the eight ride for an extra trick.

   Is there anything easier than this? No, yet duplicate bridge players continue to make "can't win" plays like the ◇6, sometimes called *nullo* plays, and wonder why they can't get good partners unless they hire professionals.

Here is another easy problem, but this one has two parts. The first part requires you to ask, "How good is my hand?" The second part requires you to ask, "How good a hand do I need to open?"

Matchpoints, Both vul.

♠ J 6 4   ♡ A K 3 2   ◇ J 8   ♣ K 8 4 3

WEST	NORTH	EAST	SOUTH
			?

First, how good is your hand?

   The commonly used measure of strength for balanced hands is *high card points* ("HCP"). Other counts than the familiar 4-3-2-1 are more accurate, but even if you use some other formula, you must translate your count into "points" that others, partners and opponents alike, will understand — which means expressing your rating of a hand on a scale in which 10 represents a hand of average high-card strength. If you rate this hand as 12, that's a sensible start, but among

Learn to think in terms of "good" and "bad" HCP. Here are some guidelines for applying this concept.

(a) The 4-3-2-1 count is imprecise (what a fluke it would be if it reflected the values of high cards *exactly*!). It undervalues aces and overvalues jacks (and to an extent queens).

(b) Whereas aces have a constant value (except when partner has a void in the suit), lower honors are worth more together than apart. Queens and jacks combined with other honors of the same suit are worth more than queens and jacks alone.

(c) Honors in short suits pull less weight than honors in long suits. Honors in suits with *no* low cards at all should be discounted a bit. Here's why. If you're declarer, and dummy has J54 in the suit, you'll take four tricks with AKQ2 but only three with AKQ. If dummy has two low cards in the suit, you'll take three tricks with AKQ, but you have a chance to take four tricks with AKQ2.

(d) Spot cards count for something. Promote hands that have tens and nines; demote hands that do not.

An alternative to thinking "good" and "bad" is to think in terms of *half*-points. You might count

♠ J 6 4   ♡ A K 3 2   ◇ J 8   ♣ K 8 4 3

as only 11½ HCP because of its stray jacks in relatively short suits. However,

♠ 6 4 3   ♡ A K J 2   ◇ 8 3   ♣ K J 8 4

would be worth 12½ HCP because both jacks are working synergistically with honors in longer suits.

12-HCP hands there are significant variations. You can judge some hands as "good" 12-HCP hands, others as ordinary, and still others as "bad" 12-HCP hands. Furthermore, if you see a hand that you count initially as 12, but it *looks stronger* than most 13-HCP hands, you may want to *promote* your rating to 13. By the same token, a hand that you count initially as 12 may *look weaker* than most 11-HCP hands. When that happens, *demote* your rating to 11.

♠ J 6 4   ♡ A K 3 2   ◇ J 8   ♣ K 8 4 3

is only 11 HCP because of its stray jacks in relatively short suits. However,

♠ 6 4 3   ♡ A K J 2   ◇ 8 3   ♣ K J 8 4

would be worth 12 HCP because both jacks are working synergistically with honors in longer suits.

Should you open?

This question is more complex. Before answering, you should decide *what* you will open, and how you plan to rebid if you do. Attractive and unattractive choices of openings and rebids should affect your decision in close cases.

With

♠ J 6 4   ♡ A K 3 2   ◇ J 8   ♣ K 8 4 3

your choice of openings is clear. Playing strong notrumps and generally avoiding opening four-card majors, your bid, if you open, is 1♣. You have no reason to be either proud or ashamed of your club suit. Though it is not strong, it is headed by a high honor. Though it is not long, at least you have four cards in it.

Your rebidding plan is also clear. If partner raises to 2♣ or (playing limit raises) 3♣, you will pass. If partner responds in diamonds, you have a happy rebid in hearts. If partner responds in hearts, you have a happy single raise. If partner responds in spades, you will not be particularly happy to raise on jack-third, but neither will you be embarrassed to do so. If partner responds in notrump, you will pass (or raise a forcing 2NT to 3NT).

Your choice of opening and your plan for rebidding should leave you with only the slightest misgivings, not nearly enough to sway you in either direction. You now have a narrowed question: 1♣ or pass?

In fact, you still do not know enough to decide because I've omitted one crucial question: *What, exactly, is your 1NT range?*

The normal threshold for opening minimum balanced hands is 3 HCP below your threshold for opening 1NT. If any balanced 15-HCP hand qualifies, you *might* open. If you require 16, or at least a *good* 15, HCP for 1NT, you should pass. With a slightly different hand,

♠ K 8 4 3   ♡ A K 3 2   ◇ J 8   ♣ J 6 4

you should certainly pass, as 1♣ on a *weak three-card suit* would be very sorry indeed.

How many points do you need for an overcall?

3

You may as well ask how many credits in Biochemistry a person needs to teach English Composition.

Some unnamed person at the Memphis headquarters of the American Contract Bridge League ("ACBL") devised the ACBL's "Yellow Card" which specifies the range for a one-level overcall as "8 to 16 HCP" — as if "points" were the relevant feature of your hand when contemplating an overcall. I say it's a mistake even to have a space for point-count range in the section of the convention card for overcalls.

An overcall should be based on playing strength, not point-count. When an opponent announces high-card strength by opening, "points" won't help you much to make a contract of your own. What you need for an overcall is a good suit and a desire to have partner lead that suit — or a hand with so many high cards that you have high hopes for game despite opener's promise of high cards of his own. Ordinarily, you need some *shape*. You need *tricks*. And *three small* in the suit bid in front of you is the death holding, presaging three fast losers in the suit.

Above all, you need positive reasons for overcalling. Ask yourself the *Four Questions*:

(1) Do you think that the hand belongs to your side?
(2) Do you suspect that you have a profitable sacrifice against an opposing contract?
(3) Will the overcall you are contemplating keep responder from bidding what he would otherwise want to bid?
(4) Is it likely that your partner will become the opening leader, and a lead in the suit you're thinking of bidding will be essential to a successful defense?

The more "yes" answers you can give to these questions, the more eager you should be to overcall. Unless you can answer "yes" to at least two of them, you should be very reluctant to enter the auction.

Matchpoints, Neither vul.

(a) ♠ Q 10   ♡ A 7 6 4 3   ◇ Q 8 4   ♣ 8 6 3

WEST	NORTH	EAST	SOUTH
		1♣	?

The answer to all four questions is *no*. I want to dwell on (4) a bit, so I'll show you two other hands:

(b) ♠ 8 4   ♡ A J 10 5 2   ◇ 7 6 3   ♣ 8 7 5

(c) ♠ 8 4   ♡ A 8 6 5 2   ◇ 7 6 3   ♣ 8 7 5

Neither one of them is suitable for a 1♡ overcall, of course, but how would you rank (a), (b) and (c) from "best" to "worst" for purposes of bidding 1♡?

Hand (b) is better than (c), obviously, because it contains three heart honors instead of one. Less obviously, (c) is better than (a). With (c) you would *fear* a lead in any other suit but hearts. In contrast, with (a) you would welcome a spade or diamond lead if either were partner's best suit (i.e. the suit he will lead against notrump if you *don't* overcall). So the final order (best to worst) is (b), (c), (a).

Scattered honors in other suits argue *against* overcalling with a marginal hand — a paradox of which few bridge players are aware.

4

Not one bridge expert in a hundred can define "reverse" accurately. That's reminiscent of what U.S. Supreme Court Justice Potter Stewart said many years ago about pornography: "I can't define it, but I know it when I see it." (I assume Justice Stewart had enough experience viewing pornography to warrant this claim.)

Matchpoints, E-W vul.

♠ K Q J 8 4   ♡ 7 6 3   ◇ Q J 5   ♣ 10 7

WEST	NORTH	EAST	SOUTH
			pass
pass	1♣	pass	1♠
pass	2◇	pass	?

Partner's 2◇ rebid introduces a new suit while *bypassing* a cheaper rebid in his first suit. Knowledgeable bridge players recognize this rebid and others like it as a "reverse".

Some bridge players say, "We don't play reverses." However, you can't "not play reverses", just as you can't "not speak in prose" — unless, that is, you speak only in poetry or don't speak at all. By its very nature, partner's 2◇ bid forces the partnership to 3♣ when you have at least as many clubs as diamonds (though the partnership may be able to stop in 2NT under certain conditions). So 2◇ requires a hand *strong enough* to have jumped to 3♣ (or 2NT). Many years ago, such a 2◇ bid was considered strong but not forcing. Though a few experts still hold out for the old-fashioned treatment, the modern (and superior) treatment of opener's "reverses" is not only as forcing but as *promising a third bid*. What does that mean for you as responder here?

If you bid 3♣ or 3◇, partner still has to deliver his promised third bid, so you must not bid either of these with a bare minimum responding hand. To bid 2NT, you need more than a stopper in the fourth suit (hearts) — you also need a little extra high-card strength in case the third bid that partner has planned is in notrump. In that case, he'll be raising 2NT to 3NT. Your only acceptable bids with a bare minimum are a rebid of your first suit (spades), and the fourth suit if you can bid it below three of opener's suits. In this case, rebidding spades merely requires five cards (though in a pinch a strong four, like ♠KQJx, may have to do). A bid in the fourth suit here is nondescript, saying nothing about that suit. Very strange indeed, and quite the opposite of responder's procedures in other (non-reverse) auctions, where a fourth-suit bid suggests extra strength. Note that 2♡ or 2♠ here doesn't deny extras, it merely doesn't show them at this time.

You do have *modest* extras (9 HCP and a good 5-bagger). After all, your 1♠ response might have been based on 6 or 7 HCP and a poorer suit. You can show your extras with any of three bids — 2NT, 3♣ or 3◇ — but you have none of the right holdings for any of these bids. You lack a heart stopper for 2NT, a third club for a 3♣ preference, and a fourth diamond for a 3◇ raise. Even if you had a hand adequate for one of these three bids, you would be happy to rebid your *strong* five-card major. Bid 2♠.

Two general principles apply here. One is well known even to non-experts — avoid raising partner's *second* suit with fewer than four-card support. (There are rare exceptions which we won't discuss here.) Except in unusual circumstances, partner's second suit is presumably a four-bagger, and your goal in the early auction is to find a trump suit with at least *eight* cards in the two hands combined.

The second general principle, known by few except experts, is that when all else is nearly equal, you should choose the *cheaper* of two plausible alternatives.

Matchpoints, N-S vul.

♠ A K J 10 6 2   ♡ 10 7 4 3   ◇ 5   ♣ J 4

WEST	NORTH	EAST	SOUTH
	1♣	pass	1♠
2◇	3NT	pass	?

North's 3NT shows a hand with long running clubs and diamonds stopped — almost as it would had West passed — not a balanced 19-HCP hand. With a balanced 19 HCP, he would have bid 2NT instead. You must pass here: to bid 4♠ would be very wrong. When partner bids 3NT, he often has a singleton spade, and in a spade contract you may not be able to draw trumps in time to utilize dummy's clubs before the defenders take some heart tricks and perhaps get a ruff in clubs or hearts.

6

Incidentally, "Hamilton over 1NT Overcalls" does not make nearly as much sense as ordinary Hamilton. There's a *point* to having 1NT-2♠ show an unspecified minor side suit: if advancer is short in spades but has support for both minors, he has a safety-valve in three of a minor. However, to play 1♠-1NT-2♠ as Hamilton has *no* merit: a spade fit being assured, no safety-valve in three of a minor is necessary. The worst part of this ill-conceived convention is that if responder has an ordinary raise to 2♠, he must bid 2♣ rather than 2♠ in the above auction. Advancer now has a chance to show his suit at the two-level, while at other tables a standard 1♠-1NT-2♠ shuts advancer out. "Hamilton over 1NT Overcall" is a "convention for convention's sake" — worse than bad.

1. Hamilton.
2. Hearts.

The Law of Total Tricks suggests that you should have a nine-card trump fit for safety at the three-level. While I'm not an advocate of the Law, there is a grain of truth in it.

Hamilton over Opponents' Notrump was invented independently by Fred Hamilton, one of the great players, and several others (Mike Cappelletti, Julian Pottage and Jerry Helms) whose names it bears in different parts of the world. Its main distinguishing feature is its 2◇ overcall, which shows both majors. Other distinguishing features are its 2♡ and 2♠ overcalls, which show the bid major and an unspecified minor suit (which partner can ask for by replying 2NT). To enter with a one-suiter, Hamilton users must start with an artificial 2♣ overcall. The player who initially intervenes with an overcall or double is called the *intervener.* Advancer (intervener's partner) can then bid 2◇ if he wants to play in intervener's suit. Intervener will then either pass with diamonds or bid his suit. The "Unusual" 2NT overcall is still available for hands with both minors.

I won't attempt a critique of Hamilton here, but I will mention its three main merits: it is comprehensive; it is simple; it is popular. It is so popular, in fact, that some like to play it even when the 1NT bid is an opposing overcall. Assume you have agreed to do so with your partner on this deal:

Matchpoints, Both vul.

♠ K J 8   ♡ —   ◇ 10 9 7 6 4 3 2   ♣ 8 5 4

WEST	NORTH	EAST	SOUTH
pass	1♠	1NT	2♠[1]
3◇[2]	pass	3♡	?

This is a most unusual auction. You and your partner are playing Hamilton over intervening 1NT overcalls. Your opponents are playing *transfer advances of 1NT overcalls,* even at the three-level.

You must pass. You do not have three-level values (especially vul.). To bid you would require (at the minimum) a *fourth* trump.

Your heart void is worth relatively little when you have only three trumps, especially when the second and third heart ruffs will use up *trump honors* instead of *low trumps* (or the defenders could lead trumps to stop the ruffs). When you bid 2♠, you have already bid the full value of your hand.

To bid 3♠ now is to beg to be doubled, and West, having heard East's 1NT overcall, is in a fine position to double. Down one doubled, or down two not doubled, costs more than the value of an opposing partscore. In short, 3♠ shuts out nothing and gives the opponents a "Fielder's Choice": they can bid game, or double you for more than the value of their partial.

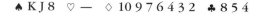

Matchpoints, Both vul.

♠ K J 8   ♡ —   ◇ 10 9 7 6 4 3 2   ♣ 8 5 4

WEST	NORTH	EAST	SOUTH	
pass	1♠	1NT	2♠[1]	1. Hamilton.
3◇[2]	pass	3♡	3♠ (!)	2. Hearts.
3NT	pass	4♡	all pass	

What should you lead?

Perhaps the fact that both opponents bid notrump should steer you to a diamond lead, but suppose you want to lead spades. The normal lead is your low spade, and there is no reason to make an exception here. If partner has the ♠Q, then whichever spade you choose makes little difference. If, however, partner has the ♠A and declarer has ♠Qxx (fairly likely), leading the ♠8 lets partner take the ♠A. He can then return a low spade through the ♠Q, thereby keeping declarer from taking a trick with it.

A ♠K lead harms in another way: it misleads partner about the ♠Q. Partner will place you with ♠ KQx (in light of your 3♠ rebid, perhaps ♠ KQxx). A bad 3♠ bid and the wrong opening lead make it much harder for partner to get an accurate picture of the hands.

Matchpoints, Neither vul.

♠ 9   ♡ A K 8 7   ◇ A K 6 4   ♣ K 10 6 2

WEST	NORTH	EAST	SOUTH
pass	pass	pass	1◇
1♠	pass	pass	dbl
pass	pass	2♣	?

You should double. You have four good trumps, four top tricks on the side, a spade to lead through dummy's strength up to partner (who made a penalty pass of your takeout double), and a chance for a huge penalty even if partner has nothing but a spade stack. The deal is a *misfit* for both sides. Don't let your opponents off the hook by bidding, and don't expect partner to be able to double if you pass.

However, if you do pass, you face this auction:

WEST	NORTH	EAST	SOUTH
pass	pass	pass	1◇
1♠	pass	pass	dbl
pass	pass	2♣	pass (!)
pass	2♠	pass	?

Pass. Playing in notrump, you have four tricks in your own hand, maybe five if you get a club trick. Where do you expect to get more? Not from partner's hand, which might be entryless, producing *no* spade tricks and no tricks anywhere else. In spades, however, partner, who has a spade stack, figures to score at least three, maybe four or five, trump tricks. A strong hand facing a misfitting weak hand belongs not in notrump but in the weak hand's long (non-solid and entryless) suit.

This is a basic concept of bidding.

Leading the wrong card in a suit can blow not only a trick in that suit but the entire defense — as on the deal where this problem arose:

Matchpoints, E-W vul.

♠ A 10 9 7 5 4   ♡ J 8 3   ◇ 5 3   ♣ K 10

WEST	NORTH	EAST	SOUTH
	3♣	pass	pass
3◇	pass	3NT	all pass

What should you lead?

Suppose that instead of leading partner's suit (the ♣K is my choice), you decide to lead spades. Then the normal lead (best) is the ♠10 (top of an internal sequence), with the ♠7 (fourth highest) not quite as good.

Look what happens if you lead the ♠5. Partner, who has ♠32, will place you with at most five spades. When you show up with three hearts and two clubs, partner will have a complete count on your hand — a *false* 5-3-3-2 count. In consequence, partner may blow a trick in diamonds.

A defensive falsecard, especially on opening lead, can harm the defense in ways you can hardly imagine in advance.

As soon as dummy appears, declarer knows the combined assets of the partnership hands. The defenders do not. This is sometimes called *Declarer's Advantage*. To overcome it, each defender must figure out, to the extent that he can, what cards the other defender has. Signals (attitude, count, and in rare circumstances suit-preference) can help, but *carding* (the choice of which card to play when not giving one of the "signals") is even more important.

Matchpoints, Both vul.

10

NORTH (dummy)
♠ K 9 3
♡ J 10 9 5 4
◇ A 6 2
♣ 7 5

WEST (you)
♠ Q 5
♡ K 3
◇ 9 5 4 3
♣ K J 9 6 2

WEST	NORTH	EAST	SOUTH
	pass	pass	1NT[1]
pass	2◇[2]	pass	2♡
pass	2NT	pass	4♡
all pass			

1. 15-17 HCP
2. Transfer

You lead the ♣6 and declarer takes partner's queen with the ace. Declarer crosses to dummy's ◇A to lead the ♡J, which rides to your king. Now what?

Take your club trick (the jack is best, as when it holds partner will know you have the king) and then exit *passively* with your last trump. *Passive* defense is the default strategy unless and until the bidding or the sight of dummy tells you otherwise. Breaking a new suit would be dangerous; shifting to the ♠Q would be very bad. If declarer has ♠AJx or ♠AJxx, left to his own devices he may be about to lose a finesse to your queen. If he has ♠Jxxx, he may be about to lose *three* spade tricks.

Matchpoints, E-W vul.

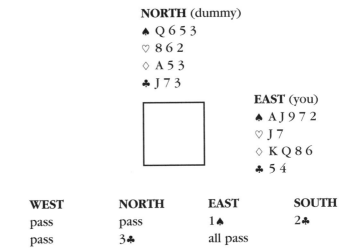

NORTH (dummy)
♠ Q 6 5 3
♡ 8 6 2
◇ A 5 3
♣ J 7 3

EAST (you)
♠ A J 9 7 2
♡ J 7
◇ K Q 8 6
♣ 5 4

WEST	NORTH	EAST	SOUTH
pass	pass	1♠	2♣
pass	3♣	all pass	

Partner leads the ♠10. Low from dummy — and you?

There is no need to play quickly to Trick 1. Take as long as you need to absorb and digest the fourteen new pieces of information that you have received: dummy's thirteen cards and partner's opening lead.

Can it be right to play the ♠A? Suppose partner's ♠10 is a single-ton. In that case, you will be able to give him a ruff.

That's only two tricks, however, and the ruff might use up a trump trick. Meanwhile, you're giving declarer two spade tricks when he's entitled to only one, and the second spade trick may provide a useful discard for him.

If you don't play the ♠A, you have two spade tricks coming any-how — without wasting any of partner's trumps. Even if your partner has three low trumps, making him ruff is harmful, because it allows declarer to draw trumps in two rounds instead of three.

Grabbing the ♠A here is a "can't gain, may cost" play. Don't be in a hurry to take that ace: in the absence of a long side suit, any spade losers that declarer has can't go away. As usual, passive defense suc-ceeds. Give declarer the tricks you can't keep him from taking (his ♠K), but don't let him score tricks you can stop him from scoring (dummy's ♠Q).

Matchpoints, Both vul.

12

NORTH (dummy)
♠ A K 6 5
♡ A J 7 3
◇ 7
♣ Q 7 4 2

EAST (you)
♠ J 7 2
♡ 4
◇ Q 6 5 2
♣ A K J 8 3

WEST	NORTH	EAST	SOUTH
		pass	pass
pass	1♣	pass	1♡
pass	3♡	all pass	

Partner leads the ◇4 and declarer takes your queen with the ace. Declarer leads the ♡2; partner plays the eight, and dummy's jack wins. Next, declarer calls for a low club from dummy. Not knowing who has the ♣10, you play the jack. Partner follows with the ten. You cash the ♣K; declarer follows again, and partner plays the nine. What now?

Return the ◇2. You dare not play a third club. If you lead the ♣A, declarer will ruff; although partner can overruff with a natural trump trick, dummy's ♣Q will take a trick later. Even if you lead a low club, declarer can discard a spade loser as partner ruffs with a natural trump trick.

Once again, the path to success lies in *passive* defense.

What do you think partner's trumps are?

That's right, ♡K108.

Matchpoints, E-W vul.

13

♠ A J 10 6   ♡ A K 4   ◇ 7 6 3   ♣ 9 4 3

WEST	NORTH	EAST	SOUTH
	pass	pass	?

Open 1♠, with the intention of passing any response except a jump shift. Bidding 1♠ is *much* better than 1♣. Sometimes fourth hand will enter, perhaps at a high level. When he does, you have two things to fear after opening 1♣: that partner will raise clubs with a decent hand, and that partner will lead clubs if fourth hand becomes declarer. Either can prove disastrous.

Here's a very useful tip. Do not count "points" as such, but count *points for a specific purpose* (such as opening 1♣ or opening 1♠). In doing so, adjust up or down according to whether the suit you contemplate opening is strong or weak. Add a point for strong suits (KJ10 or better); subtract a point for weak suits (headed by the jack or lower). Also subtract a point if your suit is short (three-card minor or a four-card major).

Applying this tip, you will count your hand as *two points better* for purposes of opening 1♠ than for purposes of opening 1♣. Of course if you don't count points but just look at and think about your hand, 1♣ is repulsive and 1♠ is attractive. If your system does not permit you to open a *good* four-card major even in third or fourth seat, you'll do better to *pass* than to open 1♣.

There are suits, there are miniskirts, and there are bikinis. Your clubs are an *itsy-bitsy, teeny-weeny, yellow polka-dot bikini*. Be afraid to come out of the water with them.

14

Matchpoints, Neither vul.

NORTH (dummy)
♠ 10 6 4
♡ Q 8 6
◇ 6 5 3
♣ A K 7 4

EAST (you)
♠ A 7 5 2
♡ 5 4 2
◇ Q 10 4
♣ 8 6 3

WEST	NORTH	EAST	SOUTH
			1♡
pass	2♡	pass	4♡
all pass			

Partner leads the ♠Q and declarer's king falls under your ace. Take it from here.

If you have more tricks coming, it looks like they'll be in diamonds. You'll need three diamond tricks to beat 4♡ if declarer's hand is

♠ K   ♡ A K J x x x   ◇ K x x   ♣ Q x x

or similar. You won't be getting in again, so you must hope partner has ◇AJxx. Your correct play is a diamond honor, but which one?

Play the ten, not the queen. Why not the ◇Q? Because it doesn't cater for certain other possibilities. Partner might have

♠ Q J 9 8 3   ♡ A   ◇ K 9 x x   ♣ x x x

for example. In that case, if you lead the ◇Q, declarer will take the ◇A and knock out partner's ♡A. Now, if partner continues diamonds, he'll be giving declarer a trick with his remaining ◇Jx; and if partner doesn't continue diamonds, declarer can discard a diamond on dummy's fourth club. You might try leading low with the ◇4, but then partner will play you for ◇K84, a holding from which the four is right, not your actual holding of ◇Q104, which demands the ten. So lead the ◇10. Declarer must still rise with the ace and you'll get your two diamond tricks.

Matchpoints, N-S vul.

♠ A K 4   ♡ K Q J 5   ◇ A Q 9 8 2   ♣ 6

WEST	NORTH	EAST	SOUTH
			1◇
pass	1♡	pass	?

If you play ordinary splinters, bid 4♣ (for which you have a fine maximum). If you play some fancier kind of splinters (of which several are possible), use whatever you play. But *do not* bid 4♡, which denies shortness. Failure to splinter may result in missing a laydown slam facing as little as

♠ 8 6 2   ♡ A 10 9 4 3   ◇ K 4   ♣ 7 3 2

Do you ever wonder how experts bid before anyone thought of splinters? An alternative to splintering is to jump-shift, 2♠, then over partner's rebid (e.g. 2NT or 3◇) bid 4♡ (usually a second jump). If by some chance partner rebids 3♡, then your bid of the fourth suit, 4♣, conventionally shows a singleton in that suit and a jump shift based on heart support. Bidding three suits strongly (including a jump) implies a singleton in the fourth. For this reason, *singleton* splinters are relatively unimportant in auctions like this. It's reasonable to play *void* splinters and bid "three suits strongly including a jump" with singletons, but for that, of course, you need a partnership agreement.

Matchpoints, Neither vul.

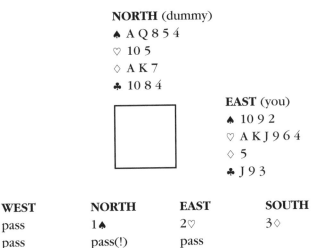

NORTH (dummy)
♠ A Q 8 5 4
♡ 10 5
◇ A K 7
♣ 10 8 4

EAST (you)
♠ 10 9 2
♡ A K J 9 6 4
◇ 5
♣ J 9 3

WEST	NORTH	EAST	SOUTH
pass	1♠	2♡	3◇
pass	pass(!)	pass	

Never mind the (quite awful) bidding. Partner leads the ♡8. You take the king, on which declarer plays the seven. You then cash the ♡A, on which declarer plays the queen and partner plays the three. You shift to the ♣3, and partner takes declarer's queen with the ace. Partner returns the ♣2 (a count card, showing an initial four-card club holding) to dummy's eight, your nine, and declarer's king.

The missing heart is the deuce: who has it?

Partner has the ♡2. If declarer had it, he would not have dropped the queen under your ace. But suppose dummy had held ♡Qx and declarer had dropped the ♡10 under your ace. The ♡10 could be a false-card, so you wouldn't know who had the deuce.

Continuing with the hypothetical play, declarer draws the ◇Q and ◇K, to which partner follows first with the deuce, then the four (count again, reverse count being standard in the trump suit). Next declarer plays the ♠A and ruffs a spade, crosses to dummy's ◇A (on which partner discards the missing ♡2), ruffs a second spade and runs the rest of her seven-card diamond suit.

Now suppose further that you haven't been watching partner's discards and haven't notice that he's pitched the only missing heart. Suddenly, at Trick 12, you have the ♡J and the ♣J left and must choose which to keep. Is there any way you can tell whether declarer's last card is a low heart or a low club?

Absolutely! It's a low club. Why? Because if declarer had a low heart, he would have ruffed it with dummy's ◇A instead of leading a trump to dummy's ◇A. Tip: when declarer plays extra trumps, he has either miscounted or he has no losers in a suit he could have ruffed with one of dummy's extra trumps. Don't play him to have miscounted, even if he has.

Matchpoints, N-S vul.

♠ 7 5 4   ♡ A Q 6 3   ◇ 10 5 4   ♣ J 8 2

WEST	NORTH	EAST	SOUTH
		pass	pass
1NT[1]	dbl[2]	pass	?

1. 11-14 HCP.
2. Penalty.

Pass. Removing a penalty double of 1NT is right only with a long suit in a weak hand. You have a hand that is as balanced as possible and 7 HCP. If partner has the expected strong hand and a good lead, you figure to collect a healthy penalty (down *four* would not be surprising). Passing would be right even if partner doubled a strong notrump (the range of the doubled 1NT is not relevant).

Let's say you do mistakenly pull partner's penalty double, leading to this auction:

Matchpoints, N-S vul.

NORTH (dummy)
♠ A K 8 6 2
♡ 8 5
◇ A Q 3
♣ K 7 4

SOUTH (you)
♠ 7 5 4
♡ A Q 6 3
◇ 10 5 4
♣ J 8 2

WEST	NORTH	EAST	SOUTH
		pass	pass
1NT[1]	dbl[2]	pass	2♡ (!)
all pass			

1. 11-14 HCP.
2. Penalty.

In general, I don't think it's a good idea to play penalty doubles of 1NT. Part of the reason is that the doubler's partner seldom knows whether to pass or pull. On this deal, a player with the clearest of passes pulled. If you have even the slightest impulse to pull on a hand like South's, you should use a double of 1NT for *something else*. (Simplest, but not optimal, is to double to show both majors.)

West leads the ◇6. What should you play from dummy at Trick 1?

Play the ◇3. You have no place to discard your third diamond. Even if West is leading from ◇Kxxx, playing dummy's queen still leaves you with a sure diamond loser; if he is leading from ◇Jxxx, playing dummy's queen leaves you with two diamond losers.

In contrast, playing low from dummy leaves you with only one diamond loser no matter which of the two missing diamond honors West has. If he has ◇KJxx, you'll have no diamond losers at all. Once West has led from the ◇J, your ten is worth a trick. Don't squander that trick by playing dummy's queen "on air"!

18

Matchpoints, N-S vul.

♠ A J 7 6 2   ♡ K Q 9 8   ◇ 3   ♣ A 8 6

WEST	NORTH	EAST	SOUTH
	1◇	pass	1♠
pass	2♠	pass	?

There is no indication that you're in the slam zone, that you're safe in 5♠, or even that you belong in spades. If partner is 3-4-4-2, for example, you belong in your 4-4 heart fit. Bid 3♡. If partner raises to 4♡, that's where you belong. If partner retreats to 3♠ or bids 3NT, you can still bid 4♣ to try for slam — but respect partner's 4♠ signoff. If partner jumps to 4♠ or cuebids 4◇, you can also try for slam. A Roman Keycard Blackwood 4NT is wrong (as most Blackwood bids are).

19

Matchpoints, Both vul.

NORTH (dummy)
♠ A Q J 5
♡ Q 10 4
◇ Q 3
♣ A 10 6 4

WEST (you)
♠ K 8 7 4 3
♡ K 7 2
◇ J 6 4
♣ J 5

WEST	NORTH	EAST	SOUTH
		pass	1◇
pass	1♠	pass	2◇
pass	3NT	pass	5◇
all pass			

You lead the ♡2 to partner's ace and declarer plays the five. Partner returns the ♡6, followed by declarer's jack and your king. What now?

Declarer didn't run from 3NT for fear of a heart lead (he's shown up with ♡J5). He's likely to be void somewhere, and it won't be in clubs, else he would have supported spades. So just continue hearts: you can't stop declarer from getting a discard on dummy's ♡Q anyway. Don't break a new suit unless there's a clear reason to do so, and don't be reluctant to concede a trick to declarer immediately when you can't stop him from taking it eventually.

Matchpoints, Both vul.

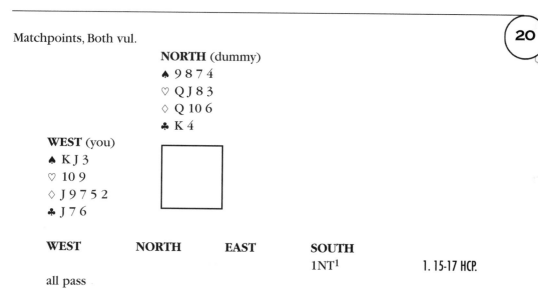

NORTH (dummy)
♠ 9 8 7 4
♡ Q J 8 3
◇ Q 10 6
♣ K 4

WEST (you)
♠ K J 3
♡ 10 9
◇ J 9 7 5 2
♣ J 7 6

WEST	NORTH	EAST	SOUTH
			1NT[1]
all pass			

1. 15-17 HCP.

You lead the ◇5 to partner's ace, as declarer plays the three. Partner returns the ◇4 and declarer plays the eight. What will you play?

This is an appropriate situation for suit preference. You see 14 HCP between your hand and dummy. Declarer has 15-17 HCP, so partner has 9-11 HCP. Partner has shown up with a doubleton ace of diamonds and figures to get in again with his remaining 5-7 HCP worth of high cards. Follow with the ◇J to request a spade shift.

21

Matchpoints, Neither vul.

♠ K 9 6 4   ♡ 7 3   ◇ A J 7 2   ♣ A K 8

	WEST	NORTH	EAST	SOUTH
1. 15-17 HCP.	pass	1NT[1]	pass	?

The "magic point-count" for 6NT is 33, just as the magic point-count for 3NT is 26. That means you should not invite to these contracts unless partner's maximum brings the partnership total up to (or one higher than) the target number of points.

You're a hair short of an invitation to 6NT. Your 15 HCP added to opener's maximum (in this case 17) brings the partnership total to only 32. But there's an even more important reason not to jump to 4NT: you may belong in spades. Start with Stayman: if you locate a spade fit, then you are in the slam zone. An extra trick is usually available by ruffing and you have prime cards (better suited for suit play than notrump). For slam purposes, it's good to have a partnership agreement that this auction

Opener	Responder
1NT	2♣
2♠	3♡

is forcing and agrees spades.

22

Matchpoints, Both vul.

♠ A Q 10 8 6   ♡ 10 7 5   ◇ Q 9 7 2   ♣ J

WEST	NORTH	EAST	SOUTH
			?

You open a weak 2♠. Partner goes wrong in the defense against East's club contract, blowing a trick to give declarer an overtrick. What do you say in the post-mortem?

Partner blew the trick because he miscounted the hand, playing you for the sixth spade you needed to justify opening 2♠. Do you defend your five-card Weak Two? Or do you say, "Sorry, partner. I had the jack of clubs mixed in with my spades"?

Better not to say either. It's a bad idea to open Weak Twos on five-baggers, though you might make an exception for a suit like ♠AQJ102 in third seat not vulnerable. Once you permit Weak Twos on five-baggers, you'll find that about 70% of your Weak Twos are based on five-baggers, for five-card suits are much more common than six-card suits. To open 2♠ on

♠ A Q J 10 8 6   ♡ 10 7 5   ◇ Q 9 7 2   ♣ —

(the hand you'd have if you'd really missorted) is almost as bad, because it has an inappropriate shape. In first or second seat, Weak Twos should be disciplined — which means, among other things, no void.

Matchpoints, N-S vul.

23

NORTH (dummy)
♠ Q 9 7 5
♡ Q J 6 3
◇ A
♣ A K Q 5

EAST (you)
♠ K 10 6 2
♡ 8 7 5 4 2
◇ 8 4
♣ 6 3

WEST	NORTH	EAST	SOUTH
			pass
pass	1♣	pass	2NT
pass	3NT	all pass	

Partner leads the ♠8 and declarer calls for dummy's five. From what do you think partner is leading?

If partner's lead is from length, he has ♠AJ8, making the ♠8 a very bad lead. Tip: don't play partner to have made a bad lead. *Partnership trust* requires you to assume that partner has made a good lead until shown otherwise. Actually, partner has made a very good lead, top of nothing from ♠843. That leaves declarer with ♠AJ. (If he had ♠AJx, he would have called for dummy's ♠9.)

Now what do you play?

Don't squander the ♠10 (a trick) when partner's ♠8 will force the jack. The ♠6 is encouraging enough. If partner is good enough to lead from ♠843, assume he is good enough to continue spades when he gets in again. When he does, he plays the ♠4. Once again it falls to you *not* to cover dummy's ♠7 with the ♠10. It would be throwing away a trick. Declarer's ♠A is now singleton and about to be played "on air" anyway. *Trick Preservation* is your first priority, and each of your spade honors is a trick.

Matchpoints, N-S vul.

NORTH (dummy)
♠ A K Q
♡ Q 10 9 4 3
♢ —
♣ K 6 5 4 2

WEST (you)
♠ 10 8 6 5 4
♡ J 6
♢ K 9 4 3
♣ Q 10

WEST	NORTH	EAST	SOUTH
			pass
pass	1♡	pass	1NT
pass	2♣	pass	2NT
all pass			

You lead the ♠5 to dummy's queen. Partner plays the nine and declarer the deuce. The ♡A followed by a low heart to dummy's queen puts partner in with the ♡K. He shifts to the ♢2, and you take declarer's ten with your king. What now?

Stop to think why partner shifted to the ♢2. *A good defender doesn't play low spot cards at random.* It was his fourth-highest diamond. Since he can have none lower, you can count him for four diamonds and declarer for five. A diamond continuation from you will help declarer set up his long suit!

Matchpoints, N-S vul.

NORTH (dummy)
♠ Q J 10 3
♡ J 5 4
♢ A 5 2
♣ 9 8 3

WEST (you)
♠ 9 8 7 6 5
♡ Q 7 2
♢ K 7
♣ Q 6 4

WEST	NORTH	EAST	SOUTH
pass	pass	pass	1♣
pass	1♠	pass	2♡
pass	3♣	pass	3NT
all pass			

You lead the ♠9. Partner takes dummy's ten with the king and declarer plays the deuce. Partner shifts to the ◇10, which declarer covers with the jack, and you play the king. What should you return?

First, wait for declarer to call a card from dummy! If you assume your king will hold the trick, declarer can call for dummy's ace, and whatever card you "return" out of turn will become a penalty card.

Suppose declarer does let your ◇K hold. What then?

Continue with the ♠8. The second spade lead must come from your side, else dummy has two spade stoppers. It appears that declarer's ♠2 is singleton; otherwise partner could have falsecarded by winning with the ♠A at Trick 1 to discourage a spade continuation.

What, a defensive falsecard? Mike Lawrence wrote a book called *Falsecards* in which, before saying anything, he says "Don't!" to warn defenders against falsecarding at all. I agree with Mike, almost entirely. I will modify his advice by saying, "Don't falsecard as a defender unless you *want* to fool your partner, or are certain that fooling your partner can't induce him to go wrong."

In the unlikely event that declarer had bid 3NT with only ◇Jx as his diamond "stopper" and partner held

$$\spadesuit A K \quad \heartsuit x x x \quad \diamond Q 10 9 x x x \quad \clubsuit x x$$

a defensive falsecard would have been necessary to ensure a diamond continuation.

Matchpoints, E-W vul.

NORTH (dummy)
♠ 7 5 3
♡ A
◇ 9 8 6 3 2
♣ Q J 9 5

EAST (you)
♠ A K J 6
♡ 7 5 4
◇ J 7 4
♣ 10 8 7

WEST	NORTH	EAST	SOUTH
pass	pass	pass	1♡
pass	1NT	pass	4♡
all pass			

Partner leads the ◇K and declarer wins with the ◇A. He then cashes the ♣A and the ♣K as partner follows high-low. Declarer crosses to dummy's ♡A and discards a spade on dummy's ♣J. Next comes dummy's ♣Q. Oops, you have forgotten: is the ♣Q high or does partner still have the ♣K? What should you do?

Memory plays a much smaller role in bridge than most people think. You don't have to remember that the ♣K appeared at Trick 3 on the second round of clubs. All you need to notice is that partner didn't take the king on the third round of clubs; therefore he doesn't have it. Ruff, else declarer will discard another spade.

Matchpoints, N-S vul.

♠ Q J 2   ♡ K 2   ◇ 10 6 2   ♣ A 7 6 4 2

WEST	NORTH	EAST	SOUTH
		pass	pass
1♠	2♡	2♠	?

You have several reasonable calls: 2NT (my first choice), 3♡, 3NT and 4♡. 3♣ is not among them.

Even if you play that new-suit advances of overcalls are forcing, why would you want to bid 3♣ on a thin five-card suit? And could 3♣

be forcing even by a passed hand? Suppose it were: would you know what to do next turn over partner's 3♡ rebid or 4♣ raise? Either 2NT or 3♡ tells a more accurate story and lets partner decide whether to play in game or a partial.

Matchpoints, Both vul.

NORTH (dummy)
♠ J 10 7 5 4
♡ J 10 7 6
♢ J
♣ A Q 10

WEST (you)
♠ —
♡ A
♢ A 9 6 5 3
♣ K J 9 8 6 5 2

WEST	NORTH	EAST	SOUTH
		pass	1♢
2♣	dbl[1]	2♡	2♠
pass	4♠	all pass	

1. Negative.

You lead the ♡A, to which declarer follows with the nine. What now?

Watch as partner plays the deuce. It should be no surprise to him that your ♡A is singleton. Therefore his card should be suit-preference. Shift to clubs to give partner a ruff. You too should choose a suit-preference card, standard procedure when giving partner ruffs. Lead the ♣2 to tell partner that you'd welcome a diamond return.

Suppose that instead of returning a club, you cash the ♢A and lead another diamond to partner's ten and declarer's king. Declarer cashes the ♠A, gets the bad news, and continues by leading the ♣3. Which club should you play?

Certainly don't play a club honor. Partner has not yet shown out in clubs, and declarer may not realize he's void. If you play low, declarer, who has ♣743, may fear that partner has the ♣J singleton and call for dummy's queen. Remember, although you know that declarer can finesse dummy's ♣10 successfully, declarer doesn't — not unless you tilt your hand forward to let him see, or play an honor (which is almost the same thing).

29

Matchpoints, N-S vul.

NORTH (dummy)
♠ Q J 8 7 5
♡ 10 8
◇ Q J 10 9 7
♣ 6

WEST (you)
♠ 9 2
♡ K J 7 6
◇ A 6 4
♣ A Q 7 5

WEST	NORTH	EAST	SOUTH
			pass
1♣	pass	2◇	2♡
dbl	all pass		

You lead the ◇A, which holds, fetching the ◇3 from partner and the ◇2 from declarer. Are you surprised that partner jump-shifted in a four-card suit headed only by the king? Why do you think he did that?

You should be surprised, but there is a simple explanation. Responder's jump shift can be based on three hand types, for which the mnemonic is "FBI": (F) a big Fit for opener's suit, (B) a huge Balanced hand or (I) an Independent suit. Here he can have only (F) — a big fit for your suit.

You shift to the ♠9 and partner tops dummy's ♠J with the king. He then returns the ♡Q to declarer's ace. Why the heart shift? To prevent club ruffs in dummy. So, when declarer leads the ♣8 to the next trick, you should win and cash a high heart. Suppose, however, that you continue with the ♠2. Partner takes the ♠A, on which declarer falsecards the ten, but partner gives you a spade ruff anyway. What now?

This is your last chance to cash a high heart and prevent declarer from ruffing one losing club in dummy and discarding another on one of dummy's good spades. Two tricks down the tubes if you do anything else: +500 instead of +1100 when the normal score is +920 for the cold 6♣ slam.

NORTH (dummy)
♠ —
♡ J 10
◇ 6 5 4 3
♣ A J 9 7 5 4 2

☐

SOUTH (you)
♠ A K 8 7 3
♡ K 8
◇ A K Q 10 7 2
♣ —

WEST	NORTH	EAST	SOUTH
1♠	pass	pass	2◇ (!)
2♡	3♣	pass	3NT
pass	4◇	pass	5◇
all pass			

West leads the ♣K. Plan the play.

West has at least five spades. You cannot cash your top spades and ruff three spades in dummy. You have two reasonable lines.

One is to ruff three spades in dummy without cashing any. Take the ♣A, discarding a heart, and lead to the ◇A. West will show out. Then ruff a spade, ruff a club, ruff a second spade and ruff a second club. Both defenders follow. Ruff a third spade, and East must ruff when you lead an established club from dummy. You can then over-ruff, finish trumps, cash two spades and lose only a heart at the end.

The other line is to try for *one* spade ruff and *two* heart ruffs in dummy. To do this, you must discard a spade on dummy's ♣A. Next play the ◇A and two top spades, discarding dummy's hearts. Then ruff a heart, ruff a club, ruff a second heart, ruff another club and ruff a spade. Your only loser is a spade at the end.

Matchpoints, Neither vul.

♠ J 9 7 6 2   ♡ Q 7 3   ◇ K 10 4   ♣ J 5

WEST	NORTH	EAST	SOUTH
		pass	pass
1◇	pass	1♡	pass
2♡	dbl	pass	?

Do you know how to tell whether a double is for takeout or penalty?

Penalty doubles of low-level suit contracts are almost always based on *knowledge of partner's values.* When they are not, they are based on *trap passes* — passes with strong hands including length and strength in the suit bid in front of you. You have not shown any values, and if partner has a trap pass, it is of diamonds, not hearts. So you can tell this is a takeout double, even without looking at your hand and noticing that you have three cards in the opponents' heart suit. Partner has spades, clubs and perhaps diamonds, but he cannot have as many as three hearts (else he'd have doubled 1◇ for takeout). You must not pass. Bid 2♠. You should be happy do to so. You have more spades and more high-card strength than partner could rely on you to have when he made his takeout double. They can make 2♡ doubled, and you'll make 2♠.

Matchpoints, N-S vul.

♠ 10 7 6 3   ♡ 10 9   ◇ K J 8 4 3   ♣ K 8

WEST	NORTH	EAST	SOUTH
		pass	pass
pass	1♡	pass	1NT
pass	2♣	pass	2♡
pass	3♣	pass	?

If partner was only able to bid 2♣ over your 1NT, then you can't make 3NT with your mediocre hand. Partner's sequence shows five hearts, five (possibly six) clubs, and extra values, but less than game values. Bid 3♡. At IMPs, you should pass and let partner play 3♣.

Matchpoints, E-W vul.

♠ K 8 6 2 ♡ A K Q 10 5 ♢ 8 7 ♣ K 4

WEST	NORTH	EAST	SOUTH
	pass	pass	1♡
pass	2♡	pass	?

If you decide to try for game, bid 2♠, your most descriptive try. Partner will know that lower honors in spades are valuable but lower honors in clubs and diamonds might be worth little. The question is, "Is this hand worth a game try?"

It is close. I can visualize 7-point hands for partner that make game *almost* laydown, but no 6-point hands that make game *actually* laydown. For example, the perfect

♠ Q J ♡ 8 7 4 3 ♢ 6 5 2 ♣ A 7 6 3

makes game *almost* laydown, but the fourth trump makes it better than a minimum. The slightly weaker

♠ Q 5 ♡ 8 7 4 3 ♢ 6 5 2 ♣ A 7 6 3

which is a perfect *minimum*, requires the defender with the shorter spades to have only one or two hearts.

Though trying for game isn't horrible, it's best to pass 2♡.

A good guideline appears on page 45 of Jeff Rubens' 1969 book *The Secrets of Winning Bridge* (my second-favorite bridge book after S.J. Simon's *Why You Lose at Bridge*): "General Principle of Evaluation by Visualization: Your hand is worth an invitation to game (or slam) if a perfect minimum holding for partner will make it laydown."

Matchpoints, Both vul.

♠ K 10 4 2 ♡ A 7 6 3 ♢ 8 4 ♣ K Q 6

WEST	NORTH	EAST	SOUTH
		pass	1♣
pass	1♢	pass	1♡
pass	2♢	pass	?

You have nothing to spare for your opening bid, and partner's sequence shows a minimum responding hand with six diamonds. In notrump, partner's diamonds figure to go to waste. The problem with bidding 2NT is that if partner has enough for you to make 2NT, he'll raise to 3NT (2NT is invitational, not merely an attempt at a higher-scoring partial). You must pass.

You bid 2NT, however, and soon face this auction:

WEST	NORTH	EAST	SOUTH
		pass	1♣
pass	1♦	pass	1♡
pass	2♦	pass	2NT
pass	3♣	pass	?

Partner's sequence shows a weak hand with six diamonds and three clubs (with four, he'd have supported clubs earlier). You must correct to 3♦. If you pass, you'll be in a 3-3 fit: down four in 3♣ instead of down one in 3♦ (which might make on a lucky day).

Suppose that in the previous auction partner had jumped to 3♦ instead of rebidding 2♦. You should pass that too. To bid 3NT, you would need a hand at least as good as

♠ K 10 4 2   ♡ A 7 6 3   ♦ K 4   ♣ K 8 6

(the ♦K instead of the ♣Q), which qualifies only because the ♦K is worth its weight in gold.

Matchpoints, N-S vul.

♠ K 8 7 4   ♡ A K Q 9 4   ♦ J 7   ♣ A 3

WEST	NORTH	EAST	SOUTH
pass	pass	1♣	?

You must plan to bid hearts, if you can do so at the one-level or the two-level. One plan is to overcall 1♡. If West raises to 2♣ and North and East pass, you can double at your next turn to show extra strength and bring spades into the picture. Another plan is to start with a double, and bid hearts next turn (unless partner bids spades). Either plan is reasonable. I recommend 1♡, if only to help you get it out of your head that a simple overcall is limited to 16 HCP.

In this scenario, you choose to double, leading to this auction:

WEST	NORTH	EAST	SOUTH
pass	pass	1♣	dbl
1♠	pass	pass	?

Now you must bid 2♡. You dare not sell out to 1♠ at matchpoints. Even if you beat 1♠, +50 will be a very bad score when the field is earning +110 or +140 in 2♡.

Matchpoints, Neither vul.

♠ K Q 7 4   ♡ A 9 3   ◇ Q J 6 5   ♣ A 3

WEST	NORTH	EAST	SOUTH
	pass	pass	?

Your 1NT range is 15-17. What should you bid?

No one would criticize you for opening 1NT (as almost everybody else will), but 1◇ is better than 1NT for several reasons:

(1) The hand is more oriented to suit play than notrumps (honors in the four-card suits, and unsupported aces in the shorter suits).

(2) You have no particular reason to want the opening lead to come up to this hand. If a major-suit contract is reached via Jacoby Transfers or Stayman after a 1NT opening, it is more likely to be wrong-sided than right-sided.

(3) A 1NT opening precludes finding a 4-4 major-suit fit unless responder is strong enough to invite, or force to, game.

(4) The hand contains a four-card spade suit and a four-card minor. Such hands can be opened in the minor without creating a rebid problem over a red-suit response. (Hands with 4-2-3-4 and 4-3-2-4 shape should often be opened 1♣. Hands with 4-2-4-3 and 4-3-4-2 shape should sometimes be opened 1◇. Hands with 4-4-3-2 and 4-4-2-3 shape should almost always be opened 1NT if in the appropriate range of strength.)

(5) The suit you'll open if you don't open 1NT is a decent one in which you have two honors.

However, if you *don't* play that 1◊-2♣; 2NT shows extra strength, then you're better off opening 1NT. A 2♣ response can handcuff you if you open 1◊ (jumping to 3NT shows a hand that is too strong to open 1NT but not strong enough to open 2NT).

37

Matchpoints, E-W vul.

♠ A 10 4   ♡ Q 8 7 6 5   ◊ J 9   ♣ Q 9 3

WEST	NORTH	EAST	SOUTH
	1♠	pass	?

This hand, with its stray queens and jacks, is not worth more than 9 points in support of spades. Your ◊J9, though better than two small diamonds, should not be counted as both a high-card and a ruffing value. This hand is not a "three-card limit raise" suitable for 2♡ followed by a spade raise. Bid 2♠.

The maximum single raise is one of the most overlooked bids in bridge. There's no such thing as a raise to "2½" spades, and with a hand that appears to be worth that mythical raise, you should not stretch to portray a hand better than a simple 2♠ raise. How comfortable it is to have moderate extra values! You can accept partner's game invitation if he bids again over 2♠. If, instead, an opponent bids 3♣ or 3◊, you can bid 3♡ quite happily at your next turn.

38

Matchpoints, E-W vul.

NORTH (dummy)
♠ A J 8 5 4
♡ 6 2
◊ Q 3
♣ K 10 6 3

WEST (you)
♠ K Q 9 3 2
♡ 8 5
◊ A 8 2
♣ A 7 2

WEST	NORTH	EAST	SOUTH
	pass	pass	4♡
all pass			

You lead the ♠K, taken by dummy's ace, as partner plays the ten (which can be either a singleton or the start of a high-low to give count with a doubleton) and declarer puts in the seven. Next declarer plays five rounds of high hearts. You discard three times: one spade and two clubs. Dummy discards the same. Partner follows only to the first heart, then discards the ♣5 and the ♣4 (count without encouragement) and finally the ♣Q (implying the ♣J) and the ♣8. By now, you should know that declarer started with eight hearts, no clubs, one or two spades, and therefore three or four diamonds.

Next declarer leads the ◇4. What should you play?

You must play low. Do not play the ◇A 'on air'. There's no way the ◇A can gain: at best it can break even. You must wait to capture an honor with your ◇A. If partner doesn't have the ◇K, you cannot keep dummy's ◇Q from scoring, so don't make a futile attempt to do so. You *can* keep declarer's ◇K from scoring if partner has ◇J10xxx. Play low, and dummy's ◇Q will win, but you'll retain the ◇A to keep declarer's king from scoring.

What if partner has the ◇K? Then dummy's queen won't score regardless, as partner will take it with his king while you wait with your ◇A to capture an *honor* from declarer instead of a low diamond. Partner has been hanging on to all his diamonds, so he's likely to have some valuable diamond spot cards. By ducking the first diamond, you let him score two diamond tricks, the ◇K and the ◇9, when he has ◇K9xx (his actual holding).

This theme recurs often for defenders, so often that it has a name: "Second hand low". While "second hand low" is not a rule, you need a reason to make an exception, and the deals that call for making an exception usually find a way into newspaper bridge columns. When you see a deal reported in a newspaper, it's usually an exceptional one.

Commonplace deals are the ones that you will find here, in just about the proportion you'll encounter them at the table.

Matchpoints, E-W vul.

♠ Q J 9 8 2 ♡ 8 ◇ A Q 7 6 ♣ A Q 5

WEST	NORTH	EAST	SOUTH
		pass	1♠
pass	2♠	pass	?

It's questionable whether this hand is worth a game try at all. A standard 3◇ try is slightly pushy. A *Short Suit Game Try*, if you play that convention (or the more complex *Two-Way Game Tries* that lets you show either shortness or length as desired) might work better. Or you might simply use 2NT as an artificial game try to which responder can reply by bidding the cheapest suit in which he has strength. Let's suppose that you have such a 2NT bid available. Then you might face this problem:

WEST	NORTH	EAST	SOUTH
		pass	1♠
pass	2♠	pass	2NT[1]
pass	3◊[2]	pass	?

1. Artificial game try: "If you're undecided whether to bid game, tell me more!"
2. "I'm undecided, but I've got 'stuff' in diamonds."

Partner shows the ◊K and a decent hand for his raise. He's unlikely to have wasted honors in hearts. That's enough information to justify venturing 4♠. By bidding 4♠ on this auction, you have a better chance of making it than you'd have if you'd been playing *Short Suit Game Tries* and reached 4♠ after a short-suit try in hearts: now West may not know whether a heart lead or a club lead is best. Wouldn't you like West to lead clubs, perhaps away from the king?

Something to take into account in choosing your conventions: if you have a choice of methods, pick the one that lets dummy (not declarer) describe his hand.

The convention that describes your hand perfectly (*Short Suit Game Tries*) gets you to the good games and avoids the bad games, but the convention that solicits further information from partner lets you *make* more of the games you bid. Isn't that better?

Suppose you reach 4♠ on the auction suggested.

NORTH (dummy)
♠ A 7 6 3
♡ 10 7 6
◊ K 8 3
♣ J 10 4

SOUTH (you)
♠ Q J 9 8 2
♡ 8
◊ A Q 7 6
♣ A Q 5

Plan the play on an opening lead of the ♣2 (lowest from three or five, a modern opening-lead convention that should be marked on the convention card of the sophisticated pairs who play it).

Look at your opponents' convention card – don't assume you know what their agreements are!

Before playing from dummy at Trick 1, think where you want to be after winning the trick. Don't you want to be in your hand, to start trumps by finessing against West's possible ♠K? So play low from dummy, winning with the ♣Q when East doesn't produce the ♣K.

Which spade honor should you lead from your hand at Trick 2?

Lead the ♠Q if you want to induce West to cover with the king, or the ♠J if you want West to duck.

This time, either line will work (West has ♠K5). After drawing trumps, play the ace, king and queen of diamonds, in that order. (It's a bad general practice to play the ace and queen before the king, blocking the suit and requiring you to burn an entry to get to your fourth diamond.) When diamonds split 3-3, your fourth diamond provides a discard for one of dummy's clubs. Making six, a lucky result for you indeed!

Matchpoints, E-W vul.

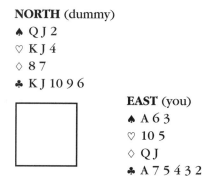

NORTH (dummy)
♠ Q J 2
♡ K J 4
◊ 8 7
♣ K J 10 9 6

EAST (you)
♠ A 6 3
♡ 10 5
◊ Q J
♣ A 7 5 4 3 2

WEST	NORTH	EAST	SOUTH
	pass	1♣	3♠
pass	4♠	all pass	

Partner leads the ♡7. Declarer, who is not very competent, puts up dummy's king and follows with the ♡8. He then leads the ♠2 to his ♠K and continues with the ♠4 to dummy's ♠J and your ♠A. Partner discards two diamonds: the six and the deuce. Declarer covers your ◊Q with the king; partner takes the ace and returns the ◊5 to your jack as declarer follows with the ◊4. What now?

You can place declarer with

♠ K 10 9 8 7 5 4   ♡ A Q 8   ◊ K 4

That's twelve cards, but what's the thirteenth? If it's a club, your ♣A will be a trick, but there's no need to take it now (no discards are available to declarer). If it's a diamond, declarer can ruff it in dummy — unless you return your last trump to remove dummy's last trump, guaranteeing the defeat of the contract.

By the way, do you know whether declarer's thirteenth card is a club or a diamond?

You should know. Partner has given you a clue with his order of diamond discards: high spot card then low spot card. He's giving count, showing an even number, which can only be six. Therefore declarer started with three diamonds, making his thirteenth card a diamond.

41

Matchpoints, Both vul.

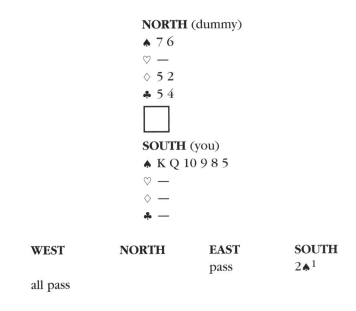

NORTH (dummy)

♠ 7 6
♡ —
♢ 5 2
♣ 5 4

SOUTH (you)

♠ K Q 10 9 8 5
♡ —
♢ —
♣ —

WEST	NORTH	EAST	SOUTH
		pass	2♠[1]
all pass			

1. Weak Two-bid.

You are declarer in 2♠. All have followed to three rounds of hearts and two rounds of each minor. The lead is in dummy. You lead spades for the first time and East follows small. How should you proceed?

Line A. Rise with the king. If it holds, continue with the queen. This succeeds against seven possible holdings: West's possible ♠J (one holding) or ♠Jx (three holdings) and East's possible ♠Jx (three holdings).

Line B. Rise with the king. If it holds, continue with a low spade. This won't succeed against West's possible ♠A or ♠Ax, for West will take the ace on the first round and East's guarded jack will score. It succeeds *only* against East's ♠Ax (three holdings) and then only slightly less than half the time, because East may have the thirteenth heart to lead through you and West will score the ♠J regardless. That's three possible holdings half the time; in effect, one-and-a-half holdings. Line A is clearly much better than Line B.

Line C. Let dummy's six ride. This succeeds against twelve possible holdings in all: East's ♠Jx (three holdings), ♠Jxx (three holdings), ♠AJx (three holdings) or ♠AJxx (three holdings). Line C is better than Line A by 12 to 7.

There's another, simpler way to look at it. Line C is essentially a simple finesse against the jack (about 50%). Line A is essentially playing for the drop of the jack-doubleton in either hand. In the absence of other information or other considerations, "eight ever, nine never": in other words, *finesse*.

Matchpoints, Neither vul.

♠ Q 7 5 4 3 ♡ A K 5 ◇ A 10 ♣ 6 4 3

WEST	NORTH	EAST	SOUTH
			1♠
pass	4♡[1]	pass	4♠
pass	4NT[2]	pass	?

1. Splinter.
2. Roman Keycard.

A splinter raise has a narrow range, telling a reasonably precise story and leaving the rest up to partner, who can see if he has wasted honors facing shortness, or whether to seek a slam.

The only exception occurs when the splinter bidder has a hand with a void plus enough strength to take control. The inference here, when partner takes control via RKCB next, is that he has such a hand. If he didn't, he'd have asked for keycards with 4NT directly over 1♠. You should really credit partner with having *planned* to ask for keycards on the second round, and not count your ♡A in replying to RKCB here. The right bid is 5◇ (one keycard).

In this auction, however, you decide to bid 5♠ (two keycards with the ♠Q) and you reach 7♠.

If you play Exclusion Blackwood partner can bid 5♡ directly over 1♠, asking for keycards *excluding* the ♡A. Obviously there is less bidding room in this sequence.

NORTH (dummy)
♠ A K J 9 8 2
♡ —
◇ Q 9 3
♣ A K 8 7

SOUTH (you)
♠ Q 7 5 4 3
♡ A K 5
◇ A 10
♣ 6 4 3

Plan the play on the lead of the ◇4.

Your play to Trick 1 matters only if the diamond honors are split, so assume they are. From which honor do you think West is leading, the ◇K or the ◇J?

Almost nobody leads from a king against a grand slam. West (an experienced and reasonably competent player) is almost surely leading from the jack (if from an honor at all). Play low from dummy, making this poor grand slam.

What should West have led?

Not a diamond away from the jack (as he did). Not a heart away from the queen (you might have had ♡AKJ). Not a club from some small ones, nor from a queen, jack or ten. Against nearly every grand slam, extreme safety is called for. The safest lead is a trump when, as here, the declaring side has shown every keycard (including the *queen* of trumps).

43

Matchpoints, N-S vul.

♠ J 3   ♡ K Q 7   ◇ Q J 10 4   ♣ A K 8 6

WEST	NORTH	EAST	SOUTH
	1♠	pass	?

The old-fashioned "standard" 3NT response shows a balanced 16-18 HCP hand, with stoppers in all unbid suits, no five-card suit, fewer than three cards in opener's major suit, and no four-card major that can be bid at the one-level: a hand just like this!

This standard 3NT response does not belong in your bidding arsenal. It takes away too much bidding space when the right trump suit has not yet been found. *Reserve big jumps for hands on which you know in which strain you belong.*

To see more specifically what is wrong with this 3NT response, ask yourself how you will proceed if partner rebids 4♡. Does partner have four hearts or five? Does he have slam hopes, or merely a distributional hand with which he is trying to reach the right game contract? Would you know what to do? I wouldn't.

Either 2♣ or 2◇ figures to work well on this deal. When partner rebids 2♡, you can force by bidding the other minor. Then, if partner bids 3♡, you can play him for an ordinary minimum opening with 5-5 in the majors and raise to 4♡. It's not a perfect plan — partner still won't know you have a balanced hand with 16 HCP rather than 13 to 15 — but it's reasonably good.

As for the "standard" 3NT response (which I call "the Old Slam Killer"), get it out of your system. Agree with your partner on some other meaning for a 3NT response. Which meaning? That depends a lot on the rest of your system, but as a minimum requirement I suggest that a 3NT response *describe your hand sufficiently for opener to know* in which suit (if any) there might be a slam.

NORTH (dummy)
♠ J 6 5
♡ 8 7 4
◇ K 10 4 2
♣ A 8 3

EAST (you)
♠ 7 3
♡ A 10 6 5 2
◇ J 9 5
♣ Q 10 2

WEST	NORTH	EAST	SOUTH
pass	pass	pass	1♠
pass	2♠[1]	all pass	

1. Semi-constructive (8-10 points).

Partner leads a low spade. Declarer draws trumps in three rounds, ending in hand. Partner follows with another low spade and the ten; you discard with the ♡5. There is one lower heart spot outstanding, so partner can read your five neither as discouraging nor encouraging (as he could if *two* lower spots were outstanding).

Declarer starts diamonds with the ◇3. Partner plays ◇6, the lowest outstanding spot card, and dummy's king wins. On the next play, the ◇2 from dummy, your ◇9 holds as declarer hesitates before playing the eight, and partner follows with the seven. What's going on in the diamond suit?

Partner's up-the-line play and declarer's second-round low diamond reveals that partner started with ◇A76 and declarer with ◇Q83. Declarer certainly has a heart honor, for with ♡KQJ or longer partner would have led the ♡K, not a low spade from ♠10xx. If declarer has two heart honors, that gives him

♠ A K Q x x   ♡ Q J   ◇ Q x x   ♣ ? ? ?

or better; he can't have the ♣K, for that would give him enough to try for game. If declarer has *one* heart honor, which do you think it is?

It's the queen. Useful tip: if declarer can be assumed to have one of three consecutive honors in a suit that partner did not lead, it is the *middle* of the three (else partner, with two *touching* honors, would have led the suit). As declarer is marked with ♡Qx or better, partner is marked with the ♣K from declarer's failure to try for game.

Declarer's actual hand:

♠ A K Q 9 2 ♡ Q 9 ◇ Q 8 3 ♣ J 7 4

Do you see why declarer (not gifted, but not incompetent) attacked diamonds after drawing trumps? He wanted to set up a long diamond to discard a loser (in this case, either a heart loser or a club loser). Dummy's ♣A is the lone remaining dummy entry. You must try to knock it out: shift to clubs. If you shift to hearts instead, partner will get in and have to break clubs from his side. He may be reluctant to lead from the ♣K when he doesn't know that you have the ♣Q.

45

Matchpoints, Both vul.

West (you)
♠ 10 6 5 ♡ 10 9 ◇ A J 10 7 ♣ Q 9 5 2

WEST	NORTH	EAST	SOUTH
			pass
pass	pass	2NT[1]	all pass

1. 20-21 HCP.

You'd be surprised how many tricks are blown through sheer inattention. When the auction ends and a player asks, "My lead?" or "Who's the notrump bidder?" he is probably about to make a bad lead, for he has not been figuring out what there is to figure out about the deal during the auction.

What should you lead?

Don't lead the ◇J or any other diamond. The ◇J would be a good lead from ◇AJ1072 (the fifth diamond makes the risk of blowing a diamond trick worth taking, since you have hopes of taking *four* tricks in the suit if you attack it early). Underleads of aces, even against notrump, are usually bad from *four-card* suits, as there is at most one long-card trick to be established in the suit, often none.

For an *active* lead, your fourth-best club is better (a lead from a non-ace suit). However, there is nothing about your hand or the auction that suggests getting active. Your best lead is your most *passive*, the ♡10, allowing you to wait for partner to get in and lead diamonds through declarer. I would recommend leading from ♡102 as well as ♡109.

46

This is a similar problem to the previous one and shows an even easier error to avoid:

Matchpoints, Both vul.

NORTH (dummy)
♠ A 7 4
♡ 8 4
◇ 9 8 5 3
♣ 10 6 4

WEST (you)
♠ 10 6 5
♡ 10 9
◇ A J 10 7
◇ Q 9 5 2

WEST	NORTH	EAST	SOUTH
pass	pass	pass	2NT[1]
all pass			

1. 20-21 HCP.

Misguidedly, you lead the ◇J. (The ♡10 would be my choice.) Declarer inexpertly wins with the ◇Q, as partner follows with the deuce. Then declarer crosses to dummy's ♠A and leads the ◇5 from dummy. Partner discards the ♡6 and declarer plays the ◇6 — a hope-lessly wrong card. What now?

The first thing you must do is look at the cards. Your ◇7 will take the trick if you play it. Playing the ◇10 lets declarer establish a sec-ond diamond trick by force. Of course, he could always have achieved that without your help by playing the ◇K.

Nothing difficult about *this* defense, yet an experienced player blew it.

Matchpoints, E-W vul.

47

♠ A 7 5 3   ♡ K Q 10 7 6 2   ◇ 6 5   ♣ J

WEST	NORTH	EAST	SOUTH
pass	1◇	pass	1♡
pass	2♣	pass	?

You have a textbook (though minimum) invitational 3♡. There's no point in bidding 2♠: if partner had four spades, he would have rebid 1♠ rather than 2♣. Moreover, the effect of bidding 2♠ (which is not only "fourth suit forcing" but also a reverse) is to create a game force when you bid 3♡ next turn over partner's 2NT or other minimum third bid. For that you would need a stronger hand — in point-count terms at least 2 points more.

48

Matchpoints, Neither vul.

♠ A 5 3　♡ A 9 2　◇ K 5 3　♣ J 6 4 3

WEST	NORTH	EAST	SOUTH
			1♣
1♡	pass	pass	?

Your 1♣ opening was marginal. You have a bad 12 HCP: a square hand with a weak suit and an unbolstered jack. In some partnerships, you would be too weak to open.

Partner couldn't raise clubs and couldn't bid 1♠, 1NT or 2◇. You are playing negative doubles and partner couldn't make one. Partner probably has a very bad hand.

Of course it is possible that partner has a good hand with five strong hearts. Bad opponents have been known to overcall on pure trash, a five-card suit to nothing, and partner *might* be trapping with something like

♠ K 10 4　♡ K Q 10 7 6　◇ Q J 4 2　♣ 7

(a good hand for a *penalty* double). However, it is much more likely that East has values to raise but failed to do so (failure to advance over-calls is a common error of bad players). In our modern era of weak jump overcalls and weak (Michaels) cuebids, it is not unlikely that West has an excellent hand (for example, one that would qualify for a strong jump overcall).

Pass. You are not close to reopening. If you reopen with a double, partner will play you for extra strength and shape with heart shortness. If you reopen with 1NT, partner will play you for a hand *too strong* (instead of much too weak) for a 1NT opening.

Whenever you are contemplating doing anything but passing in a non-forcing situation, ask yourself, "What is the typical normal minimum that my partner will picture for the call I am contemplating? And how does my actual hand compare to what he will picture?"

49

Matchpoints, Neither vul.

♠ A K 10　♡ A 10 7 4 3　◇ J　♣ K 7 5 4

WEST	NORTH	EAST	SOUTH
3♠	pass	pass	?

Pass. You have stoppers, not tricks. Yes, 3NT might work out well, but what is the "typical normal minimum" that partner will picture? Perhaps

♠ A 10 6   ♡ A 6   ◇ A K Q 8 5   ♣ J 7 5

a hand with a likely seven tricks (if diamonds split well, which the preempt does not suggest), needing only two more tricks from dummy. That's a far cry from the actual four or five tricks you will need from dummy to make 3NT. Where do you think you can get six more tricks to go with your two spades and a heart? And do you think you can get them before the defenders can set up and take enough diamond tricks to beat 3NT?

Matchpoints, Neither vul.

♠ A K 10   ♡ A 10 7 4 3   ◇ J   ♣ K 7 5 4

WEST	NORTH	EAST	SOUTH
3♠	pass	pass	3NT (?)
pass	pass	4♠	?

What a surprising development! What should you do about it?

Well, how many tricks do your expect to take against 4♠? Three? Then you shouldn't double. It's up to your partner to double if he has any defense. If he can't double, then you weren't about to make 3NT and you may not be able to beat 4♠. Perhaps 4♠ is a normal contract and the opponents should have reached it on their own steam. But if it isn't, and it goes down, you're slated for a very good score even if you don't double because you already "won the board" by pushing the opponents one higher.

Pass.

After you've made a mistake in the auction (such as bidding 3NT at your previous turn), *do nothing*; assume that your bad call has turned out well. Occasionally it will have, but even if it hasn't, trying to "correct" your mistake is likely to make things worse, especially if partner is still involved. Why? Because calls are always made *in context*, and a good partner will interpret any subsequent call as *refining*, not *correcting*, your previous calls.

Matchpoints, Neither vul.

NORTH (dummy)
♠ K J 6 4
♡ Q 10 9 3
◇ 9 7 4
♣ A Q

SOUTH (you)
♠ A 7 2
♡ A K J
◇ K J 10 3
♣ 8 7 5

1. 15-17 HCP.
2. Stayman.

WEST	NORTH	EAST	SOUTH
			1NT[1]
pass	2♣[2]	pass	2◇
pass	3NT	all pass	

West leads the ♡8. Plan the play.

    Win with the ♡A or the ♡K, not the ♡J, in order to retain an entry to dummy in the suit. Then run the hearts to force discards from the defenders before tackling diamonds. Maybe something good will happen: you will have no problem discarding, but the defenders might.

52

Matchpoints, N-S vul.

♠ K J 4 ♡ A K 10 5 2 ◇ 6 3 ♣ 7 6 4

WEST	NORTH	EAST	SOUTH
			1♡
3◇[1]	4◇	5◇	?

1. Weak.

Partner could have jumped to 4♡ instead of cuebidding 4◇. He chose the cuebid to establish a forcing-pass situation over an anticipated 5◇ by East. A simple jump to 4♡ would not establish a force.

    Do you think you can make 5♡? I don't. So double to express your opinion. If you pass 5◇, you encourage partner to bid 5♡. And when he does, this is where you end up.

NORTH (dummy)

♠ 7 5 2
♡ Q J 8 7 3
◇ J
♣ A K 10 2

SOUTH (you)

♠ K J 4
♡ A K 10 5 2
◇ 6 3
♣ 7 6 4

WEST	NORTH	EAST	SOUTH
			1♡
3◇[1]	4◇	5◇	pass[2]
pass	5♡	all pass	

1. Weak jump overcall.
2. Forcing pass.

West leads the ◇K and shifts to the ♣J. You take dummy's ♣K and set about drawing trumps. How should you continue?

After drawing trumps, you want to lead up to your spades. So arrange to be in dummy when you finish trumps. Play low to the ♡A, then the ♡K after West shows out, and finally play a low heart to dummy's ♡Q. (In general, you should play 5-5 fits so as to retain entries to *both* hands.)

Now you can lead a spade towards your hand, hoping to catch both the ♠Q and the ♠A onside to hold the set to down one.

Matchpoints, Neither vul.

53

♠ A 9 3   ♡ K Q 8 5 2   ◇ A 10 8 6   ♣ 6

WEST	NORTH	EAST	SOUTH
			1♡
2♣	dbl[1]	pass	?

1. Penalty double.

Don't pass. Bid 2◇. Partner's double of 2♣ is a suggestion (not a command) to defend 2♣. Pulling with a singleton or void is routine at a low level. Partner should *not* have something like

(a) ♠ J 5   ♡ 9 4 ◇ 7 3 2   ♣ K Q 10 9 8 4

At low levels, penalty doubles can prove profitable, and it's worth learning how to use them. However, bridge players were right to abandon them in favor of negative doubles as the hands for low-level penalty doubles seldom occur.

He should have something like

(b) ♠ K Q 8 6 2   ♡ 4   ◇ K 9 7 2   ♣ K 10 5

— a good hand short in your suit with about 11 HCP and three or four decent cards in overcaller's suit.

Why shouldn't partner double with hand (a)? After all, he figures to take seven tricks against 2♣ doubled facing a normal sound minimum opening like yours. That's a sound +300, isn't it?

The answer to that question is threefold. First, he'll seldom get a hand like (a) when an opponent overcalls 2♣. Second, he'll seldom get to defend against 2♣ doubled when he has that hand, as the opponents are likely to run to some other suit. Not only would partner be unhappy defending 2♠, he'd be unhappy defending 4♠. A penalty double of an overcall should be based not just on trumps, but on high cards and a willingness to defend against contracts to which the opponents may run. Third, partner need not double to get a good board if the overcall is less than sound (as it probably is when he has six strong trumps). For merely beating 2♣ two, without doubling, he will probably earn a top, since, at other tables (without the overcall), players with his cards may respond 1NT and then bid 3♣ over opener's 2◇ rebid, going minus when trumps split badly.

 54

Matchpoints, N-S vul.

♠ K Q J 9 6 2   ♡ 5   ◇ A 10   ♣ A J 10 8

WEST	NORTH	EAST	SOUTH
			1♠
3♡[1]	4♡[2]	5♡	pass[3]
pass	dbl	pass	?

1. Weak.
2. Strong spade raise.
3. Forcing pass.

Your pass in a forcing situation expresses doubt about the final contract. Partner assumes, tentatively, that your doubt is about whether to play 5♠ or defend against 5♡ doubled. However, pulling partner's double shows that your doubt is about something else. In this auction, that can only be about whether to play 5♠ or 6♠, the logic behind the expert consensus that "pass and pull is strong" in forcing situations.

Don't pass. Bid 5♠. This is your way of inviting slam; a direct 5♠ over East's 4♡ would have shown less slammish values. Had partner bid 5♠ instead of doubling, you would have carried on to 6♠.

Matchpoints, E-W vul.

♠ K Q 10 9 4 2 ♡ K Q 6 ◇ Q 10 3 ♣ 2

WEST	NORTH	EAST	SOUTH
			1♠
pass	2♠	dbl	pass
3♣	dbl	pass	?

Don't pass. Bid 3♠. Partner's double of 3♣ showed a maximum three-card raise with some length in — and defense against — clubs. Again, it was a *suggestion* for you to pass, not a command. (You might have bid 3♠ directly over East's double.)

IMPs, Both vul.

♠ A 8 6 5 3 ♡ Q 9 7 ◇ 4 ♣ A 9 5 2

WEST	NORTH	EAST	SOUTH
	1♡	pass	1♠
2◇	dbl	pass	?

Don't pass. Bid 3♡. That was your plan when you responded 1♠, and partner's *suggestion* to defend 2◇ doubled should not change your plan. You have unexpected shortness in the doubled suit and unexpected length in partner's suit: these are the two key features that should induce you to pull the double.

Matchpoints, E-W vul.

♠ A K ♡ J 2 ◇ J 8 3 2 ♣ Q 10 9 8 4

WEST	NORTH	EAST	SOUTH
	pass	1♠	pass
4♣[1]	dbl	4◇	pass
4♠	pass	pass	5♣
5♠	all pass		

1. Balanced forcing raise or splinter.

When you ask East for an explanation of the auction, she says she doesn't know which meaning West's 4♣ bid has. When you call the director, he rules that you're not entitled to any further explanation. Too bad! Regardless, what should you lead?

How often do you respond 3NT to partner's 1♠ opening? And how useful is it to do so? Recall the discussion on page 36 of how to respond to a 1♠ opening with

♠ J 3 ♡ K Q 7 ◇ Q J 10 4 ♣ A K 8 6

The "standard" 3NT response gets in the way of the search for a good fit in which slam can be made. I've long advocated getting rid of it. When a double-jump response of 3NT is incorporated in the splinter system, responder can distinguish between singletons and voids. If you use

Surrogate Splinters, making a double-jump response just *under your singleton* (which reduces the opponents' ability to make lead-directing doubles), then you can use a 3NT response to 1♠ (and similarly a 3♠ response to 1♡) to show an unspecified void, and follow (if partner "relays" with the cheapest bid to ask where) by bidding just *over your void.* I call this convention *Under-and-Over Splinters.*

Lead the ♠K. This cuts down on dummy's ruffing power and prevents a strip-and-throw-in against you later. If instead you lead a club, and declarer attacks spades, cash the ace after taking the king — for exactly the same reasons.

Notice that West's artificial raise (which turns out to have been a splinter) let partner make a lead-directing double that enabled you to find a profitable save and push the opponents one level higher.

58

Matchpoints, E-W vul.

NORTH (dummy)
♠ J
♡ A J 10 7 2
◇ A 7 6
♣ K 7 4 2

WEST (you)
♠ Q 10 6 4
♡ K 4
◇ K Q 10 3
♣ 8 6 5

WEST	NORTH	EAST	SOUTH
			1♣
pass	1♡	pass	1♠
pass	2◇ [1]	pass	2NT
pass	3♣	pass	3NT
all pass			

1. Artificial force.

You lead the ◇K, which holds, as partner plays the ◇4 and declarer follows with the deuce. What now?

Partner's low diamond denies the jack, so you'd better shift. The safest shift is to clubs, which will almost never cost a trick. The only way it can cost is if declarer has ♣AJ10x and would otherwise play clubs by starting with the ace and letting the jack or ten ride. However, that won't happen if declarer is at all competent, for he can't afford to let partner in to continue diamonds, so he'll finesse partner for the ♣Q anyway.

A spade shift is more dangerous. A low spade is the worst, for it lets dummy's jack score needlessly when declarer has ♠AKxx. The ♠Q isn't as bad, but it's still risky, for it lets declarer set up an extra spade trick when he has good spade spots.

NORTH (dummy)
♠ A K 9 7 6
♡ 10 2
◇ A 6 5 4
♣ A 2

EAST (you)
♠ 10 4 3 2
♡ K Q 7 4
◇ Q J 10 2
♣ 4

WEST	NORTH	EAST	SOUTH
			pass
pass	1♠	pass	2♣
pass	2◇	pass	2NT
pass	3NT	all pass	

Partner leads the ◇9 and dummy plays low. What should you play?

Play the ◇2. Save all your honors to be able to beat dummy's spots. Partner doesn't need a signal from you. He will learn all he wants to know about the diamond suit when his ◇9 holds the trick or forces declarer's ◇K.

Declarer, a poor player, takes the ◇K and leads the ♣J. It is covered by partner's ♣Q and taken by dummy's ♣A. On the next club, you discard the ♡7; declarer takes the ♣K (partner following with the ♣8) and then abandons the suit. What do you think partner has in clubs?

You should be able to read partner for ♣Q1098. You can trust partner not to have covered the ♣J without excellent club spots, but you cannot trust the opposing declarer to have played clubs sensibly holding ♣KJ7653. Trust partner more than the opponents.

Next, declarer leads the ♠J. Partner covers with the ♠Q and dummy's ♠K wins. What do you play on the next spade lead, the ♠6 from dummy?

You'd better play low. If declarer has two spades (he's very unlikely to have three on the auction), his second spade can be either the ♠5 or the ♠8. If it's the ♠8, he has just blocked the suit, holding himself to three spade tricks rather than four, and taking your ♠10 would unblock it for him. If it's the ♠5, then partner has the ♠8 and will win the trick if you play low, holding declarer to *two* spade tricks; if you

When declarer has bid notrump naturally, you can count his HCP with considerable precision, and should do so routinely. Often that will enable you to place partner with a particular ace, king, queen, or even jack.

play the ♠10, you will give declarer *four* spade tricks. But might not it be necessary to get in quickly to cash some hearts?

You'll know it isn't necessary if you count declarer's high card points. He has 8 HCP in the three suits other than hearts: the ◇K, the ♣J, the ♣K and the ♠J. For his 2NT rebid, he needs 11 to 12 HCP. He *must* have the ♡A (and doesn't have the ♡J because that would give him 13 HCP); that being the case, there is no rush to play hearts.

60

Matchpoints, E-W vul.

♠ A K 2   ♡ 3   ◇ K Q 9 5 4 3 2   ♣ J 4

WEST	NORTH	EAST	SOUTH
	pass	pass	1◇
pass	1♡	pass	2◇
pass	3◇	pass	?

Though you can expect to have a reasonable shot at making 5◇, you shouldn't bid it. It costs nothing to bid 3♠ "on the way" to 5◇, showing where your stuff is and giving partner, who will know you are worried about clubs, a chance to bid 3NT with a suitable hand.

Would it still be right to bid 3♠ if you were playing IMPs rather than matchpoints?

Yes. You might have only ten tricks in a diamond contract while partner has nine tricks in 3NT — for example, on the layout below if West leads a club.

However, you jumped straight to 5◇.

NORTH (dummy)
♠ 7
♡ K Q 6 5 4
◇ J 10 8
♣ A 9 8 2

☐

SOUTH (you)
♠ A K 2
♡ 3
◇ K Q 9 5 4 3 2
♣ J 4

WEST	NORTH	EAST	SOUTH
	pass	pass	1◇
pass	1♡	pass	2◇
pass	3◇	pass	5◇
all pass			

West leads the ♠J — luckily for you, as a club lead would set up a third trick for the defenders before you could set up a heart trick for a club discard. You take the ♠A and correctly lead the ♡3 towards dummy, ensuring the contract. North plays low, and dummy's ♡Q wins. What now?

Why not try for an overtrick? An overtrick will let you beat the North-South pairs who reach 3NT and make nine tricks. Lead a low heart from dummy and ruff it. Then lead a low diamond towards dummy: West will play low and East will take dummy's ◇10 with the ◇A. Suppose East shifts to clubs and West's club honor knocks out dummy's ace. You can ruff a second heart high, cross to dummy's ◇8 and ruff a third heart. Next the ♠K, a spade ruff, and now the ♡K will be good for a discard of your last club — unless West, who ducked the first heart and obviously has the ♡A, started with *five* hearts.

Leading the ♡K from dummy before the ♡A appears cannot possibly gain.

Matchpoints, Neither vul.

61

NORTH (dummy)
♠ K Q 3
♡ Q
◇ A K Q 9 6 3
♣ 4 3 2

EAST (you)
♠ 5
♡ A 9 8 3
◇ J 7 5 4 2
♣ K Q 5

WEST	NORTH	EAST	SOUTH
		pass	pass
pass	1◇	pass	1♠
pass	3◇	pass	3♠
pass	4♠	all pass	

Partner leads the ♣10 to your ♣Q and declarer's ♣A. Declarer plays the ♠2 to partner's ♠9 and dummy's ♠Q. He then cashes two top diamonds to discard the ♣7 and the ♣J from his hand. Now comes the ♡Q. Should you take the ♡A?

Not if you're counting the hand. Declarer has shown up with ♣AJ7 and a void in diamonds. With seven spades to the ace, he'd have opened the bidding. So give him ace-*sixth* of spades. He can't have the ♡K, but he can have

♠ A 10 7 6 4 2 ♡ J 10 5 4 ◊ — ♣ A J 7

(as he does), and taking your ♡A sets up a ruffing finesse against partner's ♡K.

Might declarer have had the ♡K *instead of* the ♠A? Not likely on the auction, but if so, partner might well have risen with the ♠A to keep declarer from reaching dummy to discard clubs on dummy's diamonds.

Ducking dummy's ♡Q isn't a sure thing, but the odds favor it greatly.

62

Your opponents in this next problem are playing a fancy 2◊ opening called the *Mexican Two Diamonds*, with a complex set of responses and continuations designed to make the strong hand declarer. As it happens, these responses aren't quite fancy enough to achieve that purpose on this deal.

Matchpoints, Both vul.

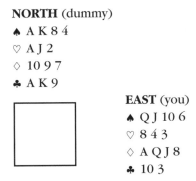

NORTH (dummy)
♠ A K 8 4
♡ A J 2
◊ 10 9 7
♣ A K 9

EAST (you)
♠ Q J 10 6
♡ 8 4 3
◊ A Q J 8
♣ 10 3

WEST	NORTH	EAST	SOUTH	
			pass	1. Balanced 19-21 HCP.
pass	2◇[1]	pass	2♠[2]	2. Puppet to 2NT.
pass	2NT	pass	3♣[3]	3. "Puppet" Stayman.
pass	3◇[4]	pass	3♡[5]	4. 1 or 2 *four-card* majors.
pass	3♠	pass	4♠	5. Spades but not hearts.
all pass				

Partner leads the ♣Q to dummy's ♣K. Plan the defense.

No, no, you mustn't drop the ♣10 under dummy's ♣K. That sets up a finesse against partner's ♣J. Preserve useful spot cards that can keep declarer's and dummy's lower spot cards (in this case, dummy's ♣9) from taking tricks. Signals, no matter what kind you and your partner use, must take a back seat to trick preservation.

If you follow with the ♣3, your partner will know that you have the ♣10 when you get in and play it, or when declarer doesn't lead a club to finesse against the ♣J. If partner sees the ♣2, either because it is in his hand or because declarer plays it, partner will know that you have ♣103 precisely, else you'd have played a higher club on the first trick. What "signal" could give partner more information about your club holding than that?

Matchpoints, Neither vul.

63

NORTH (dummy)
♠ 4 2
♡ J 8 7
◇ A 5 2
♣ J 10 9 5 3

EAST (you)
♠ A K 7
♡ A K 4 3
◇ Q 10 4 3
♣ 7 4

WEST	NORTH	EAST	SOUTH	
	pass	1NT[1]	2♠[2]	1. 15-17 HCP.
all pass				2. Spades and an unspecified minor.

Partner leads the ♡2. You take the ♡K and the ♡A as declarer follows with the ♡9 and the ♡10. What now?

Declarer's Hamilton 2♠ doesn't reveal which minor he has. It's more likely to be clubs than diamonds, however. In diamonds only the king and the jack are unseen, while in clubs the top three honors are missing. Declarer needs substantial high-card strength in his minor to justify coming in with a spade suit that is at best ♠QJ10xx.

Regardless, it can't be right to attack clubs: if declarer has losing clubs, dummy has nothing on which to discard them.

You should simply continue hearts, tapping declarer, hoping to run him out of trumps before he can establish his minor side-suit. Tapping the long hand is usually good defensive strategy. A shift to clubs, declarer's side suit, would lose timing on the hand and may give declarer the contract.

There's another danger in shifting to clubs: you probably wouldn't lead from the ♣K or ♣Q, so declarer may pick off partner's possible singleton ♣K or doubleton ♣Q, when otherwise he was about to finesse you, the 1NT opener, for any missing club honor.

64

Matchpoints, N-S vul.

NORTH (dummy)
♠ 10 6
♡ J 9 8 3
◊ Q 9 8 7 2
♣ J 8

SOUTH (you)
♠ A Q 3
♡ A K 5 4
◊ A 4 3
♣ 10 7 5

WEST	NORTH	EAST	SOUTH
			1NT[1]
pass	pass	2♣[2]	pass
2◊[3]	dbl	2♠	3◊
all pass			

1. 15-17 HCP.
2. Unspecified one-suiter.
3. "Which suit?"

West leads the ♠J and East follows small. You win with the ♠Q, and cash the ◊A, catching West's ◊5 and East's ◊10. You continue with the ♢3, and West follows with the ♢6. What should you play from dummy?

This situation is called "Restricted Choice", which says that in the absence of information to the contrary, declarer should *not* play a defender for both of two equivalent cards. However, you need not mess with the general theory behind it. Instead you can consider the holdings for East in which your play makes a difference. (If East has ♢KJ10, your play from dummy makes no difference.)

There are three such holdings: a) ♢K10, b) ♢J10, and c) ♢10. If you knew that East would *always* follow with the ten from ♢J10 (never falsecarding the jack), the odds would be about 2-to-1 in favor of inserting dummy's ♢7, ♢8 or ♢9, which works against (a) and (c). Playing dummy's ♢Q only works against (b).

"Restricted Choice" takes into account that with (a) and (c) East has *no choice* but to follow to your ♢A with the ♢10, but with (b) he can play either the ♢10 or ♢J randomly. Suppose that on six occasions you have this combination to play, and (a), (b) and (c) occur equally often (twice each). On one occasion — *one* of the two times (b) occurs — East will falsecard the ♢J, leaving only *five* occasions on which he plays the ♢10. The two times East has (a), and the two times East has (c) — a total of *four* times — playing *low* from dummy works. Only the one time that East has (b) *and doesn't falsecard* will playing dummy's ♢Q work. Thus the odds are about 4-to-1, not 2-to-1, in favor of playing low from dummy.

Suppose you make the mistake of playing dummy's ♢Q and East shows out. Now you know you have two trump losers, so abandoning trumps, you start the hearts. How should you play them?

Play from the top — the ♡A and the ♡K. The alternative, leading dummy's ♡J in an effort to "smother" West's possible ♡10, requires West to have the ♡10 singleton (one case) or doubleton (three cases) — four holdings in all. Playing hearts from the top works when *either* defender has the ♡Q singleton (two cases) or doubleton (eight cases, because ♡Q10 doubleton is included) — ten holdings in all. Thus the odds favor the straightforward play by about 10-to-4.

You don't have to be an expert mathematician or memorize charts of probabilities to be able to go with the odds on most bridge problems. Merely *counting specific holdings* for which one play works and the other fails will almost always point you to the better play.

While it's nice to have ways to show two-suiters after an opponent opens 1NT, it's more important to have ways to show one-suiters *immediately*, for one-suiters are much more common than two-suiters. I estimate that for every six times you'll have a specific two-suiter, you'll have a specific one-suiter 16 times. A good Notrump Defense caters primarily to frequent hand-types, and only secondarily to less frequent ones.

If you play Hamilton, keep track of the number of times you overcall 2♣ and 2♠. I'd guess that you'll overcall 2♣ five times as often as 2♠.

If you play DONT, an increasingly popular Notrump Defense that uses *double* artificially to show an unspecified one-suited hand while 2♣, 2♢ and 2♡ show two-suiters (the suit bid being the lower of the two), I'd guess that you'll double ten times as often as you'll overcall 2♡.

Matchpoints, Neither vul.

NORTH (dummy)
♠ 6 5
♡ J 6 3 2
◇ A 10 2
♣ K 10 8 6

EAST (you)
♠ A 9 3
♡ 5 4
◇ 9 7 6 4
♣ Q J 5 4

WEST	NORTH	EAST	SOUTH
			1♡
2♠[1]	3♡	pass	4♡
all pass			

1. Weak Jump Overcall.

Partner leads the ♠Q and your ♠A drops declarer's ♠K. What now?

There is no reason to do anything except return the ♠9. Passive defense is usually best when no suit threatens in dummy. A trump return is pointless when there is nothing to be ruffed in dummy. A diamond return risks pickling partner's possible ◇Q.

How about a trump shift? Won't that be passive too? No. Declarer, with ♡AK10xx, will figure that you wouldn't lead from the queen and he'll drop partner's doubleton queen. However, if you don't shift to a trump, a competent declarer will most likely play your partner, who has preempted with six or seven spades, for a singleton heart and finesse trumps through you.

 66

Matchpoints, N-S vul.

NORTH (dummy)
♠ K 10 7 2
♡ Q 8
◇ Q J 5
♣ Q 10 8 3

WEST (you)
♠ A 4 3
♡ J 6 5 3
◇ 9 6
♣ A K 7 2

WEST	NORTH	EAST	SOUTH
		pass	1♠
pass	3♠[1]	all pass	

1. Limit raise.

You lead the ♣K. Partner follows with the ♣4, a discouraging card. You shift to the ◇9, and partner covers dummy's ◇J with the ◇K. Declarer wins with the ◇A and leads the ♠J. You duck correctly, in case partner has a singleton ♠Q, but partner follows with the ♠9. Then declarer leads a low spade. What now?

Now you must rise with the ♠A. A defender should almost never leave himself with the high trump when his partner has none. If you duck, declarer will crossruff, getting two ruffs in dummy instead of one.

Suppose you take the ♠A on the second round. What's your best exit?

Though either a heart shift or a diamond continuation may work, neither is safe. A heart shift may blow a trick very easily: partner may have the ♡K without the ♡10. A diamond continuation may blow a trick by helping declarer pick up partner's ◇8. Your only safe exit is your third trump. That's another reason for taking the ♠A on the second round.

As a defender, be on guard against leaving yourself with the master trump: if you don't cash it when the opportunity arises, you may be thrown in with it later and find yourself without a good exit.

Matchpoints, N-S vul.

♠ — ♡ 10 8 5 2 ◇ A K Q J 9 8 5 2 ♣ 6

WEST	NORTH	EAST	SOUTH
		1♣	?

Bid 4◇. Don't worry about having four hearts. Worry more about the opponents finding a spade fit. If partner has four or five hearts, you're still unlikely to get together in hearts before the opponents get together in spades. Moreover, if by some miracle you do find a heart fit, you probably belong in diamonds anyway, lest your diamonds go to waste in a heart contract as the opponents tap dummy in a black suit.

However, you bid only 1◇, leading to this auction:

WEST	NORTH	EAST	SOUTH
		1♣	1◇ (!)
2♣	2♠[1]	3♣	3◇
4♣	pass	pass	?

1. Non-forcing, constructive.

Pass. You can't afford to bid 4◇ now when it has no preemptive effect. What tricks do you have except for your eight diamond tricks? Do you really want to risk down two (*not* doubled) or down one doubled against the opponents' partscore by bidding 4◇? Do you expect to push them to 5♣ when either opponent could have bid 5♣ voluntarily at his previous turn, but didn't? And if you do push them to 5♣, how do you expect to beat them? You'll be lucky to take *one* trick on defense.

Here's that principle again: after you've made a mistake (and I think your failure to bid 4◇ at your first turn qualifies), *do nothing* to try to catch up. *Assume that your bad call has turned out well.* Here it probably *has* turned out well. The spade suit of which you had reason to be afraid at your first turn belongs to partner, not to responder, and the opponents didn't bid the game you had reason to fear. While others may go down two, -200, with your cards, you may score -150, -130 or +50 thanks to your gross underbid at your first turn.

That explains Support Doubles roughly, but leaves many questions unanswered. I answered most of those questions in a *Bridge World* article called *Twenty Questions*, but I wouldn't swear that I covered everything. As with many conventions, Support Doubles are subject to abuse and confusion. I recommend them only for regular expert partners who have discussed them thoroughly.

As part of the modern style of avoiding low-level penalty doubles, many pairs play "Support Doubles". After a 1♡ or 1♠ response and a bid by the next player that is lower than the single raise of that response, a Support Double by opener shows a *three-card raise* of responder's major (and may temporarily conceal substantial extra values). This allows an ordinary single raise to show *four*-card support.

Some of my students insist on playing Support Doubles, which once led to the following problem.

Matchpoints, Neither vul.

♠ K 6 4 2   ♡ Q   ◇ K Q 3   ♣ A K 10 8 4

WEST	NORTH	EAST	SOUTH
			1♣
pass	1◇	2♡[1]	?

1. Weak Jump Overcall.

You and your partner play Support Doubles. However, they do not apply over jump overcalls. A double in this auction is a penalty double pure and simple, appropriate for a hand like

♠ K 4 2   ♡ Q 10 8 7   ◇ A   ♣ A K 10 8 4

Although you cannot make a Support Double on your hand, under pressure of competition you should do something. Bid 2♠, which shows a hand about as good as the one you have. You can't afford to wait for a hand strong enough for a jump shift if East had passed before you will bid 2♠ *without a jump* when the opponents are in the auction.

Matchpoints, Both vul.

NORTH (dummy)
♠ 10 2
♡ Q 9 6 2
◇ K Q 3
♣ A J 9 6

EAST (you)
♠ A J 9 6 5 3
♡ A K
◇ 7 6
♣ K 8 7

WEST	NORTH	EAST	SOUTH
pass	1♣	1♠	pass
pass	dbl	pass	1NT
all pass			

Partner leads the ♠4. What holdings can that come from, and what should you play?

Partner cannot be leading from a doubleton (there is no lower spade spot outstanding) so only from one or three. Judging from the auction, partner most likely has a singleton.

Playing the ♠A followed by the ♠J can't be right. Not only does it give you no chance to set up your ♠9 as a trick, it also relinquishes control of the suit and leads partner to believe that you have ♠AJ98xx and that your spades will soon be ready to roll. There is no bonus in bridge for taking your tricks early instead of late. Your best play is the ♠9. That will force declarer to use a dummy entry to lead up to his second spade honor. The ♠9 at Trick 1 is not only technically correct but also informs partner immediately that you don't have the ♠8.

Matchpoints, N-S vul.

♠ Q 7 6 5   ♡ Q 10 8   ◇ Q J 6   ♣ A K 3

WEST	. NORTH	EAST	SOUTH
	1◇	pass	?

When playing *standard* 2NT responses to minor-suit openings (13-15 HCP, no four-card major), the normal bid with your hand is 1♠. Notrumps can wait (you can always bid 3NT next turn).

However, this is a great hand on which to take a sensible calculated matchpoint gamble. With a 4-3-3-3 hand, weak spades, and (this is key) three queens (notrumpish values), you have much to gain by ignoring your four-card spade suit entirely. If partner has a balanced hand and four spades with you, you'll get to 3NT while the field plays in 4♠. It's a reasonable gamble that you'll take the same number of tricks in notrump as in spades. That's one way you can gain (though loss is possible). The other way is by concealment of your four spades, which may attract a more favorable opening lead than you'd otherwise receive, or cause the defenders to go wrong later in the play.

The best matchpoint strategy is usually to make "normal" calls and profit when opponents — and those who hold your cards at other tables — make errors. Once in a while, however, you can score bidding coups by deviating from "normal" action. This looks like a good time to try it, but not with an intolerant partner.

71

Matchpoints, E-W vul.

♠ K 6 5   ♡ 10 8 7 6 2   ◇ A 9 6 3   ♣ 3

WEST	NORTH	EAST	SOUTH
		pass	pass
1◇	pass	1♠	pass
pass	dbl	pass	2♡
2♠	3♡	pass	?

A player who "balances" aims to push the opponents one higher. When he does, the partnership's job is done. That's true, *if* partner is merely balancing and you don't have extremely pleasant surprises waiting for him. What about partner's bidding here?

Partner is not "merely balancing"; if he were, he would surely not raise your 2♡ to 3♡ voluntarily. Rather, he has made a takeout double of spades. He couldn't enter over 1◇, since he lacked support for spades and had no good suit of his own to bid. Bid 4♡. The ♠K may turn out to be worth little, but your fifth heart and your ◇A are wonderful surprises for partner, and your singleton club may be useful too.

Matchpoints, Both vul.

72

♠ A Q 6 5 3   ♡ 9   ◇ Q 8 7 6 5   ♣ 9 2

WEST	NORTH	EAST	SOUTH
			pass
1♡	pass	2♡	?

Having limited your hand by failure to open either 1♠ or (a weak) 2♠ as dealer, you should bid 2♠ now. This "pre-balancing" overcall has three things going for it: (1) the hand may be yours for spades; (2) you may be able to push your opponents to 3♡; (3) a spade lead will usually be good for the defense. The theory of pre-balancing is that a player with *distributional* values — shortness in the opponents' suit — should strive to enter.

Could 2♠ prove disastrous? Absolutely! But it's a good matchpoint gamble.

Matchpoints, E-W vul.

NORTH (dummy)
♠ K 8
♡ K 5 4
◇ J 5
♣ Q 9 7 5 4 2

EAST (you)
♠ 9 6 2
♡ Q 7 3 2
◇ K Q 9 8
♣ J 6

WEST	NORTH	EAST	SOUTH
			1♡
pass	2♡	pass	2♠
pass	4♡	all pass	

Partner leads the ◇6. Dummy plays the ◇5 and your ◇Q holds the trick, as declarer plays the ◇2. What now?

Clearly declarer has the ◇A, and partner must have the ◇10 else declarer would have won the first trick. Simply continue with a diamond; because you have the ◇9, you should return the ◇K, but if you didn't, a low one would do. From your perpective, partner's lead marks him with ◇1076. From declarer's perspective, however, partner could easily have ◇K1076, so declarer wouldn't let a low diamond ride to dummy's jack.

The purpose of returning a diamond is twofold. First, it prepares to tap dummy, thus protecting your ♡Q against a declarer who might otherwise finesse against it twice. Second, it does not break a new suit dangerously. A spade shift, for example, would let declarer (who has ♠Q105) make a second spade trick.

NORTH (dummy)
♠ K 8
♡ K J 10 6
◇ A Q 10 5
♣ 10 7 3

WEST (you)
♠ 7 4 3
♡ A 9
◇ 9 8 4 2
♣ K Q 4 2

WEST	NORTH	EAST	SOUTH
pass	1◇	pass	1♠
pass	1NT[1]	pass	3♠[2]
pass	4♠	all pass	

1. 12-14 HCP.
2. Invitational.

You lead the ♣K. Suppose partner follows with the ♣5 and declarer plays the ♣6. What should you play next?

You should continue with the ♣2. Partner is marked with the ♣A or the ♣J. If declarer had both missing club honors, he would have taken the ♣A and established a second club trick "by force" (because of dummy's ♣10).

When you lead the ♣2 next, partner takes the ace and returns a third club to your ♣Q as declarer follows. What now?

You'd better cash the ♡A before it gets away, as dummy's diamonds are menacing. If declarer has running spades and the ◇Kx or better, he has ten tricks as soon as he gains the lead. Down one should be a tie for top: the opponents have overbid, and most other East-West pairs figure to be -140 (or worse, if they misdefend).

Matchpoints, N-S vul.

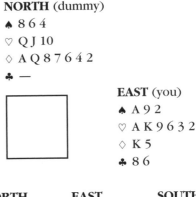

NORTH (dummy)
♠ 8 6 4
♡ Q J 10
◇ A Q 8 7 6 4 2
♣ —

EAST (you)
♠ A 9 2
♡ A K 9 6 3 2
◇ K 5
♣ 8 6

WEST	NORTH	EAST	SOUTH
		1♡	1♠
pass	4♠	pass	pass
5♣	5♠	all pass	

Partner leads the ♡5. You take the ♡K and the ♡A as declarer follows twice and partner plays the ♡4. You want to continue with a third heart to kill dummy's high heart, while hoping partner can overruff declarer. Which heart shall it be?

When you're giving partner a ruff, it's a suit-preference situation. You have four heart spots. So you can play the ♡2 to request a club shift, the ♡9 to request a diamond shift, the ♡6 or ♡3 to ask partner to use his judgment.

You play the ♡9, and partner overruffs declarer's ♠3 with the ♠J.

Guided by your request for a diamond shift and thinking that you may be void, partner shifts to the ◇J. Dummy's ◇A wins and declarer ruffs a diamond with the ♠5 as partner drops the ◇10. Declarer ruffs a club in dummy and then plays dummy's high ◇Q. What should you play now?

Don't play the the ♠A, which would shorten your own trumps while letting declarer discard a losing club. The ♠2 is acceptable, and so is your second club, which allows you to overruff dummy with the ♠9 on the second club lead and then play the ♠A and ♠2 to keep dummy from ruffing another club.

♠ A 8 5   ♡ K 9 3   ◇ Q 5 4   ♣ K 9 8 7

WEST	NORTH	EAST	SOUTH
pass	1♣	pass	?

A standard 2NT response shows a balanced 13-15 HCP. You have a poorish 12 HCP (3-3-3-4, no tens). With your present partner, you play limit minor raises, so you can bid 3♣.

If you played forcing jump raises, you would have to "manufacture" a 1◇ response with the intention of bidding 3♣ next turn.

If you played Inverted Minor Raises, you could raise to 2♣. This seems to be a hand on which Inverted Minors would work well, but would they?

I don't think so. Having made an Inverted 2♣ raise, would you know whether to pass or bid 3NT over partner's possible 2NT rebid next? You stretch to respond a 13-15 HCP 2NT, and now you must declare 3NT after partner raises to game:

NORTH (dummy)
♠ Q J 10 9
♡ J 5
◇ K 9
♣ A Q J 6 3

SOUTH (you)
♠ A 8 5
♡ K 9 3
◇ Q 5 4
♣ K 9 8 7

Incidentally, some pairs play *non-forcing* (11-12 HCP) 2NT responses to minor-suit openings. There is a reason for this treatment when the opening bid is 1◇, as otherwise responder might have to bid a very awkward 2♣. However, I can see no reason for playing a 2NT response to 1♣ as non-forcing (except for the fact that the ACBL convention card, whether by design or thoughtlessness, provides only one box to check for responses to *both* minors).

If you play a non-forcing 2NT response to 1♣, how do you think it would work here? Not well, I imagine. Square hands are not good for notrump; they are merely not as bad for notrump as they are for suit contracts, and even in notrump contracts it is often better for the partner with the square hand to be dummy than declarer.

West leads the ♠3. Dummy's ♠9 wins as East follows with the ♠4. You continue with dummy's ♠Q, on which East discards a low diamond. What now?

You can't avoid a spade loser. If you take the ♠A now, you'll have to feed West a trick with his king to set up a third spade trick anyway, and he'll have a chance to lead a fourth spade to set up a fifth spade for himself. If you duck, however, you'll force West to take the ♠K now, and you'll remain with a spade stopper even if he plays a third spade to dislodge your ace. Force West to take the ♠K while you still have ample control of the suit.

Taking the ♠A now and discontinuing spades leaves you one trick short of the nine tricks you can ensure by ducking.

77

Matchpoints, N-S vul.

♠ K Q J 7 3 ♡ J 10 4 2 ♢ K 6 3 ♣ 8

WEST	NORTH	EAST	SOUTH
			pass
pass	1♣	pass	1♠
pass	2♣	pass	2♡
pass	3♣	pass	?

Notrump is not the place for misfits unless you have a superabundance of high cards. On partscore deals, your primary objective should be to make your contract; your secondary objective should be to score +110 or more, as that will be better than the +50 or +100 others may obtain with your cards against opponents who compete and go down.

Pass. Your 2♡ at your second turn was already slightly optimistic. Partner's 3♣ bid doesn't make your hand any better. 3NT should be based on

♠ Q J 9 7 3 ♡ J 10 9 2 ♢ A 6 ♣ K 8

or similar, a hand with enough help in clubs to make you think that partner's clubs will run. Partner's sequence does not show solid clubs. Your misfit for clubs should discourage you from bidding again. In 3NT, you'd need some luck to go down only one.

78

Matchpoints, Both vul.

NORTH (dummy)
♠ 9 6 5
♡ 7 3
♢ J 5 3
♣ A 7 4 3 2

WEST (you)
♠ K Q 10
♡ K Q 4
♢ Q 7 6 4 2
♣ Q 5

WEST	NORTH	EAST	SOUTH
		pass	1NT[1]
all pass			

1. 15-17 HCP.

You lead the ◇4 and declarer takes partner's ◇8 with the ◇K. Do you know the entire layout of the diamond suit yet?

Declarer has ◇AK. Partner has ◇1098, unless declarer has ◇AK109 and is good enough to have taken pains to preserve dummy's ◇J as an entry. (Nah, this declarer isn't that good.)

Declarer leads the ♡10 to Trick 2. You win with the ♡Q and partner follows with the ♡5. You continue with the ◇2 and partner plays the ◇10 as declarer takes the ◇A perforce. You note correctly that partner, who started with ◇1098, is showing a preference for spades rather than clubs. Now declarer plays the ace and another heart to your king, discarding a club from dummy; partner follows with the ♡6 and the ♡9.

You run off three diamond tricks. Declarer discards the ♠2 on the first. On the next two, partner discards the ♣6 and the ♠J in that order; declarer discards the ♠3 and ♠7. What should you lead in this end-position?

NORTH (dummy)
♠ 9 6 5
♡ —
◇ —
♣ A 7

WEST (you)
♠ K Q 10
♡ —
◇ —
♣ Q 5

By now, declarer has turned up with

♠ x x x   ♡ A J 10 x x   ◇ A K   ♣ ? ? ?

Partner has signaled the ♠A and has kept another spade. Declarer surely has the ♣K for his 15-17 HCP notrump. You have three spade tricks coming. Make sure you get them by shifting to the ♠10. If instead you lead the king, partner should overtake and return his last spade, but will he? Don't give partner a chance to go wrong by blocking the suit.

Matchpoints, E-W vul.

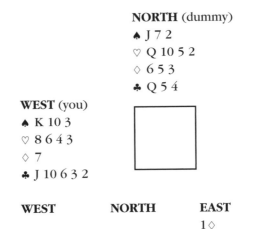

NORTH (dummy)
♠ J 7 2
♡ Q 10 5 2
◊ 6 5 3
♣ Q 5 4

WEST (you)
♠ K 10 3
♡ 8 6 4 3
◊ 7
♣ J 10 6 3 2

WEST	NORTH	EAST	SOUTH
		1◊	1NT

all pass

You lead the ◊7 of diamonds. Partner wins with the ◊K and then shifts to the ♠4. Declarer follows with the ♠6 and you take your king. What now?

    Although a club lead would have been good at the start, it's too late to shift to clubs after your outside entry is gone. Besides, if partner didn't welcome a spade return he'd have led a high spade spot, not his lowest. Continue with the ♠10 to set up more spade tricks for your side. A club shift now gives declarer time to get his diamonds rolling before partner's spades can be established and cashed.

80

Matchpoints, Both vul.

♠ Q 8 ♡ K Q 7 5 ◊ A Q 9 7 4 2 ♣ Q

WEST	NORTH	EAST	SOUTH
pass	1♡	pass	?

More than any other jump shift, the Fit Jump Shift is the royal road to slam.

Bid 3◊, a Type "F" (Fit) jump shift. Then you can bid 4♡ next turn and leave the rest to partner. If you start with 2◊ and bid 4♡ next, partner will never know you have such a fine supporting hand. If you start with 2◊ and mess around with forcing bids in the black suits, partner will have no idea what you have; you'll probably wind up overbidding because you won't have strutted your stuff early on.

Matchpoints, E-W vul.

♠ K J 6 2   ♡ K 10 4   ◇ K J 10   ♣ 9 8 4

WEST	NORTH	EAST	SOUTH
		pass	pass
pass	1♣	1◇	?

Bid 1♠, whether you play negative doubles or not. A negative double of 1◇ shows *both* majors (the only negative double that does).

Bridge theorists have invented a number of ways to cope with intervening overcalls after a 1NT opening. The most popular is called *Lebensohl* (even though nobody has ever met a person with that name). The main purpose of Lebensohl is to distinguish different grades of responding hands at the three-level. To achieve this purpose, Lebensohl uses an artificial 2NT response that asks opener to bid 3♣ but does not promise clubs.

If you play Lebensohl, all three-level bids are game-forcing, even three of an unbid minor (which is not forcing for pairs that do not play Lebensohl). To compete in clubs without forcing, responder bids a Lebensohl 2NT and then passes opener's 3♣. To compete in some other unbid suit without forcing, responder bids a Lebensohl 2NT and then bids his suit. However, if he could have bid that suit at the two-level, his 2NT-mediated bid of the suit invites game.

A secondary purpose of Lebensohl is to distinguish responding hands that have stoppers in overcaller's suit from those that do not. Most Lebensohl users play that a 2NT-mediated 3NT (or Stayman-like cuebid of overcaller's suit) confirms a stopper in overcaller's suit, but a direct 3NT or cuebid denies one. Some have the opposite agreement, so you must discuss with each partner which version you are playing, and mark your convention card accordingly. You must also discuss whether Lebensohl applies when the overcall does not identify overcaller's suit or suits; it's sensible to play that Lebensohl applies only *after* an overcaller has shown a particular suit.

Should you play Lebensohl? There are fancier and better conventions that serve the same purposes and more, but Lebensohl is much better than nothing. One caveat: you should not play Lebensohl unless you are capable of alerting and explaining the bids it involves clearly and accurately enough for even the most inexperienced and unsophisticated opponents to understand.

Matchpoints, N-S vul.

♠ K 8 5   ♡ A 6 3   ♢ Q 9   ♣ A K 10 7 2

WEST	NORTH	EAST	SOUTH
			1NT[1]
2♡	dbl[2]	3♡	pass
pass	3♠	pass	?

1. 15-17 HCP.
2. Negative double (a non-standard use thereof).

Having a non-standard agreement to play negative doubles even when the opening bid is 1NT, partner has chosen to make one, despite the availability of Lebensohl.

Look at the bids that partner could have made at his first turn: 3♠ (forcing); 2NT (Lebensohl) followed by 3♠ (highly invitational); 2♠ (mildly constructive, for West's overcall took you off the 1NT hook). Instead he made a negative double.

So, what can partner have for 3♠ in this sequence?

He likely has a moderate 5-1-4-3 or 5-1-3-4 hand with mediocre spades and an unwillingness to sell out to 3♡ at matchpoints. With a hand good enough to force, partner would have jumped to 3♠ initially. With a hand good enough to invite game, he would have bid a Lebensohl-mediated 3♠.

You have two reasonable calls. Four spades is not one of them. Pass or bid 4♣ (certainly right at IMPs, and perhaps right at matchpoints too). Your opponents will be leading hearts, and clubs figure to play better than spades, even one level higher, because you'll be taking ruffs in the hand with the short trumps.

By the way, here are two other auctions that might occur on the same board:

(a)

WEST	NORTH	EAST	SOUTH
			1NT
2♡	2♠	3♡	3♠
all pass			

(b)

WEST	NORTH	EAST	SOUTH
			1NT
2♣[1]	2♠	all pass	

1. Unspecified one-suiter.

Auction (a) will occur at tables where North and South do not play the very unusual negative doubles of two-level overcalls following a 1NT opening.

Auction (b) will occur at tables where East and West play Hamilton; North will buy the contract for 2♠, unless North and South play "system on" over 2♣ overcalls, in which case North will bid 2♡ as a "transfer" to spades, East will get a chance to double 2♡ and West will be able to bid 3♡.

Matchpoints, Both vul.

West (you)
♠ A 6   ♡ A Q J 7 2   ◇ A 5   ♣ Q J 5 4

WEST	NORTH	EAST	SOUTH
1♡	pass	1♠	2◇
3♣	dbl	redbl	3◇
pass	pass	4♡	pass
pass	5◇	dbl	all pass

What should you lead?

Partner's redouble of your second suit is a business redouble, showing a desire to play there. South figures to be short in clubs when he pulls. You have the hearts locked up. Partner has good spades, and his bidding suggests a 5-3-1-4 pattern. You are close to the slam zone, even with clubs breaking badly.

Where are the opponents going to get any tricks? Only by using their ten trumps to crossruff. The auction demands that you draw trumps. Lead the ace and another diamond and hold declarer to *seven* tricks.

However, you lead the ♠A, and partner plays the ♠2. This is what you see:

NORTH (dummy)
♠ 3
♡ 10 5 4
◇ Q 10 3 2
♣ K 10 9 8 7

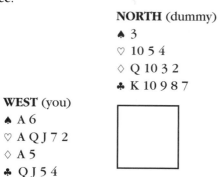

WEST (you)
♠ A 6
♡ A Q J 7 2
◇ A 5
♣ Q J 5 4

What now?

There's still time to play the ♢A and another diamond and collect 800 or 1100. You can even play the ♡A and another heart (surely partner has ♡Kxx for his jump to 4♡) and let partner shift to diamonds. What you mustn't do is lead clubs, dummy's suit, which can be a source of tricks for declarer.

A shift to the ♣Q gets the expected result: ♣K from dummy, ♣A from partner, ruffed by declarer. Spade ruff in dummy, then the ♣7, on which declarer discards a heart. Now dummy has *three* club winners, and the defenders get only one trick in each suit, down two, 500 points, less than you can make in 4♡.

84

Matchpoints, E-W vul.

♠ 6   ♡ Q J 8 7   ♢ K 9 7 5   ♣ K Q 4 3

WEST	NORTH	EAST	SOUTH
pass	1♠	pass	2♣
pass	2♠	pass	?

In most modern partnerships, a 2-over-1 response by an unpassed hand promises a rebid. Your methods with your present partner relieve you of the duty to bid again only if opener makes a single raise. You mustn't pass: bid 2NT, which shows a hand about as good as this one.

85

Matchpoints, Both vul.

NORTH (dummy)
♠ K
♡ K Q 5
♢ A K J 8 5 4 3 2
♣ 7

EAST (you)
♠ J 8 7 4
♡ A 8 3
♢ 9 6
♣ 10 5 4 3

	WEST	NORTH	EAST	SOUTH
1. Strong, artificial.		2♣[1]	pass	2♢[2]
2. Artificial waiting bid.	3♣	3♢	4♣	4♠
	pass	5♢	all pass	

Partner leads the ♣Q (which should be considered standard from AKQx), which holds, and he then shifts to the ♡6. You take dummy's ♡Q with the ♡A. What now?

If declarer has the ♠A and either a hand entry (◇Q or ◇10x) or the ♠Q, you have no more tricks coming. If partner has the ♠A, however, that's the setting trick. Can it go away? Yes, if partner's shift was from ♡1076, or from ♡J76 and you return a heart to finesse him out of his jack. In that case, declarer's fourth heart will provide a discard for dummy's spade. Return a spade to guarantee the set.

Why did partner shift to hearts from ♡J76 (his actual holding)? Because he knew you had something for your 4♣ bid and it could only be the ♡A. You might also have had the ♡10, and if so, a heart shift was necessary to beat what was probably a normal 5◇ contract *two* tricks.

Incidentally, the bidding was not normal. North might reasonably open 1◇ or 5◇, but not 2♣ with so little in high cards and so little defensive strength. An *Omnibus* 2♣ (my term for a strong artificial 2♣ opening that says nothing about suits) should deliver "more Honor Tricks than losers" according to Ely Culbertson's criterion for old-fashioned Strong Two-bids. If anything, the Omnibus 2♣ requires even stricter adherence to Culbertson's standard than a strong and natural two-bid.

Matchpoints, Both vul.

86

NORTH (dummy)
♠ K 5 3
♡ K 4
◇ K Q 10 7 2
♣ J 8 2

EAST (you)
♠ J 10 6
♡ Q J 9 2
◇ A 3
♣ 9 5 4 3

WEST	NORTH	EAST	SOUTH
pass	1◇	pass	1NT
all pass			

Partner leads the ♡8. Your ♡J holds the first trick and your ♡2 return fetches declarer's ♡10, partner's ♡7 and dummy's ♡K. Dummy's ♣J rides to partner's ♣K, and partner returns the ♡6 to declarer's ♡A. Dummy discards a spade. Declarer now cashes four club tricks, discarding two diamonds from dummy, until you have to discard in this ending:

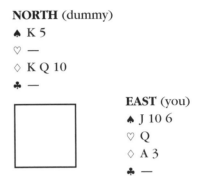

NORTH (dummy)
♠ K 5
♡ —
♢ K Q 10
♣ —

EAST (you)
♠ J 10 6
♡ Q
♢ A 3
♣ —

Having already shown up with ♡A10x and ♣AQ10xx, declarer cannot have another high card point and still have bid only 1NT. He'll soon be leading a diamond to dummy's ♢Q and your ♢A, and you'll be cashing the ♡Q in one of these two positions, depending on what you have discarded on declarer's fifth club:

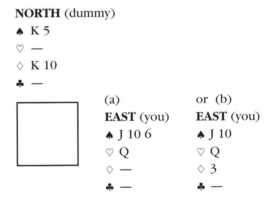

NORTH (dummy)
♠ K 5
♡ —
♢ K 10
♣ —

(a)
EAST (you)
♠ J 10 6
♡ Q
♢ —
♣ —

or (b)
EAST (you)
♠ J 10
♡ Q
♢ 3
♣ —

Dummy is squeezed and must discard the ♢10 to preserve a spade stopper. If you have (a), you must exit in spades and both dummy's kings will score. If you have (b), you can exit in diamonds and dummy will have to lead from ♠K5 into partner's ♠AQ. Therefore, on declarer's fifth club, you must keep your low diamond and discard a spade.

NORTH (dummy)
♠ J 4
♡ —
♢ A Q 10 5 2
♣ Q 10 6 5 3 2

WEST (you)
♠ K 8
♡ A K Q 8 7 2
♢ 7 6 4
♣ K 4

WEST	NORTH	EAST	SOUTH
	pass	pass	pass
1♡	2NT[1]	pass	3♢
all pass			

1. "Unusual" for the minors.

You lead the ♡K and dummy ruffs as partner plays the ♡3. A low club goes to declarer's jack and you take the ♣K. What now?

Continue hearts to shorten dummy's trumps before the clubs are set up. Second choice: play a trump. The last thing you should do is return a club, the suit that is a source of tricks for the opponents and that declarer is trying to set up, especially when you have neither the ♢9 nor the ♢J to overruff declarer.

♠ 8 7 5   ♡ A J 9 6 3   ♢ K 10   ♣ K Q 5

WEST	NORTH	EAST	SOUTH
pass	1♢	pass	1♡
pass	1♠	pass	?

Don't bid 3NT. Bid 2♣, the fourth suit. You can always bid 3NT later, and if you bid 2♣ now, you may discover that partner has three-card heart support. In that case, 4♡ figures to be the right game.

89

An overcall that comes between two opposing bidders (of different suits) is called a *sandwich*. Sandwiches are very dangerous. Each opponent has already made some promise of strength, and each knows about the other's suit. Based on knowledge of the combined partnership strength, either opponent can double for penalties (unless the opponents are playing *Support Doubles*), especially if the overcall is 1NT.

For this reason, many players prefer to use a sandwich 1NT artificially, to show 5-5 in the two unbid suits. This convention blends nicely with the usually expert treatment of a two-level overcall in opener's minor or responder's major as *natural*. By a passed hand, that's just about the only thing a sandwich 1NT can be anyway.

In general, you should overcall your *major* with a 6-5 major-minor two-suiter. If your six-card suit is a minor, you can use a two-suited overcall (if available in your system).

Matchpoints, Both vul.

♠ A 10 7 6 4 3   ♡ K 3   ◇ —   ♣ J 10 6 5 2

WEST	NORTH	EAST	SOUTH
			pass
1◇	pass	1♡	?

What do you bid here? A double would show the two unbid suits. 1NT would show a very distributional hand with the two unbid suits. Since 2NT is unnecessary to show a black two-suiter here, and forces to the three-level on what might still be a misfit, you shouldn't bid 2NT here. If you do, partner may not interpret it as showing the black suits. Instead he may conclude that West opened in a three-card diamond suit and you had a *minor* two-suiter.

You should simply bid 1♠ instead of trying to show both black suits. Your spades are both longer and stronger than your clubs, and offer the only realistic chance of buying the contract at a reasonable level. Furthermore, your void in diamonds suggests that the opponents may be headed for a diamond contract, and you'd welcome a spade lead (far more than a club lead) from partner.

90

Minor-suit partials and slams are fine even at matchpoints if they give you the best chance of a plus score. (The field may get overboard and go minus when you make a minor-suit partial, or stop in game when you make a minor-suit slam.) Minor-suit games, however, are seldom right, and when they are right, you'll usually have a clear indication from the auction that they're right.

Matchpoints, E-W vul.

♠ K J 9   ♡ A J 10 5   ◇ —   ♣ A J 8 6 3 2

WEST	NORTH	EAST	SOUTH
pass	1◇	pass	2♣
pass	2◇	pass	2♡
pass	2NT	pass	?

Partner has shown a minimum hand with a spade stopper and has twice denied club support. If you bid 3♣ now, partner won't pass, as your 2♡ rebid showed a very good hand and you can't really expect him to bid notrump a second time if his spades are only ♠Qxx. The danger in bidding 3♣ is that partner will have nothing better than to raise to 4♣. And what will you do then? Bid 5♣? Convert to 4NT and hope that partner doesn't take it as Roman Keycard Blackwood? (It's best *not* to play 4NT as RKCB in minor-suit slam auctions.) Your best bet here is to bid 3NT immediately.

Matchpoints, Neither vul.

NORTH (dummy)
♠ 5
♡ A 8 3
♢ A Q 10 6 5
♣ A K 8 2

□

SOUTH (you)
♠ A Q J 8 6 3
♡ K J 7 6 4
♢ K
♣ 4

WEST	NORTH	EAST	SOUTH
			1♠
pass	2♢	pass	2♡
pass	3♣	pass	3♡
pass	4NT[1]	pass	5♡[2]
pass	6♡	all pass	

1. RKCB (hearts).
2. Two keycards, no ♡Q.

West leads the ♣J, killing one of dummy's scarce entries. How should you play?

Take dummy's ♣K for starters. If you plan to take a heart finesse, do it now, preserving dummy's ♡A as a precious entry. Suppose you do, and your ♡J wins. Unblock the ♢K and cross to the ♡A, intending to take some pitches. When West shows out on the second heart, you know you're in trouble. Discard one spade on the ♣A and a second spade on the ♢A. When East drops the ♢J under the ♢A, you're at a crossroads. If you think East is falsecarding, you can continue with the ♢Q. If East ruffs, you can overruff and try a ruffing finesse in spades, ♠A then ♠Q, hoping that West has the ♠K. If you believe East's ♢J, you

Do you approve of your partner's bidding on this board?

I don't. North really can't tell from a 5♡ reply to Roman Keycard Blackwood whether 6♡ is a good contract. For 6♡ to be good, he needs you not only to have the requisite two keycards (or one keycard with the ♡Q), but also extra values, and only you know if you have them. Instead of bidding 4NT, North would have done better to jump to 5♡ and leave the slam decision to you.

This deal illustrates one of the drawbacks of Roman Keycard Blackwood (perhaps its worst drawback): it tempts players, even fine experts, to take charge of auctions in which they should relinquish control to partner. (Other forms of Blackwood are worse still.)

can try a straight spade finesse, then play the ♠A, ruff a spade, and finally try dummy's ◇Q, discarding your last spade if East ruffs.

A tough hand, and I wouldn't blame anyone for going down. However, there is a point in the above analysis that applies to many hands: that is, *care* and *efficient* use of scarce entries. You must use dummy's early club entry for something constructive: in this case, a heart finesse. You cannot afford to burn another entry (the ♡A) to take a heart finesse later.

Matchpoints, Both vul.

♠ Q J 8 3   ♡ 5   ◇ 6 5   ♣ K Q 9 6 5 4

WEST	NORTH	EAST	SOUTH
	pass	1♡	pass
2♡	dbl	4♡	?

Your hand is worthless defensively, and you can't play partner for more than two defensive tricks in view of his initial pass. Even if he hadn't passed initially, you wouldn't be close to a double of 4♡. Suppose he has a fine takeout double of hearts, 4-1-4-4 with *three* aces (though he'd surely have opened with such a hand). What, besides those three aces, do you think you'd get? (Actually, you might not even get the ♣A, for East might well be void.) You have three plausible calls: 4♠ (best), 5♣ (not too bad) and pass (a bit too timid, given partner's takeout double). You have a highly offensive hand: *bid*, don't double!

Matchpoints, N-S vul.

NORTH (dummy)
♠ A 10 2
♡ 7 4
◇ A K 6 5
♣ A 9 6 4

WEST (you)
♠ K Q 5 4 3
♡ 10 9 6 3
◇ J 2
♣ Q 3

WEST	NORTH	EAST	SOUTH
			pass
pass	1◇	pass	1NT
all pass			

You lead the ♠4. Partner wins with the ♠8, and returns the ♠J, which holds. You follow with the ♠3 to show that you started with five. Partner continues with the ♠9, on which declarer discards. You must choose among the ♠K, ♠Q and ♠5, which are equivalent cards now that dummy's ♠A is singleton. Which spade should you play?

The only entry you can possibly have is in hearts. You don't have one. So play your lowest spade, the ♠5, to warn partner against playing you for a heart entry. Suppose, however, that you play the ♠K. Declarer takes the ♠A and runs four diamond tricks. You must discard twice. What should you discard?

Declarer may want to take a finesse in hearts. You must make it dangerous for him by discarding hearts and saving your spades as a threat.

Matchpoints, Neither vul.

94

NORTH (dummy)
♠ K 10 4
♡ Q J 6 5 4
◇ 6
♣ Q 10 8 3

SOUTH (you)
♠ Q J 7
♡ 10 3
◇ A K 10 4
♣ A K J 5

WEST	NORTH	EAST	SOUTH	
pass	pass	pass	1◇	
pass	1♡	pass	2NT[1]	1. 18-19 HCP.
pass	3NT	all pass		

West leads a low club. You win with the ♣J (the ♣K would actually be better as it retains *two* club entries to dummy) and lead the ♡10. West takes the ♡A and shifts to a low diamond. East plays the ◇9 and you score a cheap trick with your ◊10. You lead the ♡3 to dummy's ♡J and East takes the ♡K. Then East returns a diamond and you take the ace, discarding a club from dummy. What now?

Don't cross to dummy in clubs to cash the ♡Q. A defender may have four hearts plus the ♠A as an entry to cash a heart. First you must lead one or two rounds of spades until you knock out the ♠A, and you'll lock up the ten tricks that West handed you with his diamond shift: four clubs, three diamonds, one heart and two spades.

Can it gain to cash the ♡Q? Absolutely not. If hearts are 3-3, you'll take four clubs, three diamonds and three hearts, but you'll discard three cards from your hand on dummy's hearts: one diamond and two spades. When you're finished cashing winners, you'll have only one spade left and the defenders will take the ♠A. You'll still have only ten tricks.

The right approach to notrump play is usually to establish tricks early, cash tricks late.

95

Matchpoints, N-S vul.

NORTH (dummy)
♠ Q 2
♡ A Q 4
◊ 9 6 5 4 2
♣ K J 4

EAST (you)
♠ K J 10 9 8 4
♡ 9 7 6
◊ 8 3
♣ 6 5

WEST	NORTH	EAST	SOUTH
pass	1◊	2♠[1]	3NT
all pass			

1. Weak.

Partner leads the ♠3 and dummy plays the ♠2. Which spade should you play?

This is a routine card play: play the lowest spade that is certain to keep declarer's possible ♠7 from scoring. Only the ♠8 will do. If you play the ♠J, partner will credit declarer with the ♠10. — who knows what wrong picture of the hands partner will get, and how he might go wrong.

After inattention (first) and the squandering of useful cards to signal (second), the third biggest source of blown tricks on defense is careless play from equals or equally worthless spot cards.

Matchpoints, Both vul.

♠ Q 10 6 3   ♡ K 7 6 3   ◇ 10 5 4 2   ♣ 8

WEST	NORTH	EAST	SOUTH
		pass	pass
1NT	dbl[1]	2◇[2]	?

1. Four-card major, longer minor.
2. Transfer to hearts.

If West's explanation of East's 2◇ is correct, you can diagnose the distribution. Partner is likely to have four spades and longer clubs, with a singleton heart. Your ♡K figures to lie under the ♡A and is of little value offensively. It will be useful on defense, however: if West has ♡AJx behind you, he can't pick up your ♡K. The misfit for clubs hurts (you don't figure to be able to set up and run dummy's clubs if you play in spades). You should pass, especially if you're vulnerable and -200 looms.

You should take one other thing into account: the opponents may be in a confused auction, West thinking that transfers are on over North's artificial double, East intending his 2◇ as natural. If so, partner might well have four *hearts* and longer clubs. You dare not bid 2♠.

By the way, it isn't impossible that partner's long minor is diamonds. Why can't partner be 4-1-6-2, East be 2-6-0-5 and West be 3-2-3-5?

You may have missed a ten-card fit.

Wouldn't you rather play a Notrump Defense that lets you show your six-card suits? I think that most people would do best to play a Notrump Defense in which 2◇, 2♡ and 2♠ overcalls are all natural. I can recommend a few.

Here's one I think is dynamite: I call it *TNT* (for "Touching, Non-Touching"): Double shows two *Touching* suits, not both minors (2NT shows the minors). Advancer relays with 2♣ to ask which, and doubler replies by bidding the cheaper (his 2♠ rebid, for example, showing *spades and clubs*).

2♣ shows two *Non-Touching* suits. Advancer relays with 2◇ to ask which.

Matchpoints, Neither vul.

NORTH (dummy)
♠ 6 5 3
♡ Q 9 7 4 2
◇ J 6 5
♣ J 2

WEST (you)
♠ Q 10 7 4
♡ J 6 3
◇ 8 2
♣ A Q 6 4

WEST	NORTH	EAST	SOUTH
pass	pass	pass	1NT[1]
pass	2◇[2]	dbl	2♡
all pass			

1. 15-17 HCP.
2. Jacoby Transfer.

You lead the ◇8 of diamonds, as partner urged when he doubled the 2◇ transfer bid. Partner covers dummy's ◇J with the ◇Q and declarer takes the ◇A. The ♡5 goes to dummy's ♡Q and partner's ♡A. Partner returns the ◇10 to declarer's ◇K.

Partner had a choice of diamonds to return: the ◇10 or the ◇9 (or the ◇7, as it happens, though you could not know this). He chose the higher. For all he knew, your ◇8 might have been a singleton, and he was giving you a ruff. Clearly, this was a time for suit-preference: the ◇10 showing stuff in spades; the ◇9 (or the ◇7) showing stuff in clubs.

Declarer cashes the ♡K, on which partner's ♡10 falls, and then leads the ♣3. You take the ♣Q. What now?

You must cash the ♡J (it's the master trump and you can pull two opposing trumps for one of yours), then lead the ♠4. Partner will take his ♠A, cash the ◇9 (on which you can discard a club) and return a spade to set up your ♠Q. You'll get two hearts, two spades, one diamond and two clubs for *down two*.

If instead you cash the ♣A and continue with another club, you are doing declarer's work, establishing his ♣K and high-club spot card as winners on which he can discard a diamond loser and a spade loser from dummy. And, of course, if you ruff with your high trump when declarer leads a low diamond, you let declarer discard another low spade from dummy.

98

Matchpoints, Neither vul.

♠ Q 8 7 5   ♡ A J 10 4   ◇ Q 7 6   ♣ 5 3

WEST	NORTH	EAST	SOUTH
		pass	pass
1◇	2♣	pass	?

Pass, and pass quickly. Two small clubs do not a fit make. Even ♣J3 would be significantly better. The opponents may be in trouble, especially if they, like some others nowadays, play the unannounced convention (unethical, but condoned by most directors) that opener *must* balance (unless advancer shows interest in the proceedings). Note that you dare not ask whether opener is required to balance, for that's a dead giveaway that you're hoping he will.

Matchpoints, E-W vul.

♠ A Q J 6 3 2   ♡ —   ◇ A K J 7 6 3   ♣ A

WEST	NORTH	EAST	SOUTH
		pass	?

If you were playing Strong Two-bids, you could open 2♠, but playing Weak Twos, you must open an Omnibus 2♣. It's often dangerous to do so with freakish two-suiters, for enemy preemption may keep you from showing both your suits at conveniently low levels. However, this hand is a proper Omnibus 2♣ for these reasons:

(a) You have *three aces* (defense).
(b) You have *spades* (and can therefore expect to outbid opponents who compete).
(c) Your opponents are *vulnerable* (and therefore will seldom get frisky).
(d) One opponent has already passed.

If you open with 1♠, there's a significant danger that you will play in 1♠. Even if you escape that fate, you will have a hard time convincing your partner that his yarborough with four small spades (or four small diamonds) will produce a slam.

Luckily, after partner passes your 1♠ opening, an opponent reopens the bidding for you:

WEST	NORTH	EAST	SOUTH
		pass	1♠ (!)
pass	pass	2♡	3◇ (!)
3♡	4♠	pass	?

Partner couldn't raise 1♠ to 2♠, yet he jumped to 4♠ after you bid 3◇, even though 3♠ would have been mildly constructive in view of West's intervening 3♡. What better picture could he paint for you?

Play partner for one useful high card (the ♠K or the ◇Q). Isn't that enough for slam? If you don't bid 6♠, you'll never get there, for since you didn't open 2♣, partner won't imagine that you have as good a hand as you do.

Tip: when a good bidder passes first and jumps later, it's because the bid he just heard turned him on.

100

Matchpoints, N-S vul.

NORTH (dummy)
♠ J 9 8 6 5 3
♡ K 9 6 4
♢ 9
♣ Q 4

EAST (you)
♠ 7 4
♡ J 3
♢ A K 10 8
♣ A 9 8 6 5

WEST	NORTH	EAST	SOUTH
			1♡
pass	3♢[1]	pass	3♠
pass	4♡	all pass	

1. Artificial heart raise: four hearts, 7-10 support points.

Partner leads the ♢3 to your ♢K; declarer follows with the ♢4. What now?

Recognize that after agreeing on hearts with four-card support, the search for a trump suit ended. South's 3♠ was a cuebid seeking a slam. Dummy's spades will probably be established (if necessary, by ruffing) for as many discards as declarer needs. It's cashout time. Playing the ♣A can't hurt: if declarer has the ♣K (which is likely from his strong bidding), he has eleven tricks regardless.

101

Matchpoints, E-W vul.

♠ 9 5   ♡ A J 10 9 3   ♢ Q 9   ♣ A K 8 2

WEST	NORTH	EAST	SOUTH
			1♡
2♠[1]	pass	pass	?

1. Weak.

You play negative doubles, so your partner couldn't make a penalty double if he wanted to. Should you be worried about that? What should you call?

Don't worry too much about partner being a frustrated penalty doubler. Worry more about your own hand. If you balance with a double, partner is likely to bid diamonds. If you balance with 3♣, you are unlikely to make anything: partner had a negative double available but *didn't make one*, either because he didn't have one of the minors (most likely clubs) or because, despite having both minors, he was too weak to ask you to bid at the three-level.

Pass. If partner is a frustrated penalty doubler, you should have no trouble achieving a "matchpoint magic" +200 defending against 2♠ *undoubled*. That will be better than any partscore you may be able to make.

But mightn't you be able to nail West for 500 with a balancing double and a penalty pass?

Yes, but that doesn't mean other North-South pairs will do so. Some Souths may face the same problem you do and bid 3♣, letting West off the hook. Some Wests won't bid 2♠.

At other tables, with more sensible Wests, an uncontested auction is likely to lead to a partscore for North-South, as the bidding may start 1♡-*pass*-1♠.

A few pairs don't play Weak Jump Overcalls, but among the majority who do, there is wide variation. Does anybody know what a Weak Jump Overcall should look like at *adverse vulnerability*? I haven't heard anybody say. If a vulnerable Weak Jump Overcaller has stuck his neck on the chopping block, you needn't chop it off to get a fine matchpoint score — unless your side has a game.

Matchpoints, Neither vul.

NORTH (dummy)
♠ J 9 8 7
♡ Q J 6 3
◇ 9
♣ 8 7 5 4

EAST (you)
♠ A 10
♡ A 10 7 5 4
◇ J 5
♣ A 10 9 6

WEST	NORTH	EAST	SOUTH
			1◇
pass	pass	1♡	2◇
2♡	pass	pass	2♠
all pass			

Partner leads the ♡2. You take dummy's ♡J with your ♡A, and declarer follows with the ♡9. What now?

If partner had diamonds locked up, he'd have led a trump. Declarer has six good diamonds and four spades. The bidding and the play to Trick 1 mark him with only one heart. That means he has a 4-1-6-2 pattern.

Playing the ♠A and then the ♠10 is a very bad plan. It not only clarifies the trump situation for declarer but gives the timing he needs to set up his diamonds.

Your best chance for tricks is to force declarer to lose control by running him out of trumps. Most likely he has ♣Kx. If you return a low heart, he can't gain by discarding a club and blanking his ♣K. He'll probably ruff. You may be able to keep him from setting up and running his diamonds. Notice that you can overruff dummy twice with your ♠A10, while partner will remain with his three trumps (perhaps including an honor) to stop the run of the diamonds.

What if declarer *doesn't* have the ♣K? Then he may discard a club when you lead the ♡5 at Trick 2. No matter: partner will shift to clubs and you'll tap declarer in clubs.

Even though your balancing overcall was clearly right, you should note that it wasn't without risk: it allowed the opponents to find a better trump suit and reach a higher-scoring partial. Bear that in mind for future balancing decisions, especially when 1♣ or 1♢ gets passed around to you. Think twice before balancing with *weak* hands.

103

Matchpoints, Both vul.

♠ A Q 6   ♡ 10 9   ◇ A K 9 7 2   ♣ A 10 5

WEST	NORTH	EAST	SOUTH
			1◇
pass	1♠	pass	?

You've already done well to have recognized that this is an 18-point hand (I count it closer to 19) and to have opened 1◇ instead of a 15-17 1NT.

What now? Bid 2NT without a heart stopper? That's possible, but not good, for it wrong-sides the notrump (partner may have ♡Kx). Bidding 3♠ is much better, but not without some risk, as it normally shows four-card support and you have only three spades.

You can do better still if you appreciate that in the modern style a reverse over partner's one-of-a-major response is forcing and promises a rebid, and responder normally rebids his major when he has five. This rebidding of even a mediocre five-card suit may seem strange, but it makes sense for two reasons. First, since opener has promised to bid again, he can't (or at least, shouldn't) pass. Second, in this "reversing" auction, a 2♠ rebid is the cheapest bid he can make, and cheap bids don't promise much in the suit bid.

Bid 2♡. There is no danger of winding up in hearts. If partner raises hearts, he implies not only four-card heart support but five spades (with 4-4 in the majors, he'd have responded 1♡, not 1♠), so you can safely correct a heart raise to spades.

Matchpoints, Neither vul.

104

NORTH (dummy)
♠ K 7
♡ K 8 4 3
♢ A 7 5
♣ Q 6 5 3

WEST (you)
♠ J 10 9 5 3
♡ 5
♢ 10 8 3
♣ J 10 9 4

WEST	NORTH	EAST	SOUTH
		1♢	1♡
pass	3♡	pass	4♡
all pass			

A lead from 10-8-3 is rarely good. It might pickle partner's honor if he has ♢Kxxx in front of declarer's ace or ♢Qxxx behind dummy's ♢AJx. So you lead the ♠J, adhering to the principle of remaining passive on defense when there's no reason to get active. Your ♠J wins the first trick. Good! What now?

There is no need to continue spades. The second spade trick is not in danger of disappearing. You must use the lead more constructively. It's safe to lead diamonds through dummy's ace (no diamond holding that partner might have can be pickled). However, you must be careful to cater for partner's not-unlikely ♢KQxx. If you lead the ♢3, partner may play you for the jack and return a diamond after being allowed to win the queen. So lead the ♢8, feigning three small (or a doubleton).

That's the killing defense. Without the ♠J lead, or without the ♢8 shift, declarer can execute a strip-and-endplay against partner to make 4♡.

One more point about this deal: partner has ♠AQx or ♠AQxx and he knows that you have the ♠10. If he thought it necessary or desirable to cash a second spade trick, he could have overtaken your ♠J with his ♠Q and cashed the ♠A. His failure to do so tells you that he wants you on lead to *shift*.

Matchpoints, N-S vul.

♠ A Q J 7 3   ♡ A K 9 4   ◊ 3   ♣ A K 6

WEST	NORTH	EAST	SOUTH
pass	pass	pass	?

You would have a close choice between 1♠ and an Omnibus 2♣ except for one fact: your opponents are not vulnerable, a condition mitigated only partly by the fact that they have both passed. An overcall and a preemptive raise (most likely in diamonds) would give you a tough rebid problem if you were to open 2♣. So 1♠ is much better than 2♣. It's not really close. When you have a close decision, choose a bid that shows a suit.

Luckily, you do not face interference and the auction actually goes:

	WEST	NORTH	EAST	SOUTH
1. Strong and artificial.	pass	pass	pass	2♣[1]
2. Natural positive.	pass	2♡[2]	pass	?

You and your partner have agreed to play splinters. Should you bid 4◊ here? If not, what should your plan be?

An Omnibus 2♣ opener must follow with a natural bid, so bid 3♡. You cannot jump to 4◊ as a splinter; bidding 4◊ in this auction would show a solid diamond suit.

If partner continues with 4◊, a cuebid showing the ◊A, slam is assured. If he bids 3NT, you can play him for

♠ K 8 2   ♡ Q J 7 6 3   ◊ K 8   ♣ Q 5 4

or similar, and drive to slam on that basis. If he bids 4♡, you can cuebid 4♠, so he'll realize the king of spades is a very valuable card and drive to slam if he has it.

Matchpoints, Both vul.

♠ 10 4   ♡ 9 7 6 4 3 2   ◇ Q 7   ♣ 7 6 3

WEST	NORTH	EAST	SOUTH
	pass	1NT	pass
3NT	all pass		

What should you lead?

There's nothing better than a heart, a lead that is unlikely to cost and may strike gold if partner has ♡AKx and hearts split 2-2. But which heart?

When leading from a very weak suit, lead fourth highest if you want to suggest a continuation, but lead the highest spot card you can spare if you want to suggest a shift. On this deal, you should not want to suggest a shift, so lead the ♡4. Suppose, however, you did want a shift: which heart should you lead then?

Lead the ♡7, not the ♡9. The ♡9 could blow a trick if declarer had ♡AQ8 and partner had ♡KJ or ♡K10 (among other possibilities). Indeed, the ♡9 could blow three tricks if declarer had ♡Q10 or ♡QJ and partner had ♡AK8 (among other possibilities).

Do not squander potentially useful spot cards!

Matchpoints, Neither vul.

♠ 10   ♡ Q 8 2   ◇ K Q 10 7 6 4   ♣ A 10 3

WEST	NORTH	EAST	SOUTH
	1♣	pass	1◇
1♠	pass	pass	?

You and your partner have agreed to play Support Doubles. Would a double by North have been a Support Double (showing a three-card diamond raise, any strength) in this auction?

Some advocates of Support Doubles play that it would, but most play that after a 1♣ opening followed by a 1◇ response and a 1♠ sandwich overcall (i.e. in this auction *only*), opener's double shows *four hearts*, and Support Doubles do not apply. You and your partner play that they do apply, so partner *probably* has fewer than three diamonds, and you should have alerted partner's pass.

With a good hand, responder's normal course of action, playing Support Doubles, is to reopen with an "action" double. This asks opener to bid something but caters to the possibility — very likely when the partner of the sandwich overcaller doesn't raise — that opener is a frustrated penalty doubler. Such "action" doubles are a necessary concomitant of Support Doubles. However, an "action" double of a one-level bid with a singleton in intervener's suit is wrong, as you won't be happy to see opener pass for penalties.

If you don't want to defend against 1♠ doubled when partner has four strong spades, then you should show some sign of strength by jumping to 3◊. Bidding 2♣ understates your hand, overstates your club support and fails to get the message "good diamond suit" across.

Matchpoints, N-S vul.

♠ A K 5   ♡ A 4 3   ◊ 9 7   ♣ K Q 8 7 2

WEST	NORTH	EAST	SOUTH
	pass	pass	1NT[1]
pass	2♡[2]	dbl	?

1. 15-17 HCP.
2. Transfer.

Did it occur to you to pass this double? Suppose partner has ♡Qxx, ♡Qx or ♡J10x: wouldn't you rather have a heart lead come up to him than to you?

Perhaps without having discussed the matter, you accept the transfer and become declarer in 2♠. Luckily, partner does not have a heart holding that needs protection against the opening lead:

Without any agreement to the contrary, a pass of a doubled Jacoby Transfer shows a desire to put the doubler on lead. The transfer bidder can bid two of his suit if he'd have passed opener's simple accept; otherwise he can bid as he would over a simple accept. However, some pairs play that a pass shows poor support, and an accept shows good (at least three-card) support for responder's major. In our example hand, you should pass or bid 2♠ according to your own partnership agreements.

NORTH (dummy)
♠ J 9 8 6 3
♡ 9 5
◊ A Q J 2
♣ 6 5

☐

SOUTH (you)
♠ A K 5
♡ A 4 3
◊ 9 7
♣ K Q 8 7 2

West's ♡6 lead fetches East's ♡J, and you duck. You win East's ♡K continuation and cash the ♠A, East dropping the ♠10. East discards a heart when you cash the ♠K. You take a diamond finesse and dummy's ◊J wins. You lead a club from dummy. East takes the ace and leads a third heart; West follows with the ♡10 and dummy ruffs. This is the ending, with dummy to lead:

NORTH (dummy)

♠ J 9
♡ —
◇ A Q 2
♣ 6

SOUTH (you)

♠ 5
♡ —
◇ 9
♣ K Q 8 7

What now?

You have a pretty good picture of the defenders' hands. East, who is a passed hand, has shown up with

♠ 10   ♡ K Q J x x   ◇ ? ? ?   ♣ A ? ? ?

and can't have the ◇K (which you suspected when dummy's ◇J won on the first round of diamonds). West is known to have ♠Q7 left, along with the ◇K (most likely guarded), and is probably out of hearts.

To take all the remaining tricks but one (your goal on this deal), you must score dummy's ◇Q by taking a second finesse and then ruffing dummy's ◇2.

So cross to your ♣K (hoping West will be forced to follow), repeat the diamond finesse, and ruff dummy's ◇2 with your last trump. Note that cashing dummy's ◇A first would be wrong, as that would let West overruff the fourth diamond if he started with ◇Kxx. When you lead the ♣Q next, whether West has the ◇K or a third club remaining, you can lose only one more trick — to West's ♠Q. (If West follows to the ♣Q, discard dummy's ◇A; if West ruffs, overruff and lead dummy's ◇A next.)

Matchpoints, Neither vul.

109

♠ 109873   ♡ K 3   ◇ K J 9 8 5 3   ♣ —

WEST	NORTH	EAST	SOUTH
			pass
pass	3♣	3♡	all pass

What should you lead?

Defend passively when the auction does not supply a good reason to defend actively.

Partner's 3♣ preempt doesn't promise any strength outside the club suit, so you should not play him for the ◇Q (much less the ◇A). A diamond lead figures to cost a trick. Lead a safe card, the ♠10.

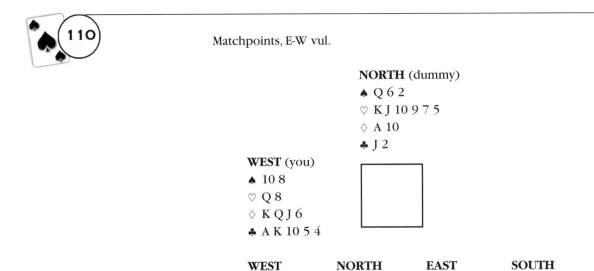

110

Matchpoints, E-W vul.

NORTH (dummy)
♠ Q 6 2
♡ K J 10 9 7 5
◇ A 10
♣ J 2

WEST (you)
♠ 10 8
♡ Q 8
◇ K Q J 6
♣ A K 10 5 4

WEST	NORTH	EAST	SOUTH
			2♠[1]
pass[2]	3♠	all pass	

1. Weak.
2. Slow pass.

You lead the ◇K to dummy's ◇A. Partner plays the ◇3 and declarer follows with the ◇7. When dummy's ◇10 is continued, partner plays the ◇9 and declarer the ◇8. You take your ◇J. What now?

The long time you took before passing 2♠ told declarer that you had a good hand, but not where your high cards were. If you cash two top clubs, as you did, declarer is extremely unlikely to play you for the ♡A. Partner's ◇3 was an attitude card, denying the ◇J, but his second diamond (the ◇9) was suit-preference (what else could it be?), requesting a heart shift, so you know he has a heart honor. You know it's the ♡A, but even an attentive declarer may not know whether it's the ♡A or the ♡Q. Shift to the ♡8 before disclosing your club strength, and there's a chance that declarer will misguess. If declarer guesses correctly, trust partner to shift to clubs after winning the ♡A. (Partner won't play you for a singleton heart, for he knows you have a doubleton spade and will figure that with ten minor-suit cards you would have entered the auction.)

Matchpoints, Both vul.

♠ Q   ♡ A Q 10 4   ◇ Q 9 3   ♣ A Q 7 6 2

WEST	NORTH	EAST	SOUTH
	pass	pass	1♣
pass	1♠[1]	pass	?

Bid 2♣. You're not nearly strong enough for a 2♡ reverse, the modern standard treatment being "forcing one round, promising a rebid." If you are truly unhappy with a 2♣ rebid, you should have opened 1NT despite your singleton ♠Q.

Once in a while, opening 1NT with a high singleton honor is the least of evils, especially when that singleton is in spades.

However, you rebid 2♡ and face yet another problem:

WEST	NORTH	EAST	SOUTH
	pass	pass	1♣
pass	1♠[1]	pass	2♡[2]
pass	2♠[3]	pass	?

1. Extra length or extra strength.
2. Forcing, promising a rebid.
3. Five or more spades.

Bid 2NT, delivering the promised rebid. You mustn't break your promise by passing. How can it be right to play in what may be a 5-1 fit anyway?

If partner bids 3♣, 3♡ or 3♠ over your 2NT, *then* you can pass cheerfully, having given your all.

Matchpoints, Neither vul.

♠ J 9 8 4   ♡ A K 5   ◇ A 6   ♣ A 9 3 2

WEST	NORTH	EAST	SOUTH
pass	1♣	pass	1♠
pass	2♠	pass	?

If you'd had

♠ A J 9 4   ♡ A K 5   ◇ 8 6   ♣ A 9 3 2

you'd have had a fine hand for a 2♠ jump shift. With your actual hand, you did well to bid only 1♠ (your spades are too weak for 2♠). Now, however, you have a difficult rebid problem, which suggests that your 1♠ response wasn't perfect. (There are superior conventional ways to bid balanced 16-18 HCP responding hands.)

It's not unreasonable to bid 3NT, offering a choice between 3NT (if partner has only three spades) and 4♠ (if he has four). You play 15-17 1NT openings with your present partner, so you know he has at most a balanced 14 HCP or unbalanced 15 Support Points. With weak trumps and only 16 HCP, you shouldn't be optimistic about 6♠. However, facing a "perfect" minimum, e.g.

$$♠ K Q 3 \quad ♡ 8 4 \quad ◇ K 7 3 \quad ♣ K Q 8 6 4$$

6♣ is possible. You might try 3◇ to force, with the plan of passing over 3NT, continuing to 4♣ over 3♠ or bidding 4NT (RKCB) over a jump to 4♠.

Bidding 3♣ risks playing a potential slam deal in a partscore. With the perfect minimum cited above, partner could and should pass 3♣, as your sequence shows a limit raise with four spades, e.g.

$$♠ J 9 8 4 \quad ♡ K Q 5 \quad ◇ 9 6 \quad ♣ A J 3 2$$

or similar.

Luckily, you get another chance:

WEST	NORTH	EAST	SOUTH
pass	1♣	pass	1♠
pass	2♠	pass	3♣ (!)
pass	3♠	pass	?

Partner's 3♠ shows a minimum, but strongly suggests a fourth spade. Bid 3NT, giving up on slam. Partner can still correct to 4♠.

It's a big mistake to ask for keycards with a Roman Keycard 4NT, as you may not be safe in 5♠. Even if partner has two keycards, e.g.

$$♠ A K 6 3 \quad ♡ 9 8 2 \quad ◇ Q 7 \quad ♣ K J 7 6$$

you need the ♠Q falling singleton or doubleton and the ♣Q on side to make 5♠. When partner can't bid game over your non-forcing 3♣, you do not belong in slam.

Can you survive yet another mistake in this auction?

♠ J 9 8 4　♡ A K 5　♢ A 6　♣ A 9 3 2

WEST	NORTH	EAST	SOUTH
pass	1♣	pass	1♠
pass	2♠	pass	3♣ (!)
pass	3♠	pass	4NT[1]
pass	5♢[2]	pass	?

1. Roman Keycard (spades).
2. 1 keycard.

A Roman Keycard 4NT bid implies a willingness to bid slam if all five keycards, or four keycards and the trump queen, are present. What's the point of asking for keycards if you're unwilling to bid slam when only one is missing? If you think you "had" your 4NT bid, you should bid 5♡, the Queen Ask, instead of signing off with 5♠.

Suppose partner had replied 5♠, two keycards and the ♠Q. Would you have been able to bid a slam then?

♠ A K Q 3　♡ Q 9 2　♢ 9 4　♣ K 7 6 4

This, a hand good enough to have jumped to 4♠ over your 3♣, would give you no play for 6♠.

Roman Keycard Blackwood is designed for hands that have all the necessary intermediates for slam but may be missing keycards, not for hands that have lots of top tricks but little else.

It is auctions like this that leave me convinced that most bridge players would be much better off without any form of Blackwood than with even the best version of RKCB (the one in my book *Not Your Daddy's Blackwood*).

Matchpoints, E-W vul.

♠ J 7 6 5 2　♡ A K 8 6 5　♢ —　♣ 8 7 2

WEST	NORTH	EAST	SOUTH
	1NT[1]	3♢	?

1. 15-17 HCP.

Game is not certain — partner figures to have some wasted high-card strength in diamonds — but it's right to want to reach game in partner's better major. The way to do so is to bid 4♢, choice of major-suit games, protecting partner's diamond honor or honors from an opening lead-through and your own hand from being tapped.

When you don't bid 4♢, you wind up having to declare the final contract:

If in response to 1NT you play four-level transfers to majors, they apply only when both are *jumps*.

NORTH (dummy)
♠ K Q
♡ 10 3
◇ A 10 8 5
♣ A Q J 10 9

SOUTH (you)
♠ J 7 6 5 2
♡ A K 8 6 5
◇ —
♣ 8 7 2

WEST	NORTH	EAST	SOUTH
	1NT[1]	3◇	3♠
pass	3NT	pass	4♡
dbl	4♠	pass	pass
dbl	all pass		

1. 15-17 HCP.

Uh oh. Partner opened a slightly off-shape 1NT and now you may have to pay a price for it. West leads the ◇6. Plan the play.

Your plan should be to set up dummy's clubs. Best is to play low from dummy (the lead may be from ◇J96, ◇Q96 or ◇K96 and East may play an honor) and ruff in hand. Then finesse clubs (losing to East's possible ♣K early) before starting trumps. Eventually you hope to discard hearts on dummy's winners.

Setting up hearts is a plan doomed to failure, as you'll be ruffing with dummy's trump *honors* — trump tricks, not small trumps.

114

Matchpoints, Neither vul.

WEST (you)
♠ Q J 6 4 2   ♡ 10 9 8 4 3   ◇ —   ♣ Q J 7

WEST	NORTH	EAST	SOUTH
pass	1◇	pass	2NT[1]
pass	4♣[2]	pass	4♡[3]
pass	5♣[2]	pass	5♠[4]
pass	6NT	all pass	

1. Non-forcing.
2. Gerber (4♣-5♣).
3. 1 ace.
4. 2 kings.

What should you lead?

Lead the safest card: the ♡10, top of a sequence. A black-suit lead is unlikely to catch partner with the king and may blow a trick. Nevertheless, you lead the ♠4. The ♠4 would be a reasonable lead against 3NT, as partner might well have the ♠A or the ♠K, but not here.

Can you survive this opening-lead error?

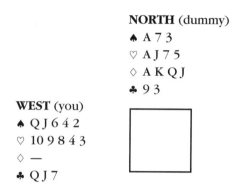

NORTH (dummy)
♠ A 7 3
♡ A J 7 5
◇ A K Q J
♣ 9 3

WEST (you)
♠ Q J 6 4 2
♡ 10 9 8 4 3
◇ —
♣ Q J 7

Your ♠4 rides to partner's ♠9 and declarer's ♠10. Declarer cashes the ♡K and then loses a finesse of dummy's ♡J to partner's ♡Q. Partner returns the ♣2 to declarer's ♣A. Here come four rounds of diamonds and you must find four discards (partner plays up the line in diamonds, showing an odd number). What should your discards be?

You can afford to discard one low heart and two low spades. Do you know why?

Partner's carding has pinpointed the distribution. He has two hearts, five diamonds (from his up-the-line plays), three or four clubs (from his return of the *deuce* of clubs rather than a random low spot) and therefore at least two spades. Partner's ♠9 of spades at Trick 1 denies the ♠8, so he can't have ♠985; he therefore has ♠95 exactly. That means partner is 2-2-5-4. Even if declarer is a bad bidder who would bypass a major as good as ♠K1085 to respond 2NT, he can't have four spades under these circumstances.

You can afford to throw a third spade. After you do, declarer leads a spade to his king, and his last spade towards dummy's ace. The ending is:

NORTH (dummy)
♠ A
♡ A 7
◇ —
♣ 9

WEST (you)
♠ —
♡ 10 9
◇ —
♣ Q J

What should you discard?

If you discard a heart, dummy is high except for the ♣9, and declarer will make the rest of the tricks if he has the ♣K. If you discard the ♣J, declarer needs to have ♣K10 remaining and drop your ♣Q to take the rest.

Now declarer has already shown up with

♠ K 10 x   ♡ K x   ◇ x x x x   ♣ A ? ? ?

If he has ♣AK10x, then he is too strong for his non-forcing 2NT (and there's nothing you can do anyway). However, it is certain from his reply to dummy's Gerber 5♣ that he has only two kings, and therefore he cannot have the ♣K. Furthermore, partner's ♣2 return showed an honor (with only low clubs he would have returned a high spot card). So you can safely discard the ♣J to beat the contract two.

Key principle: keep length with dummy (who will be on lead after you discard). Discarding a heart is certain to blow a trick. Even if you can't tell who has the ♣K, you should discard the ♣J, another play that can't lose but may gain.

It's a shame to beat a slam reached through Gerber *only one trick*.

115

Matchpoints, N-S vul.

♠ —   ♡ A 10 8 7 5   ◇ 6 5   ♣ Q 7 6 5 3 2

	WEST	NORTH	EAST	SOUTH
1. 15-17 HCP.	pass	1NT[1]	2♠	?

With your present partner you play Lebensohl, a convention whose primary use is to compete to the three-level without forcing to game.

Bid 2NT, a puppet to 3♣, and pass partner's mandatory 3♣ reply. If you don't use Lebensohl on a hand like this, there's no point in playing the convention. However, if not playing Lebensohl (or some variation thereof), you should bid 3♣, which is constructive but not forcing in standard bidding.

Might 3♡ be a better spot? It will score +140 if it makes, which is more than you'll score in clubs even with an overtrick.

Yes, but "might" doesn't make "right" in bridge. In standard bidding, you dare not bid 3♡ because (unlike three of a minor) three of a major is forcing. Playing Lebensohl, you can bid a non-forcing 3♡ over partner's 3♣ reply to 2NT, but you're better off letting partner play 3♣ than playing 3♡ yourself.

"Conventional wisdom" overemphasizes playing partscores in major suits. Your goal in competitive partscore auctions should not be to reach the highest-scoring partial. Rather, you should seek the safest contract, preferably one in which you can score +110 or more, while avoiding the "matchpoint poison" -200.

Matchpoints, Both vul.   **116**

♠ Q 9 8 7   ♡ 2   ◇ J 9 5   ♣ Q J 9 7 5

WEST	NORTH	EAST	SOUTH
pass	2♣[1]	pass	2◇[2]
pass	2♡	pass	?

1. Omnibus 2♣.
2. Neutral response.

Your collection of queens and jacks plus a misfit for partner's hearts do not add up to a positive response. Use your "second negative", whatever that is in your system.

Most experts use 3♣ over 2♡ or 2♠, and 3◇ over 3♣, as the second negative by a 2◇ responder, but have no second negative over 3◇. I recommend using 2NT over 2♡ or 2♠, and 3♡ over 3♣ or 3◇, as the second negative.

Matchpoints, E-W vul.   **117**

♠ —   ♡ K 7 4 2   ◇ K 7 5 4   ♣ Q J 10 8 5

WEST	NORTH	EAST	SOUTH
		pass	pass
1♣	dbl	1♠	?

Bid 2♡, which shows just about as good a hand as this one.

Responsive Doubles are always doubles of *raised suits*. Responsive Doubles do not apply over new-suit bids. Penalty doubles apply over suits bid (or promised) by partner.

No, a double would not be a "responsive double" asking partner to pick a red suit; a double here would be a penalty double, showing spades and a decent hand. Nowadays, responders bid weak four-card majors even over an intervening takeout double and risk getting doubled for penalties when they do. A double would be appropriate with

♠ K 7 4 2   ♡ K 4   ◇ 7 5   ♣ Q J 10 8 5

or similar.

118

Here's an accident of bridge history: Weak Two-bids were invented before transfer bids were. Had the order of invention been reversed, Weak Twos might never have become popular, for one of their effects is to wrong-side contracts when partner (an unpassed hand) has a strong 1NT or 2NT opening.

There are at least three sets of standards for suit quality when opening Weak Two-bids in first and second seats. (1) Wanton: anything goes! (2) Mainstream: "Two of the top three honors, or any three honors." (3) Sound: "Three honors including the ace or king."

Matchpoints, N-S vul.

♠ Q J 9 7 5 4   ♡ J 10   ◇ K Q   ♣ 10 6 3

WEST	NORTH	EAST	SOUTH
		pass	?

Your suit qualifies for neither a Sound nor a Mainstream 2♠. Pass.

Would it surprise you to learn that if partner declares a spade contract on this deal, he'll make at least one more trick than you will, maybe two more?

However, you're stuck with the 2♠ you open, and the auction continues:

WEST	NORTH	EAST	SOUTH
		pass	2♠[1]
pass	3♣	pass	?

1. Weak.

Unless your partnership has an explicit agreement to the contrary, a new-suit response to a Weak Two-bid is forcing by an unpassed hand. You don't have such an agreement with your present partner. Bid 3◇, 3♠, even 4♣, and hope you can survive. You must not pass, even if you didn't "have" your 2♠ bid. To pass is to violate partnership, the worst kind of bidding error because it can induce partners to jump directly to what they *guess* they can make, fearing that otherwise you may pass their forcing bids.

Matchpoints, N-S vul.

♠ A J 8 3 2   ♡ K 9 7 5   ◇ 7   ♣ Q 8 7

WEST	NORTH	EAST	SOUTH
		pass	pass
pass	1♡	2◇	?

Your partner's 1♡ opening has improved your hand. Do not cuebid 3◇; do not bid 4◇ even though you and your partner play splinters. Jump directly to 4♡. Do not make it easy for West to double to suggest a sacrifice. Remember, when faced with a close choice between a natural call and an artificial, choose the natural, especially in a competitive auction.

Matchpoints, N-S vul.

♠ J 10 9 6 4 2   ♡ A 8 7   ◇ Q 9   ♣ A 8

WEST	NORTH	EAST	SOUTH
			?

With your present partner, you play moderately wanton Weak Two-bids with non-forcing new-suit responses… for "rescue" presumably. Is this the time to trot out a Weak 2♠ bid?

Under the circumstances, yes! You'll be happy whether partner passes, raises or rescues. Finally, a hand that fits your methods.

Of course, playing either Mainstream or Sound Weak Twos, you should pass (second choice, 1♠), as you have too little strength in your suit and too much strength outside.

Matchpoints, Both vul.

♠ A K 6 4 2   ♡ A J 6 3   ◇ 6   ♣ 10 8 7

WEST	NORTH	EAST	SOUTH
		1◇	?

It's better to double, bringing hearts into the picture, than to overcall 1♠. Hands with 5-4-1-3 and 4-5-1-3 patterns are generally handled

With 5-3 in the majors (a two-card discrepancy), a singleton in opener's minor and four cards in the unbid minor, it is much better to overcall in the five-card major than to double (unless the five-card major is weak). Then, after a raise of opener's minor and two passes, you may be able to double on the second round.

better with takeout doubles of 1◇ than with overcalls in five-card majors, unless there is a large discrepancy between the quality of the two suits. Here both suits contain the ace and another honor (the discrepancy is small). Partner will look to bid a four-card major rather than 2♣ in reply to a double of 1◇, but if he does bid 2♣, your clubs will serve well to ruff diamonds, while your top tricks in the majors will be useful.

 122

Matchpoints, Neither vul.

♠ 5   ♡ K J 4 2   ◇ A 9 7 3   ♣ K J 7 6

WEST	NORTH	EAST	SOUTH
1♠	pass	1NT[1]	pass
2◇	pass	2♠	pass
pass	dbl	pass	?

1. Forcing, may contain as much as 12 HCP.

You must start digesting every call at the time it is made. When West bids 1♠, think, "Five spades."

When East responds 1NT, think, "Probably not game values, and if only normal high-card strength, at most two spades."

When West rebids 2◇, think, "Four diamonds, but in light of forcing notrumps, possibly a 5-3-3-2 pattern, since he must bid something. Less than game values."

When East takes a 2♠ preference, think, "Minimum response, doubleton spade."

When West passes, think, "Only minimum to moderate strength."

Now when partner doubles, you can conclude, "They're on a 5-2 fit, with little extra for their bids. Partner, whom the auction marks with five spades, must have strong spades stacked behind West. They're in deep trouble, for I have surprising high-card strength."

Then you won't have to rely on any misguided "rules" (e.g. "all low-level doubles are for takeout") that somebody told you. The only problem you'll have is refraining from licking your lips as you *pass*.

NORTH (dummy)
♠ A 8 7 2
♡ 7 6 4
◊ A K J 5 2
♣ 5

WEST (you)
♠ 6 5
♡ Q 8 5 2
◊ Q 8 6 3
♣ A K 4

WEST	NORTH	EAST	SOUTH
		pass	pass
pass	1◊	pass	1♠
pass	2♠	pass	pass[1]
pass			

1. After long huddle.

You lead the ♣K. Partner plays the ♣J and declarer follows with the ♣8. Now you know that partner has ♣J10x and other clubs. Time to shift, but to what?

Dummy's diamonds are a source of tricks and the only losers declarer might need to pitch on them are hearts. You should shift to the ♡2; dummy's diamonds make it an emergency.

Instead you shift to the ♠6, a dangerous move, possibly blowing a trump trick. If declarer has ♠KJ10x, he might otherwise have misguessed the queen. If he has ♠Q109x, he would otherwise have taken two finesses through you. Fortunately, it doesn't cost a trump trick, as declarer has ♠KQ103. Declarer draws trumps in three rounds, ending in hand as partner follows. Think, "Only four spades, therefore fewer than four hearts (else he'd have responded 1♡)."

You discard a heart. Declarer starts diamonds by leading the ◊10 through you. Is there anything to be gained by covering?

Yes, if partner has the ◊9, so cover.

When you follow small, declarer lets the ◊10 ride, finesses the ◊J next, and runs diamonds, pitching two hearts and a low club. What do you discard on the fifth diamond?

Declarer has shown up with only four spades and cannot have four hearts. Partner's strength, besides the ♣J and ♠J that have already appeared, must be in hearts. Therefore you needn't keep a guard for your ♡Q. Keep length with declarer in clubs and come down to

♡Q8 ♣A4. If you discard a club, declarer can cross to his ♡A, ruff out your ♣A, ruff a heart with his last trump and take a trick with the ♣Q. Declarer's hand was

♠ K Q 10 3   ♡ A 9 3   ◇ 10 7   ♣ Q 8 7 6

No wonder he hesitated before passing his partner's 2♠ raise. He might have bid 2NT to try for game.

124

There are three boxes on the convention card to check for jump shifts over an opponent's takeout double: for "forcing," "invitational" and "weak". I've never seen anyone check the box for "forcing"; I favor playing these jump shifts as invitational. However, if you play that a new-suit response at the one-level is forcing, then it's reasonable to play a jump shift at the two-level as weak.

Matchpoints, E-W vul.

♠ A J 10 7 6 4   ♡ 5 4   ◇ 10 3   ♣ 8 3 2

WEST	NORTH	EAST	SOUTH
pass	1◇	dbl	?

With your present partner, you play Weak Jump Shifts over an intervening takeout double. This is a perfect hand for one. Bid 2♠. A 1♠ bid lets West bid 2♡ or 2♣ — or show extra values by jumping to 3♡ or 3♣. What's the point of playing a convention or treatment if you don't use it when the hands for it arise?

However, you neglect to bid 2♠ now, with a predictable outcome:

NORTH (dummy)
♠ 9 5 3
♡ K 7 3
◇ A 9 6 4
♣ A K 4

☐

SOUTH (you)
♠ A J 10 7 6 4
♡ 5 4
◇ 10 3
♣ 8 3 2

WEST	NORTH	EAST	SOUTH
pass	1◊	dbl	1♠
2♡	dbl[1]	pass	2♠
pass	pass	3♡	3♠
all pass			

1. Support Double (three-card raise).

West leads the ♡6 and you correctly cover with dummy's ♡7. East wins with the ♡10 and returns the ♠Q. What now?

East's ♠Q shift looks strange. Apparently he didn't know he could afford to break clubs. You should take the ♠A and return the ♠J, hoping he started with ♠KQ doubleton and will think himself endplayed. If he exits in diamonds, you may be able to set up dummy's ◊9 for a club discard.

By the way, do you see the effect of your failure to use the Weak Jump Shift? You let West bid at the two-level, which in turn let East push you to the three-level. Most likely, an immediate 2♠ would have bought the contract.

Matchpoints, N-S vul.

125

♠ A K J 3 ♡ A Q 8 3 ◊ 6 ♣ Q J 7 6

WEST	NORTH	EAST	SOUTH
	1◊	pass	1♡
pass	2♣	pass	2♠[1]
pass	3♣	pass	?

1. Fourth suit artificial and forcing (to game if a reverse or at the three-level).

Well, now that you've learned that partner is 5-5 in the minors, do you like your hand? You should. You're in the slam zone. Bid 4♣ to settle the trump suit. Won't you love to see partner cuebid 4◊ (showing the ◊A) or 4♡ (showing the ♡K)?

Experts disagree whether a king or a singleton should be cuebid when the ace of the suit has not been cuebid previously. I say *no*, except that the *king of partner's first suit* may be cuebid as freely as an ace.

Matchpoints, Both vul.

NORTH (dummy)
♠ A K Q 10 6
♡ Q 6 3
◇ K 9 6
♣ 5 4

WEST (you)
♠ J 3
♡ K 8 5 2
◇ Q J 10 8 4
♣ Q 7

WEST	NORTH	EAST	SOUTH
			1♣
pass	1♠	pass	2◇
pass	2♡	pass	2NT
pass	3NT	all pass	

You lead the ◇Q to dummy's ◇K; partner plays the ◇2 and declarer plays the ◇3. The ♣4 goes to partner's ♣6, declarer's ♣9 and your ♣Q. You continue with the diamond ◇10 to drive out declarer's ◇A as partner discards the ♡4. Now declarer cashes four high clubs. You can afford to discard two hearts and your low diamond, so you do. Dummy discards a diamond and two hearts; partner, who has followed to four clubs, discards the ♡7.

Here come the spades. South discards the ◇5 on the second spade and the ◇7 on the third spade. You discard a diamond too. On the fourth spade, declarer discards the ◇9. You must discard in this ending:

NORTH (dummy)
♠ 6
♡ Q
◇ —
♣ —

WEST (you)
♠ —
♡ K 8
◇ J
♣ —

Your ◇J is the thirteenth diamond and partner is known to have the high spade and one heart left, while declarer is known to have two hearts left. If partner's remaining heart is the ace, your play won't matter. Partner will take the last two tricks with the ♡A and the high spade. If partner's remaining heart is not the ace, then you must keep both your hearts to stop declarer's low heart from taking a trick.

You must discard the thirteenth diamond. Even if you knew that partner had the ♡A, discarding the ◇J couldn't hurt. However, it's virtually certain that declarer has the ♡A, as he wouldn't "have" his 2◇ reverse without it. Discarding a heart is a "can't gain, almost sure to lose" play.

Matchpoints, Neither vul.

127

♠ A 5   ♡ A K Q 10 9 3   ◇ A J 10   ♣ A 7

WEST	NORTH	EAST	SOUTH
			2♣[1]
pass	2◇[2]	pass	?

1. Omnibus 2♣.
2. Neutral response.

Bid 2♡. You'll soon find out what kind of hand partner has. With a very weak hand, he'll rebid 2NT, your conventional "second negative". With a positive response with heart support, he'll raise to 3♡. With a positive response in some other suit, he'll rebid 2♠, 3♣ or 3◇.

You've already jumped when you opened 2♣. You don't have to jump again to show a powerhouse. Besides, any jump bid you make now will crowd the auction. The hand could belong in any of the four suits or notrump. Take it slow and find out.

A jump to 3♡ or 3♠ by an Omnibus 2♣ opener has a special meaning. It shows a solid suit, sets that suit as trumps and asks responder to show aces and kings. With an ace, responder bids the suit of his ace. With no ace but at least one king, responder bids 3NT. With neither an ace nor a king, responder raises opener's major.

You jump to 3♡ and the auction continues:

WEST	NORTH	EAST	SOUTH
			2♣[1]
pass	2◇[2]	pass	3♡[3]
pass	3NT[4]	pass	?

1. Omnibus 2♣.
2. Neutral response.
3. Solid hearts, triggering cuebids.
4. No ace, at least one king.

Don't pass. Bid 4♣. Wouldn't you like to hear more about partner's hand? He's unlimited; you could be cold for a grand slam. It's senseless to ask if partner has an ace when you can tell from your own hand that he doesn't, and then pass 3NT, knowing that he has at least one king, but knowing nothing else about his hand.

Partner might have:

(a) ♠ K 7 3   ♡ J 8 7 2   ◇ 3   ♣ K 8 5 4 2

(b) ♠ K 7 3   ♡ 2   ◇ K Q 9 8 5 2   ♣ 8 5 4

(c) ♠ K Q J 3   ♡ 2   ◇ K Q 5 2   ♣ K 8 5 4

(d) ♠ J 10 9 8 7 3 2   ♡ 2   ◇ K Q 5   ♣ 5 4

(a) will produce 7♡, (b) will produce 7◇, (c) will produce 7NT, (d) may not suffice for 3NT but can produce 4♡ or 6♠.

128

The Lebensohl convention (see #82 and #115) can be adapted to advancing partner's takeout doubles of Weak Two-bids.

When partner doubles a Weak Two, the need for distinguishing different grades of responding hand is even greater than when an opponent intervenes over an opening 1NT. Why? Two reasons:

(1) A takeout double of a Weak Two-bid encompasses a much wider variety of hands than a 1NT opening.

(2) With a very weak hand, responder can always pass after an opponent overcalls a 1NT opening, but advancer doesn't have the option of passing a takeout double of a Weak Two-bid.

Although fancy versions of Lebensohl in reply to doubles of Weak Twos exist, and have technical advantages, I can recommend a simple version wholeheartedly. You can play that direct non-jump suit bids at the three-level show "constructive" hands: in point-count terms, they show about 8 to 11. Lebensohl 2NT asks doubler to bid 3♣, which advancer will pass with a weak club hand; any subsequent bid by the Lebensohl 2NT bidder shows a weaker hand than the same bid would show if made directly.

Matchpoints, Both vul.

In contrast to *Lebensohl Responses*, *Lebensohl Advances* are so simple that partner figures to have no trouble alerting and explaining adequately.

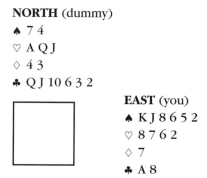

NORTH (dummy)
♠ 7 4
♡ A Q J
♢ 4 3
♣ Q J 10 6 3 2

EAST (you)
♠ K J 8 6 5 2
♡ 8 7 6 2
♢ 7
♣ A 8

WEST	NORTH	EAST	SOUTH
2♢ [1]	pass	pass	dbl
pass	3♣ [2]	pass	3♡
pass	4♡	all pass	

1. Weak Two-bid.
2. Alerted as forcing.

Apparently, your opponents agreed to play Lebensohl Advances, but thought that Lebensohl Advances work the same way as Lebensohl Responses. That explains the strange treatment of North's 3♣ as forcing, which it would be after 1NT-2♢.

Partner leads the ♣5 to dummy's ♣Q and your ♣A. Surprisingly, declarer ruffs and leads the ♡5 to dummy's ♡J as partner follows with the ♡4. Next comes a successful finesse of the ♠Q, on which partner drops the ♠10. Declarer then plays the ♠A, on which partner discards the ♢10.

Declarer ruffs a spade in dummy and leads dummy's ♣J. He then discards a low diamond and partner takes the ♣K. Partner exits with the ♣9; dummy plays the ♣10 — and you?

You must trump. Discarding will only give declarer a trick he could not otherwise get. True, declarer will overruff, but he'll do so with a trump that will score anyway.

However, you discard a spade and declarer discards another low diamond. He then leads a low club from dummy. You discard a spade and so does declarer. Partner wins cheaply and plays the ♢A and a low diamond. What now?

This is your last chance to ruff, else declarer will score the ♢K, finish drawing trumps and make his contract. How many chances to trump his winners do you need?

Partner's Weak 2♦ bid with a 1-1-6-5 pattern was certainly unorthodox, and I would not recommend it. Nonetheless, on this deal it had a chance of working, as it somehow prodded the opponents to bid a very shaky game. Nowadays, preempts have that effect more often than not. For this reason, promiscuous preemptors and their partners need to be good defenders.

 129

Matchpoints, N-S vul.

NORTH (dummy)
♠ J 10 9 7 6
♡ 5 2
◇ 10 8 4
♣ Q 10 3

SOUTH (you)
♠ A 8
♡ A K 7 6
◇ K Q 9 6
♣ 8 6 5

WEST	NORTH	EAST	SOUTH
			1NT
pass	2♡[1]	pass	2♠
all pass			

1. Jacoby Transfer.

Ruffing gains in a number of situations:
+ When you ruff with trumps in the short hand that you don't need for drawing trumps.
+ When you ruff with low trumps in the long hand that might not otherwise take tricks.
+ When ruffing lets you score your own trumps and dummy's separately.
+ When ruffing helps you establish tricks in a side suit.
+ When you need to shorten yourself in trumps to prepare for a Trump Coup.

West leads the ♡4 to East's ♡J, and you win with the ♡A. What now?

Draw trumps with the ♠A and the ♠8. You have nothing you need to ruff in the short hand, but a defender may be able to ruff one of your diamond tricks. You gain nothing by ruffing hearts in dummy: the spades with which you ruff are winners regardless.

♠ Q 9 7 6 5 2 ♡ 3 ◊ K 9 2 ♣ J 8 7

WEST	NORTH	EAST	SOUTH
	1♣	pass	1♠[1]
2♡	2♠[2]	3♡	?

1. Extra length or strength.
2. Playing Support Doubles, four-card support.

In view of your use of Support Doubles in this auction, you know that partner has four spades. (Did you remember to alert his raise?) You also know that you have little defense against 4♡. So bid 4♠ right away. The opponents may not know whether you are bidding it to make or as a premature save. Moreover, West won't have a forcing pass available and may have to guess whether to double or bid 5♡ instead of being able to shunt the decision to East.

♠ 8 6 ♡ 5 4 2 ◊ A K Q J 8 4 ♣ J 8

WEST	NORTH	EAST	SOUTH
		pass	?

If you play Weak 2◊ Bids, open 2◊. You have an ideal hand for one in second seat vulnerable. Otherwise you must pass or open a shaded 1◊. To open 3◊ vulnerable is to overbid by one trick.

In the following problem, you have twisted your partner's arm so hard that he has agreed that opener *must* reopen after responder passes in an auction where negative doubles apply. Partner, who is a choco-holic, has named this convention *OREO*, an acronym for Opener Relies Entirely on Opponents: that is, on his LHO *not* to have substantial extras for his overcall and on his RHO *not* to have passed with either a good fit or a decent hand.

At your partner's insistence, you have agreed to alert both responder's passes and opener's balancing calls.

As an incentive to play OREO, you have an ancillary agreement that after every deal in which you use the convention, successfully or unsuccessfully, each of you will march to the refreshment table of the bridge club and eat one of the Oreo cookies to be found there.

Many bridge players think that opener is *obliged* to reopen when responder passes an opponent's overcall... just to cater for responder's possible trump stack.

Disabuse yourself of that misconception. Not only are hands for penalty doubles of low-level overcalls rare, but the penalty pass cannot substitute fully for the forsaken penalty double. Opener can pull a low-level penalty double if short in overcaller's suit, but he cannot pull a penalty pass.

Matchpoints, E-W vul.

♠ Q 8 5 3 2   ♡ 6   ◇ 8 7   ♣ K Q 9 4 2

1. By partnership agreement, *requires* partner to reopen if West passes.
2. By partnership agreement, says *nothing* about his hand.

WEST	NORTH	EAST	SOUTH
pass	1◇	1♠	pass[1]
pass	dbl[2]	pass	?

.

You have one trump trick defending against spades. Partner may have club length (he *might* have a normal takeout double with a 1-4-4-4 pattern). If so, your ♣K and ♣Q may be of little value on defense. Bid 2♣. You must not pass for penalties.

Would it surprise you to learn that your side can make a slam, yet you can't beat 1♠?

Matchpoints, Neither vul.

NORTH (dummy)
♠ A 8 3
♡ K 5
◇ J 4 3
♣ K J 9 6 5

SOUTH (you)
♠ K Q J
♡ A 7
◇ A K 8 6 2
♣ A 4 3

WEST	NORTH	EAST	SOUTH
		pass	2NT
pass	6NT	all pass	

West leads the ♡Q. How should you play?

You have nine top tricks and need three more to make 6NT. If either minor runs for five tricks without loss, you're home. If you lose a club trick, you can hope you have no diamond loser. If you lose a diamond trick, you can hope you have no club loser. Which minor should you try first?

Clubs, for three reasons. First, the defenders can see the long clubs in dummy, and won't discard any if you start (and run) diamonds, but they can't see your long diamonds and may discard diamonds while you're running clubs.

Second, you can more often "change horses" in mid-play if the clubs don't run than if diamonds don't run. Your best play for five club tricks is a second-round finesse against West's possible guarded ♣Q. Suppose, for example, you win the ♡K at Trick 1, lead a club to your ace at Trick 2, finesse the ♣J at Trick 3 and learn that East started with a small singleton club (3 holdings). Or suppose West follows to the first club with the queen but shows out on the second (1 holding). That's a total of 4 holdings. In either case, you have three club tricks without losing a club, and can play diamonds for four winners and one loser. Your best play for five diamond tricks is to play diamonds from the top, hoping that the ◇Q will fall doubleton. You can change horses only if the ◇Q is singleton in either hand (2 holdings).

Third, you risk going down by more when diamonds split badly than when clubs split badly. If you play two top diamonds but West shows out on the second round, you'll be down two when you lose a finesse to East's doubleton or tripleton ♣Q. Playing the ◇A and a low diamond towards dummy's ◇J gives up any chance to run five diamond tricks, and settles for at most four diamond tricks no matter how the diamonds lie; you still need to get lucky in clubs to come to twelve tricks. If you do play on diamonds first, you must play them from the top, else you're committed to picking up the ♣Q regardless.

Do you think playing the ◇A and a low diamond is a "safety" play? Safety plays are for rubber bridge, IMPs, and sound games and slams that the field won't reach at matchpoints — not skinny, precarious games and slams.

Playing the ◇A and a low diamond towards the jack never succeeds when starting on clubs fails. The best line is to play the ♡K and the ♣A and then finesse the ♣J. If the clubs are running, run them, discarding two diamonds. When you do so, a defender with ◇Qxx may discard one, hanging on to ♠10xxx or a guarded ♡J instead. Then cash your spades. Once again, West may discard from ◇Qxx in order to keep hearts. You might even make an overtrick.

If dummy's ♣J loses to East's ♣Q, East will probably return a heart. Take the ace and run clubs as before, hoping for either the fall of the ◇Q or a pseudo-squeeze and defensive error.

Matchpoints, Neither vul.

NORTH (dummy)
♠ 9
♡ Q 6 5
◇ A J 10 8 2
♣ Q 9 5 4

EAST (you)
♠ A Q 10 3
♡ 10 9 7
◇ K 9 5
♣ A K 10

WEST	NORTH	EAST	SOUTH
pass	pass	1NT	pass
pass	2♣¹	pass	2◇²
all pass			

1. Unspecified minor, perhaps with an unspecified major.
2. Bid a major if you have one, else pass with diamonds or correct to 3♣ with clubs.

Partner leads the ♣8. You take the ♣K as declarer follows small and make a good shift to the ♡10. Partner plays the ♡8 and dummy's ♡Q wins. You rise with the ♠A when dummy's ♠9 is led and continue with the ♡9. Declarer takes the ♡K and partner follows with the ♡3. Declarer discards a club from dummy on the ♠K as partner's ♠J falls. Next comes a spade ruff (while partner discards the ♣7), a heart to declarer's ace and another spade ruff (while partner discards the ♡J). Declarer calls for dummy's ♣9 in this ending:

NORTH (dummy)
♠ —
♡ —
◇ A J 10
♣ Q 9

EAST (you)
♠ —
♡ —
◇ K 9 5
♣ A 10

Who has the ♣J?

From partner's opening lead of the ♣8, you know he doesn't. Actually, you know more: when partner discarded the ♣7 next, you could read him for at most three clubs. (With four, he'd have discarded his lowest club, and then another.) So, partner started with ♠Jx ♡Jxxx ♣87x and ... what in diamonds?

Four diamonds. If you don't take the ♣A now, declarer's ♣J will score and then, with nothing but diamonds left, partner will ruff your ♣A (instead of ruffing declarer's ♣J).

Matchpoints, N-S vul.

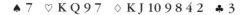

(135)

♠ 7   ♡ K Q 9 7   ◇ K J 10 9 8 4 2   ♣ 3

WEST	NORTH	EAST	SOUTH
		1♣	?

Bid a bold 4◇ or a cautious 3◇, but don't pass.

Do you think that if you pass, you will find a heart fit and reach 4♡? Just about the only way that will happen is if West passes and partner bids 1♡. That's very unlikely, for even if West passes, partner will probably have club length and pass also. However, the most likely candidate for the next bid is a spade bid, whether by West or by North. The next most likely bid is a club raise by West.

You may want to adjust your preempt to your opponents' negative double range. If they play negative doubles of preempts as high as 4◇, that's what you should bid. Look at their convention card to decide.

Your four-card heart suit makes a diamond preempt more potent. If West lacks heart support he may decline to make a negative double, and if East lacks heart support he's unlikely to make a reopening double, so the opponents may not be able to find their spade fit.

After you pass, the auction continues:

WEST	NORTH	EAST	SOUTH
		1♣	pass (!)
1♠	pass	4◇[1]	?

1. Splinter raise.

What lead would you like? Not a diamond, which can't set up a trick for you when dummy has a singleton. You want a heart through dummy's likely ♡A, to set up a heart trick or tricks before declarer can

Note that at adverse vulnerability, a double of an opposing splinter suggests only an opening lead. It does not suggest a sacrifice — especially if the doubler had a chance to bid at a low level and did not.

set up dummy's clubs to discard his heart losers. What's partner's normal lead against a spade contract on this auction? A heart. So why beg for a diamond lead and stop him from leading hearts? *Pass*, don't double. Before making a lead-directing bid or double, look at your holding not only in the suit but also in the suit or suits that partner might lead without your help.

136

Matchpoints, N-S vul.

♠ A 9 8 7 4 2   ♡ Q   ◇ K   ♣ Q 9 7 6 2

WEST	NORTH	EAST	SOUTH
pass	1◇	3♡	?

(a)   What do you call if you have negative doubles in your bidding arsenal?

(b)   What do you call if you *don't*?

(a) The literature on negative doubles is surprisingly sparse, and there are very few examples of negative doubles of 3♡ after a minor-suit opening. But even if you search that literature, you won't find any examples of negative doubles with hands like yours, because there are none. Nobody who writes about negative doubles would classify your hand as suitable, not even as close.

If you make a negative double, you can't expect partner to bid spades with ♠Kx or ♠Qxx, can you? You can expect him to bid 4◇, or pass for penalties.

Live dangerously: bid 3♠. You don't need partner to have four spades in order to want to play in spades. Or live cautiously: pass (not my choice). Don't double — not unless you relish the thought of defending 3♡ doubled if partner is balanced.

(b) If you *don't* play negative doubles, or play them only through 2♠, then the advice in (a) is doubly applicable.

"Since negative doubles at the one-level are never left in unless opener has five of the suit (and how often will opener have five of a higher-ranking suit than the one he opened?), responder doesn't have to worry about doubling with a void or a singleton. At the two-level, opener may well pass if the opponents happen to have bid his second suit, so responder should not make a negative double with a void or a weak two-suiter. At the three-level, responder should not double unless he is willing to have opener pass with a balanced hand." (Marshall Miles, *Competitive Bidding in the 21st Century*, p. 151)

Matchpoints, Both vul.

♠ K 10 6　♡ A K 10 5　◊ 10 9 7 4　♣ J 4

WEST	NORTH	EAST	SOUTH
	1♣	1♡	?

Should you bid 2NT, or should you bid 3NT to make sure of reaching game?

Bid 2NT. Your good spot cards make your hand worth 12 points, but that's not enough to insist on game by jumping to 3NT. You *probably* belong in game, but partner will *probably* bid game. Your ♡10 confers added protection in the suit, but it's not as valuable as the ♣10 would be if partner has a six-card suit with a hole in it (e.g. ♣ AQ9762).

2NT is also a more flexible bid than 3NT. Would your partner bid 4♠ over 3NT with

♠ Q J 9 8 2　♡ 7 3　◊ 3　♣ A K Q 9 2

or a minimum opening hand with six clubs and five spades? 2NT lets him bid 3♠ with a black two-suiter.

It's a good idea to play a 2NT response in competition as invitational, not forcing, even if it's a jump.

"Hamman's Law" says to bid 3NT whenever that's one of your choices. I disagree. When it's close between 2NT and 3NT and your partnership's hands haven't yet been defined very narrowly, choose 2NT. The extra level of bidding space will come in handy for finding the best strain for game.

Matchpoints, N-S vul.

NORTH (dummy)
♠ A K
♡ 7 6 4
◊ Q J 5 3 2
♣ J 8 6

WEST (you)
♠ 9 8 3 2
♡ A 2
◊ 9 8 6 4
♣ A 9 4

WEST	NORTH	EAST	SOUTH
			1♡
pass	1NT[1]	pass	2♣
pass	3♡	all pass	

1. Forcing, may conceal extras.

You lead the ♠9 to dummy's ♠K as partner follows with the ♠7 and declarer plays the ♠4. A low heart goes to partner's ♡J, declarer's ♡Q, and your ♡A. You return the ♡2 to partner's ♡9 and declarer's ♡K. Declarer plays the ◇A, dropping partner's ◇10, and then plays the ◇7 to dummy's ◇J and partner's ◇K. Partner cashes the ♡10. What should you discard?

Despite the 3-5-2-3 pattern that is possible for opener when playing "forcing notrumps", declarer's pattern is probably 2-5-2-4. Partner is about to exit in spades to kill dummy's last entry and keep declarer from establishing and cashing a long diamond. Eventually, declarer will have to attack clubs.

Don't give declarer any help. Don't signal your club holding. Partner knows you have something good in clubs, the ♣A or the ♣K, because if South, who has already shown up with 9 HCP in the red suits, had both top clubs, he would have accepted North's game invitation gladly.

Discard the ♠2. To signal with the ♣9 not only helps declarer play the suit (you surely wouldn't discard from ♣Q9x) but also surrenders a spot card that may take a trick. Yes, declarer has ♣K1072.

139

Matchpoints, Neither vul.

♠ Q J 3   ♡ 9   ◇ A 9 8 5 2   ♣ Q 9 6 2

WEST	NORTH	EAST	SOUTH
	1NT[1]	pass	?

1. 15-17 HCP.

In the notrump structure that you play with your present partner, a 2NT response is a puppet to 3♣, showing either a club bust or a strong three-suiter. Your only way to offer partner a choice between 2NT and 3NT is to "go through Stayman" en route to 2NT. What should you do when a natural raise to 2NT is unavailable?

If you start with a Stayman 2♣, you'll give West a chance to bid 2♡ and direct a lead. Most of the time, however, it will be partner who bids 2♡, or makes some other reply to Stayman that reveals something about his hand-pattern, either denying or affirming a four-card spade suit. The information won't help you, but it may help the opponents.

You'll do better to gamble 3NT than to bid a Stayman 2♣ with this hand. Second choice: pass.

You pass, but the auction is not over:

It's more important to make the contracts you bid than to bid only "percentage" contracts. Many an "anti-percentage" contract succeeds when reached via a route that tells the defenders little about declarer's hand. Likewise, many a "percentage" contract fails when reached via a route that needlessly gives the defenders information about declarer's hand.

WEST	NORTH	EAST	SOUTH	
	1NT[1]	pass	pass	1. 15-17 HCP.
2♣[2]	pass	2♡	?	2. Both majors.

What a revolting development this is! Bid 2NT, and hope that partner reads it as you intend, a request for him to bid his longer or stronger minor.

You bid 2NT, but it's too late for your side to buy the contract:

WEST	NORTH	EAST	SOUTH	
	1NT[1]	pass	pass	1. 15-17 HCP.
2♣[2]	pass	2♡	2NT	2. Both majors.
3♡	all pass			

What should you lead?

Best bet: the ♡9, in case declarer needs to ruff spades. Second best: the ♣2. Worst choice: any spade. Leading dummy's side suit helps declarer set it up. If you have spade tricks coming, they won't be going away (on what could declarer possibly discard spades?). This is a key concept for defenders to remember.

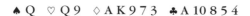

Matchpoints, N-S vul.

♠ Q   ♡ Q 9   ◇ A K 9 7 3   ♣ A 10 8 5 4

WEST	NORTH	EAST	SOUTH
pass	pass	4♠	?

Let's take a look at the options. In standard bidding, a double shows a strong hand, presumably balanced with two-way values (defensive and offensive) and is a final action unless partner has a long suit. 4NT is a strong distributional takeout, presumably three-suited, but conceivably may be based on diamonds and hearts because overcaller can correct 5♣ to 5◇ (implying hearts).

Here you should pass. You dare not bid 4NT "for the minors", because it isn't.

Suppose, however, that 4NT were for the minors. This would be the wrong hand for it. Your clubs and diamonds may well provide three fast defensive tricks. Your major-suit queens may be worth something on defense (partner may have jack-third or jack-fourth, for example).

I favor a defense against 4♠ preempts that uses the double for takeout (support for all three suits) and 4NT as a strong "Michaels" cuebid showing hearts and an unspecified minor. This requires partnership agreement, of course.

Ideally, a hand for a two-suited takeout contains suits like KQJ94 and QJ1076 — suits that are worth a lot on offense but don't figure to be worth much on defense. The orientation of a hand is a key concept: is your hand good only for offense, only for defense, or for both? The higher the level to which your bid drives the bidding, the more closely your hand should approximate the ideal.

Matchpoints, N-S vul.

♠ Q 6 3   ♡ K Q 7 5 4   ◇ A 8 5   ♣ K 6

WEST	NORTH	EAST	SOUTH
		1♣	1♡
1♠	2◇	pass	?

Bid 3◇. Your single club stopper and doubtful spade stopper do not give you a 2NT rebid. Your hearts aren't even close to establishment. From where do you expect to get eight tricks in notrump if the defenders start clubs and knock out your ♣K (for example)? You have only ordinary overcalling values, not extras.

However, you overbid slightly, and trouble follows:

WEST	NORTH	EAST	SOUTH
		1♣	1♡
1♠	2◇	pass	2NT (!)
3♠	4♣	pass	4◇
dbl	pass	4♠	?

Pass. Do not double. You've already shown your values. Partner will expect you to have at least as good a hand as you do, and he can double if it's right to do so. On this auction, your ♠Q figures to be worthless (though it might have been worth something if you had bid 3◇ instead of 2NT) and your ♣K won't be worth much if West is short in clubs.

Matchpoints, Both vul.

NORTH (dummy)
♠ A 8 7
♡ Q 6 3
◇ K 8 4
♣ A 9 7 6

WEST (you)
♠ J 6 4
♡ A
◇ A 10 9 5 3 2
♣ Q J 4

WEST	NORTH	EAST	SOUTH
1♢	dbl	1NT	2♡
all pass			

You lead the ♣Q to dummy's ace. Partner follows with the ♣2 and plays the ♢6 on dummy's subsequent ♢4. How should you continue after taking declarer's ♢Q with your ♢A?

Obviously, declarer is eager to discard something on dummy's ♢K. What do you suppose that something is? That's right, a club. How many clubs do you suppose partner has?

You should assume he has four. A 1NT response to 1♢ shows at least four clubs (if your partner has chosen to bypass a weak four-card major, that's his business, not something you should expect).

An exception arises among pairs that play Inverted Minor Raises. Their 1NT responses to 1♢ may be based on 3-3-4-3 or even 3-3-5-2 distribution, for their system keeps them from making simple 2♢ raises.

For this reason, when you're on opening lead against a declarer who has responded 1NT to his partner's 1♢, you should seldom lead clubs — and you should always check to see if the opponents are playing Inverted Minors no matter what you lead.

It can't hurt to continue with the ♣J at Trick 3. Partner's ♣2 was not a discouraging signal. Third hand can't afford to signal with a high card that he may need later to take a trick or keep declarer from taking a trick. For all partner knew at Trick 1, your ♣Q may have been a singleton or doubleton. If that were the case, to signal with the ♣8 from ♣ K1082 would subject him to a finesse against his ♣10.

A good defender signals only with cards he can spare, not potential tricks or stoppers.

Matchpoints, Neither vul.

143

♠ K J 4   ♡ Q J 9 5   ♢ J 8 7   ♣ 6 4 3

WEST	NORTH	EAST	SOUTH
1♠	2♣	pass	?

You really don't have enough information to solve this problem. I neglected to tell you about your partnership agreements and your partner's style. Here are the relevant questions.

(1) Do you play Weak Jump Overcalls or Strong Jump Overcalls?

If you play Strong Jump Overcalls, you have an easy pass. You have a balanced hand with one king, one queen and three jacks. You don't have any club honors that might help bring the suit home. Your partner didn't bid 3♣; if he couldn't make a Strong Jump Overcall, you won't have good play for game.

> (2) If you play Weak Jump Overcalls, are your partner's simple overcalls virtually unlimited? If not, does he routinely make off-shape takeout doubles with "Strong Jump Overcall" type hands?

If the latter, you also have an easy pass, for partner didn't start with a takeout double, so his simple overcalls are limited. However, off-shape takeout doubles create other, more severe problems; the "unlimited simple overcall" school may be right.

Unfortunately, if you play unlimited simple overcalls, you have an insoluble dilemma. The "unlimited simple overcall" school teaches players to reply to overcalls "as if they were opening bids"; you'd keep partner's 1♣ open, so this implies that you should bid 2NT over his 2♣ overcall. However, 2NT here shows more than a one-level response to an opening bid. You really aren't strong enough for 2NT; it's a constructive, invitational bid, akin to a minimum 2-over-1 response. I can't solve this dilemma, which is one of the reasons I abhor Weak Jump Overcalls.

The only good solution (which is unavailable mid-auction) is to persuade your partner to play Strong Jump Overcalls. Or must I first persuade you?

144

Matchpoints, N-S vul.

♠ 4 3   ♡ 7   ♢ Q 9 8 5 3 2   ♢ 9 8 6 2

WEST	NORTH	EAST	SOUTH
1♡	1NT[1]	pass	?

1. 15-17 HCP with "system on".

"System on" over 1NT overcalls of *major-suit* openings (or over 2NT overcalls of Weak Two-bids) is crazy. It relinquishes two natural bids, 2♣ and 2♢, meaning all too often advancer will be unable to get out

This is another insoluble problem, because I haven't told you *which* system is on. Suppose you are playing the popular "Walsh" system of responses to 1NT, in which your only way to get out in diamonds is to bid 2♠ ("Minor-Suit Stayman") and then pass partner's 3♢ reply or "correct" his 2NT or 3♣ reply to 3♢.

Do you really want to get to the three-level with this hand? East, who has some assurance of strength from West's opening bid, may double, turning what might be a mere -100 after an uncontested "system" auction into a "matchpoint poison" -200.

Your guess is as good as mine. If West is about to double 1NT, you should pass, for then you can run to 2◊. If West is about to bid 2♣ or 2♡, you should pass and let him take partner off the hook. But if West is about to pass, by all means bid 2♠ (Minor-Suit Stayman).

"System on" over 1NT overcalls of *minor-suit* openings has arguable merits. It relinquishes only one natural bid: two of the unbid minor.

cheaply in a long minor. He seldom needs to seek a 4-4 fit in the unbid major (which requires game-invitational or better values) and there is never any use in being able to transfer to opener's major (nowadays, almost always at least five cards long).

If you can cure your partner of the psychosis that makes him insist on "System On", you're a better psychiatrist than I am.

Matchpoints, E-W vul.

145

NORTH (dummy)
♠ A Q J 8 5 3
♡ 10 4
◊ 7 3 2
♣ K 4

EAST (you)
♠ 6 4
♡ J 9 6 3
◊ 8 5
♣ 10 8 7 6 2

WEST	NORTH	EAST	SOUTH
			1◊
pass	1♠	pass	2♣
pass	3♠	pass	3NT
all pass			

Partner leads the ♡2. You cover dummy's ♡10 with your ♡J, which holds the trick. You return the ♡3; partner takes declarer's ♡K with the ♡A and continues with the ♡8, on which dummy discards the ◊2. You follow with the ♡6 and declarer takes the ♡Q. As you can see, declarer is not very skillful.

Declarer leads the ♠2; partner plays the ♠7, and dummy wins with the ♠J. Declarer discards the ◊4 on dummy's ♠A and continues with a low spade from dummy. What do you discard?

Keep winners, throw losers. Often it's as simple as that.

The ♡7 is missing and your ♡9 beats it. If declarer has the ♡7, you must save the ♡9 (it's a stopper). If partner has the ♡7, you need the ♡9 as an entry (you don't want partner to be endplayed and forced to lead from the ◇AQ or the ♣Q). So don't discard the ♡9.

At this point, you don't know declarer's distribution. He may be 1-3-5-4, but he may also be 1-4-4-4 or 1-3-4-5. You can't afford to discard a club, lest declarer have five clubs. Even when declarer has only four clubs, a club discard from you may dissuade him from taking a losing finesse if he has ♣AJxx. Discard the ◇5.

146

Matchpoints, E-W vul.

♠ A   ♡ J 10 7 6   ◇ A K 10 8 3 2   ♣ J 4

WEST	NORTH	EAST	SOUTH
pass	pass	1♡	2◇¹
dbl²	3◇	pass	?

1. Limited: you play Strong Jump Overcalls.
2. Negative double.

What is your opinion about your defensive prospects if, for example, West makes a repeat negative double? Do you think you're a favorite to beat 3♠, and would you compete to 4◇ over 3♠? For that matter, do you think you're a favorite to beat 4♠?

If your answer is *no*, then you should bid 4◇ now, or better yet, 3NT. When you're not vulnerable and you don't expect to get doubled, down two may be good bridge.

However, you allow West to balance at the three-level, and now *you* must decide whether to balance:

WEST	NORTH	EAST	SOUTH
pass	pass	1♡	2◇¹
dbl²	3◇	pass	pass
3♠	pass	pass	?

1. Limited: you play Strong Jump Overcalls.
2. Negative double.

Do you think you can beat 4♠? If not, are you confident they won't bid it if given a second chance? It's a big gamble to bid 4◇ now.

NORTH (dummy)
♠ 10
♡ A 10 4 3
♢ Q 8 7 4 3
♣ K 10 6

☐

SOUTH (you)
♠ K J 7 4
♡ K 8 7 2
♢ J 5
♣ A J 3

WEST	NORTH	EAST	SOUTH
			1♣
pass	1♢	pass	1♡
pass	3♡	all pass	

West leads the ♢K, and East plays the ♢2.

Encouraging or discouraging? A count card showing an odd number, or a count card showing an even number?

How can you tell if you don't look at the opponents' convention card? ACBL rules require each partnership to display two conforming convention cards on the table.

West shifts to the ♡5 and East's ♡Q falls to your king. You lead the ♡2 and West's ♡J appears, so you take dummy's ♡A. What now?

Draw the last trump with dummy's ♡10 and lead a low diamond to your ♢J. West will take his ♢A but have no good return. There's no reason to leave East's ♡9 outstanding.

Instead, however, you lead a low diamond to your jack and West's ace without drawing the last trump. West continues with the ♢10. What do you play from dummy?

If you've noticed that the opponents use Upside-Down Signals, you'll realize that East started with exactly ♢62; West's diamond continuation makes little sense otherwise. Even if you play low from dummy, East is about to trump with his ♡9; he knows that if he doesn't, you'll ruff, lead to dummy's ♡10 and take two discards on dummy's diamonds. So don't squander dummy's ♢Q on this trick.

Matchpoints, E-W vul.

NORTH (dummy)
♠ 9 6 5
♡ 4
♢ A J 9 6 2
♣ A K J 2

☐

SOUTH (you)
♠ A 3
♡ A K J 10 7 6
♢ 3
♣ 9 5 4 3

WEST	NORTH	EAST	SOUTH
pass	1♢	pass	1♡
pass	2♣	pass	2♠[1]
dbl	pass	pass	4♡
all pass			

1. Fourth suit artificial.

It would have been better to jump to 4♡ at your second turn, but that matters little now. West leads the ♡3. East plays the ♡Q. Take it from there.

You should finish drawing trumps (which divide 3-3) and discard two spades from dummy. Now you can count ten tricks. If the ♣Q is onside, that's one more; if clubs split 3-2, that's one more too. Yet another possible overtrick may come if you can set up dummy's diamonds. So play the ♢A and ruff a diamond. Cash the ♣K (West's ♣Q appears!) and ruff a second diamond as both defenders follow. Play the ♣J (West discards a spade) and ruff a third diamond (East discards a spade). Follow up with the ♣A, dummy's long diamond and the ♠A, making twelve tricks.

Running off your three long trumps doesn't gain anything; those trumps are better used to ruff out the diamonds.

NORTH (dummy)
♠ K 9 3
♡ 8 6 5 2
◇ Q
♣ A 10 8 7 5

WEST (you)
♠ Q 8 6 5
♡ 10 4 3
◇ J 6 4
♣ 4 3 2

A defender who holds the master trump almost always does best to cash it, thus extracting a low trump from declarer that declarer could otherwise score by ruffing, and sometimes preventing declarer from throwing him in with the master trump for an unpleasant endplay later. When the defender can draw two trumps (one of dummy's and one of declarer's) with his one high trump, the benefit of cashing the master trump is greater still.

WEST	NORTH	EAST	SOUTH
			1◇
pass	1♡	pass	1♠
all pass			

You lead the ♣4 and partner's ♣Q falls to declarer's ♣K. Declarer leads the ♠2 to dummy's ♠9 and partner's ♠10. Partner returns the ♡7 and declarer's ♡Q wins. South leads the ♠4 to dummy's ♠K and partner's ♠A. Partner exits with the ♡9 to declarer's ♡A. Next comes the ♠7, and your ♠8 holds the trick; partner discards the ◇9. This is the position:

NORTH (dummy)
♠ —
♡ 8 6
◇ Q
♣ A 10 8 7

WEST (you)
♠ Q
♡ 10
◇ J 6 4
♣ 3 2

What now?

Partner's ◇9 signals his ownership of the ◇A all right, but if you lead a diamond now, all you and your partner will get is his ◇A and your ♠Q; declarer will trump the third round of hearts.

You must cash your high trump first and then put partner in with your last heart. That will get you four tricks instead of two and beat the contract.

150

Matchpoints, Neither vul.

♠ 10 4 3   ♡ K 10 4   ◇ A J 9 3   ♣ K 8 6

WEST	NORTH	EAST	SOUTH
			pass
pass	1♠	pass	2♣[1]
pass	3♡	pass	?

1. Reverse Drury.

The Drury convention is a passed-hand 2♣ response that is designed to cater for light third- and fourth-seat openings in major suits. In the original version, a 2◇ reply by opener indicated that he didn't have a "genuine" opening bid. In the modern version, called Reverse Drury, the passed-hand 2♣ response to a major-suit opening shows a limit raise (but possibly only three-card support). Opener's retreat to two of his major rejects game, and opener's 2◇ rebid shows at least some game aspirations.

When you've told one story with your first bid, look for a second story to tell with your next bid. Don't tell the same story twice.

Have you discussed with your partner what continuations after a "Reverse Drury" 2♣ mean? Most who play the convention haven't, and there are several conflicting versions of Reverse Drury.

As you play it with your present partner, opener's 2♡ reply always shows a weak hand, even if the opening bid was 1♠. This permits the partnership to stop in 2♡ on a 4-4, 5-4 or 5-5 fit instead of 2♠ on a 5-3 or 4-3 fit. Opener's jump to 3♡, which should also be discussed, may be played either as a natural game force or as a game try, akin to a 3♡ game try over a simple raise to 2♠.

Regardless, you should bid 3NT. You have a "high-card maximum", but three very weak spades, a flat hand and stoppers. Partner already knows you have at least three spades, so why rebid spades when you have a much more descriptive bid available? If you bid 3NT, partner can always bid 4♠ himself, but if you bid 3♠ he may not be able to bid 3NT with an unstopped suit (e.g. a doubleton ♣Q or a singleton ◇K).

151

Matchpoints, Neither vul.

♠ 8 5 4   ♡ J 5 3   ◇ A J 8 7 6   ♣ A 7

WEST	NORTH	EAST	SOUTH
			pass
pass	1♠	pass	?

(a) What should you call if you play Reverse Drury?
(b) What should you call if you don't?

I've placed these questions in the wrong order. Many conventional bids (and sequences) replace natural bids in the supposed interest of greater efficiency. Before deciding to make a conventional bid, it's a good idea to ask yourself, "What would I do if the convention were unavailable?"

A Reverse Drury 2♣ replaces a passed-hand limit raise of partner's 1♡ or 1♠ opening. So…

(b) In borderline cases, look at your trump quality. Bad trumps call for conservatism. So does the helpful maxim, "Invite cautiously, accept aggressively". The logic behind the first clause is that if you invite and partner rejects, things may go very wrong and you'll have turned a plus into a minus. The logic behind the second clause applies primarily to IMPs, but it also applies to matchpoints; if at some other tables, North-South collect +300 against rambunctious opponents, your +170 won't be very good, but your +420 will. Your hand is borderline and your trumps are wretched. Bid 2♠, not 3♠.

(a) If you'd bid 2♠ without Reverse Drury, you should bid 2♠ playing Reverse Drury also. Though Reverse Drury does let you stop in 2♠, which a 3♠ limit raise does not, it also lets the next hand compete far more easily. Would you like it, for example, if West doubled a 2♣ response and East raised to 3♣? That can't happen if you bid 2♠.

Matchpoints, Both vul.

152

♠ K   ♡ A 10 7 2   ◇ A Q 6 5 3   ♣ K 8 3

WEST	NORTH	EAST	SOUTH
	pass	pass	?

A 1◇ opening is surely acceptable, but what will you do over a 1♠ response? If your system permits opening 1NT with a mediocre 15 HCP (what your hand is worth if you downgrade your singleton king), you should consider opening 1NT.

A singleton king is almost as good for notrump purposes as a small doubleton. Though it shouldn't be routine to open 1NT with a singleton king, you'll do well to consider doing so when the hand is awkward to bid otherwise.

As you should have expected (other players having the annoying habit of bidding the suits in which you are shortest), partner responds in your singleton:

WEST	NORTH	EAST	SOUTH
	pass	pass	1◇
pass	1♠	pass	?

Your notrump range is 15-17, so a 1NT rebid would show a weaker (12-14 HCP) hand. You have too much for it. You're not strong enough to force (and promise a rebid) with a 2♡ reverse. You need a constructive second bid from partner to be interested in game. Wouldn't you like to see partner raise 2◇ to 3◇? Then you could bid 3NT (or 3♡). So bid 2◇. You have no choice.

153

Matchpoints, N-S vul.

NORTH (dummy)
♠ 6 5 3
♡ K 10 9 3
◇ A 9 5
♣ 9 5 4

EAST (you)
♠ —
♡ A Q 6 5
◇ K Q 8 3
♣ K J 10 6 2

WEST	NORTH	EAST	SOUTH
		1◇	1♠
pass	2♠	dbl	pass
3♡	pass	pass	3♠
dbl	all pass		

Partner leads the ♣8 and dummy plays low. Which club should you play?

Play the ♣6. Partner's ♣8 will force declarer's ♣Q. If you play the ♣J, partner will infer that you don't have the ♣10 (else you'd have let the ♣8 ride).

Eventually, you reach this ending:

NORTH (dummy)
♠ 6 5
♡ K 10 9 3
◇ —
♣ —

EAST (you)
♠ —
♡ A Q 6 5
◇ 8
♣ 10

Partner has turned up with three diamonds, one club and has discarded the ♡7. You are on lead, having played one round of spades (on which you discarded the ♣2), three rounds of diamonds and three rounds of clubs (partner having ruffed one club). It's clear that partner can't have heart strength, and can't want you to lead hearts. So what does his high spot card mean?

It's a count card. Now you know that partner is 5-4-3-1. Thus declarer is 5-1-3-4, with one low heart, one high club and four spades remaining.

Lead your last club for partner to ruff with a high spade spot. Then he can put you back in with a heart so you can give him an overruff, or a trump promotion, by leading the thirteenth diamond.

Suppose you cash the ♡A instead and partner drops the ♡J. Why would he do that?

He dropped the ♡J to make it clear that continuing hearts will let dummy score two heart tricks and to beg you to revert to clubs or diamonds.

Matchpoints, Both vul.

154

♠ A K Q J 9 6 5 3 2 ♡ A 7 2 ◇ 6 ♣ —

WEST	NORTH	EAST	SOUTH
pass	pass	3♣	?

You have ten playing tricks, which is more than the eight or nine playing tricks that a jump to 4♠ would show. Should you double?

No. When you double an opposing three-level or four-level preempt, you must consider the possibility that partner will make a penalty pass. Should your club void alone deter you from doubling?

No. With

♠ A K 9 6 5 ♡ K Q 1 0 7 ◇ A 8 6 3 ♣ —

for example, you would surely double. Despite the club void, that hand figures to contribute three or four tricks to the defense. Your actual hand figures to contribute only one or two tricks to the defense; with nine spades, you can't count the ♠K as a trick and you may not even be able to score the ♠A.

Bid 4♠, even though that doesn't show the great offensive strength of your hand.

Luckily, even though you err by doubling, you get another turn and reach the right contract:

NORTH (dummy)
♠ 8 4
♡ Q 6
◇ Q J 10 8 5 3
♣ 8 3 2

SOUTH (you)
♠ A K Q J 9 6 5 3 2
♡ A 7 2
◇ 6
♣ —

WEST	NORTH	EAST	SOUTH
pass	pass	3♣	dbl(!)
pass	3◇	pass	4♠
all pass			

You ruff the opening club lead. How should you proceed?

Lead a low heart immediately. If the king is offside you dare not draw even one round of trumps first, lest the defenders maneuver to draw dummy's last trump before you can use it to ruff a heart.

155

Matchpoints, Neither vul.

♠ 5   ♡ A J 10 7 6 2   ◇ A 4   ♣ A 9 7 6

WEST	NORTH	EAST	SOUTH
	pass	pass	1♡
3◇[1]	3♠	pass	?

1. Weak Jump Overcall.

You have a close decision between 4♣ and 4♡. The ♡10 should sway you to bid 4♡. If partner has four strong clubs and two low hearts, you figure to take the same tricks playing in both suits. Conceivably, you'll take one more trick in hearts if partner's clubs are not so strong: you may be able to discard a club loser on dummy's spades if partner has a hand like

♠ K Q 10 7 2   ♡ Q 4   ◇ 8 3   ♣ K 8 5 2

You bid 4♣ and catch a good fit as everone passes:

NORTH (dummy)
♠ K J 9 6 2
♡ 5 3
◇ J 7
♣ K Q J 5

SOUTH (you)
♠ 5
♡ A J 10 7 6 2
◇ A 4
♣ A 9 7 6

West leads the ◇K. Plan the play.

   Take the ◇A and lead a club to the ♣J to start the hearts. When you lead to your ♡J, West wins with the ♡K and cashes the ◇Q. He continues with the ◇10. What now?

   Ruff high in dummy and discard your spade. Then take another heart finesse. If it works, lead a second low club to dummy's remaining honor. Even if West shows out, you can still take the proven finesse against East's remaining ♣10x, draw the last trump and run the rest of your hearts.

Matchpoints, E-W vul.

(156)

♠ A K Q 6   ♡ K 5 3   ◇ 8 3   ♣ Q 7 6 4

WEST	NORTH	EAST	SOUTH
		3♡	pass
pass	4♣	pass	?

Should you bid a four-card spade suit? No, not even a strong one. You needn't bid spades to find a 4-4 fit (if you have one). Cuebid 4♡, showing a strong raise to 5♣. If partner has a four-card spade suit, he'll bid it "on the way" to 5♣, and you can pass.

   Note that finding the right strain (choice of games) takes priority over trying for slam.

157

Matchpoints, N-S vul.

♠ A 8 6   ♡ K 7 6   ◇ J 7   ♣ Q 9 5 4 2

WEST	NORTH	EAST	SOUTH
			pass
pass	1◇	1♠	1NT
pass	2♣	pass	?

Your 1NT showed a spade stopper and a balanced 8-10 HCP. Now that partner has rebid 2♣, your hand is worth 12 points (no longer 8-10). You might have had

♠ Q J 8 6   ♡ K 7   ◇ 8 7 2   ♣ Q 5 4 2

Look how much better your actual hand is:

  (a) Instead of four clubs, you have five.

  (b) Instead of the worst holding (three small) in diamonds, part-ner's first suit, you have a useful jack.

  (c) Instead of lower spade honors facing partner's shortness, you have the ♠A, which covers partner's singleton without any wastage.

Bidding 3♣ doesn't do justice to all these pleasant surprises. There is a bid that does, however: a 2♠ cuebid.

158

Matchpoints, Both vul.

NORTH (dummy)
♠ K 10 6 4
♡ Q 6
◇ 9 6 5
♣ 9 7 4 2

EAST (you)
♠ Q 9 7 2
♡ A 7 5
◇ K 10 4
♣ Q J 6

WEST	NORTH	EAST	SOUTH
			1♡
pass	1♠	pass	1NT[1]
all pass			

1. 12-14 HCP.

Partner leads the ◇Q, which holds, as you play the ◇4 and declarer plays the ◇7. Partner continues with the ◇J. You overtake, and declarer wins with the ◇A. How many diamonds do you think partner has?

Three. From ◇QJxx, he'd have led fourth-highest (standard against notrump) rather than the ◇Q (standard against suit contracts), and even more surely, he'd have continued with his fourth-highest if for some esoteric reason he'd started with the queen.

Now declarer leads a low heart to dummy's ♡Q and you take the ♡A. How should you continue?

You must not cash the ◇10, which is sure to set up declarer's fourth diamond as a winner. Instead, you must shift to clubs: the ♣Q, not the ♣6. Declarer has no guess in the club suit, but to partner the ♣6 might appear to be top of a doubleton, inducing him to place declarer with ♣KQJ and credit you with the ♠A and the ♠Q.

Matchpoints, Neither vul.

159

♠J76 ♡AKJ8 ◇A2 ♣AQJ5

WEST	NORTH	EAST	SOUTH
	1♠	pass	?

With this hand, you have two reasonable plans. One is to start with 2♣, then keep forcing with new suits until partner has described his hand sufficiently for you to place the contract. The other, which I prefer, is to jump to 3♣ immediately. If you adopt this plan, however, you must show a Type (B) jump-shift, not a Type (F). This is usually achieved by rebidding in notrump. Because your hand is slightly better than the minimum for a Type (B) jump shift, it is reasonable to plan to rebid 4NT.

Remember: responder's jump shift may be based on (F) a big *Fit* for opener's suit, (B) a big *Balanced* hand or (I) an *Independent* suit in a good 8-winner (or better) hand. It says, "Slam may be laydown opposite the *right minimum*."

You jump to 3♣ and the auction continues:

WEST	NORTH	EAST	SOUTH
	1♠	pass	3♣
pass	3◇	pass	?

Now what? You have more than minimum values for a Type (B) jump shift. You dare not bid 3NT to show your Type (B) jump shift because 3NT is a game bid that partner can pass.

You can, however, rebid 3♡. If partner understands the three types of jump shift, he won't misread 3♡ as showing a club-heart two-suiter. Instead, he will read 3♡ as showing extra values, and most likely a Type (B) jump shift.

Mistakenly, you rebid 3♠, leading to:

WEST	NORTH	EAST	SOUTH
	1♠	pass	3♣
pass	3◇	pass	3♠ (!)
pass	4♣	pass	4◇
pass	4♡	pass	?

What does partner's 4♡ show? Hearts not having been bid previously, it shows specifically first-round control. This late in the game, at partner's fourth turn after he has bid three suits, the first-round control is apt to be a void. What else can it be when you have the ♡A? Your ♡AKJ8 thus represents 8 HCP in the least useful place.

Partner might have

♠ A Q 8 7 4   ♡ —   ◇ Q J 7 6 3   ♣ K 10 8

a very poor mesh with your actual hand.

♠ K 6 3 2   ♡ 8 5 4   ◇ A 2   ♣ A Q J 5

would be a much better hand on this auction.

Do not try to take control with Roman Keycard Blackwood. What you need for a small slam is a specific king, the ◇K, and RKCB cannot reveal whether partner has it without committing to slam. Slow things down by bidding 4♠. If partner has

♠ A Q 8 7 4   ♡ —   ◇ K 8 7 6 3   ♣ K 10 8

or similar, he won't pass 4♠, for he'll have one more cuebid left in his quiver: 5◇, after which you will reach the good slam.

NORTH (dummy)

♠ Q 10 8 7 3

♡ A J 9 8

◇ K 4

♣ 6 5

WEST (you)

♠ K J 6 2

♡ Q 7 6

◇ Q 9 7 2

♣ 9 4

WEST	NORTH	EAST	SOUTH
	pass	pass	1♣
pass	1♠	pass	1NT
pass	2♡	pass	2NT
all pass			

Although the normal opening lead is the ◇2, you lead the ♡6, and partner's ♡10 falls to declarer's ♡K. Declarer leads the ◇10. What should you play?

You must play low. Declarer may have ◇AJ10 and wonder which defender to play for the ◇Q. Note that covering cannot possibly promote a trick for your side; it can only take the guess out of the suit for declarer. Even if declarer leads the ◇J, you should not cover, for he wouldn't lead the ◇J without the ◇10 (unless he is a beginner).

The advice given to beginners, traditionally, is in the form of a so-called rule: "Always cover an honor with an honor." Then newspaper columnists make a big deal out of it when covering is wrong: "Rules are made to be broken. Sometimes it's right *not* to cover an honor."

The truth is actually much simpler. Rules are not made to be broken, but must be correctly stated. Here's my advice:

Cover a card that declarer (or dummy) leads when you think that by doing so you can promote another card in the suit as a trick for your side. Try to anticipate what you will do before the crucial play arises. Start planning as soon as you see dummy. Stop to think before turning Trick 1.

Matchpoints, Both vul. 161

♠ A Q 7 5   ♡ A J 10 3   ◇ 10   ♣ A Q J 10

WEST	NORTH	EAST	SOUTH
			1♣
pass	2♣	pass	2♡
pass	3♣	pass	3♠
pass	4♣	pass	?

So far you've bid well. Your 2♡ was a game try showing four hearts. Partner's 3♣ denied game interest and denied having a four-card major. He probably doesn't have the ♠K among his (limited) goodies, else he might have bid 2NT instead of 3♣. Your 3♠ was another good bid, showing game interest despite partner's rejection of game, and pin-pointing your singleton diamond. Partner's 4♣ showed a very bad hand for game (he declined to bid 3NT or 5♣).

It's close, but you should pass. Many pairs will reach 3NT, and they figure to go down. (The field hates minor-suit contracts.) For this reason, just making 4♣ will probably be a fine result, though of course you should try for an overtrick if you can do so without risking your contract.

Matchpoints, E-W vul.

NORTH (dummy)
♠ 8 3
♡ K Q 10 5
◇ Q 8 6 5 3
♣ J 6

WEST (you)
♠ J 9 2
♡ A 6 3
◇ A 7 4
♣ 9 5 4 2

WEST	NORTH	EAST	SOUTH
			1♠
pass	1NT	pass	2♡
all pass			

You lead the ♣2. Partner takes the ♣K and ♣A, as declarer follows with the ♣8 and the ♣10. Partner shifts to the ◇9 at Trick 3 and declarer plays the ◇2. What's declarer's exact hand?

Declarer has the ♣Q, else partner would have played the ♣Q at Trick 1. Partner has the ♣7, because declarer wouldn't release the ♣10 unnecessarily. Declarer is 5-4-1-3,

♠ A K Q x x   ♡ J x x x   ◇ 2   ♣ Q 10 8

(but conceivably no ♡J). With less, he wouldn't have opened. How should you proceed?

Take the ◇A and continue a diamond for declarer to ruff. Declarer will probably start trumps. Win the second trump and continue diamonds to remove declarer's last trump. You still have a trump to interrupt the run of the spades.

Matchpoints, E-W vul.

♠ A 10 8 6 5 2   ♡ K 8   ◇ —   ♣ K 10 7 6 4

WEST	NORTH	EAST	SOUTH
pass	pass	pass	1♠
pass	2♣[1]	pass	?

1. Reverse Drury (artificial limit raise).

Bid 4♠. Do not splinter with 4◇, for to splinter shows more than shortness — it implies that slam is possible. To try for slam is to look at this hand through rose-colored glasses. So long as you're going to play 4♠, bid it without telling the defenders anything about your hand.

I've heard some bridge players say, "The purpose of bidding is to describe your hand." That's wrong. The purposes of bidding are (a) to reach good contracts, (b) to avoid bad contracts and (c) to help you *make* more of the contracts you reach. You should describe your hand when doing so will further (a) and (b) more than it will hinder (c). When you *know* what the right contract is, and partner will no longer be involved, just bid it.

Matchpoints, Both vul.

♠ A 8 3   ♡ 9 7   ◇ 10 4   ♣ K J 10 7 5 4

WEST	NORTH	EAST	SOUTH
		1◇	pass
1♠	2♡	pass	?

Bid 3♣, which is constructive but not forcing as most pairs (including you and your present partner) play. It shows a hand and suit about as good as yours.

You pass, but you get another chance to bid clubs. Should you?

WEST	NORTH	EAST	SOUTH
		1◇	pass
1♠	2♡	pass	pass
3◇	pass	pass	?

You must pass. To bid either 4♣ or 3♡ would be inconsistent with your previous pass.

Look at the difference between direct action last turn and delayed action now. If you had bid 3♣ last turn, partner would know whether to compete further over West's 3◇. If you had bid 3♡ last turn, West would not have been able to bid 3◇ at all.

It's too late and too risky to try to "correct" the error you made last turn.

The standard meaning of simple new-suit bids after partner overcalls is natural, constructive and non-forcing. The ACBL convention card provides a box to check if you and your partner play this way. Two other boxes list alternative treatments: non-forcing (by which is meant *merely corrective*) and forcing. Only *forcing* and *non-forcing* constructive are reasonable. To play a new suit as merely *corrective* is seldom useful, as you can usually wait until an opponent doubles to "rescue" partner.

Matchpoints, Neither vul.

♠ A 9 6 5 4 ♡ A Q 7 ◇ 8 ♣ Q 9 8 3

WEST	NORTH	EAST	SOUTH
			1♠
pass	1NT	pass	2♣
pass	2♠	dbl	pass
3♣	pass	pass	?

Don't bother trying to figure out the hand when you don't have near-ly enough information to do so. Get one thing straight. A 1NT response to a minimum opening bid is not a favorite to make. Neither is a two-level contract reached after a 1NT response to a minimum opening bid unless your side has an eight-card or longer fit. Your expectation in 2♠ was to go down. Be happy that the opponents took you off the hook.

Here's a much better and much easier way to bid: when you've already shown your values and partner has not forced you to bid, just pass. You have a normal minimum for your auction. Pass. You're not close to doubling, and you certainly can't bid 3♠ with a one-honor five-card suit.

If the opponents had bid up to 5♣, it would still be wrong to dou ble. You've told your story, and if 5♣ should be doubled, partner wil know enough to do so.

Matchpoints, E-W vul.

NORTH (dummy)
♠ J
♡ 7 5 2
◇ A 6 3
♣ A K J 9 4 3

WEST (you)
♠ 8 6 3
♡ Q 9 8 4
◇ K J 9 7
♣ 6 5

WEST	NORTH	EAST	SOUTH
	1♣	pass	1♡
pass	2♣	pass	3NT
all pass			

You lead the ◇7. Dummy plays low and partner follows with the ◇5, declarer taking the trick with the ◇10. A finesse of dummy's ♣J loses to partner's ♣Q. Partner returns the ◇8. Declarer follows with the ◇2, and dummy wins with the ◇A. That's dummy's last entry outside the club suit.

What do you think the diamond layout is?

Partner started with ◇85. (If he had ◇854, he'd have played the ◇4 at Trick 1 instead of the ◇5.) So declarer started with ◇Q1042 and has ◇Q4 left.

Declarer discards two low spades on dummy's ♣A and ♣K, and you discard a low spade too. Then declarer leads a heart to his ♡10 and you take your ♡Q. What now?

Don't cash the ◇K; that will set up declarer's ◇Q. Declarer has no way to get rid of his two diamond losers without your help. (Dummy's clubs are not yet set up and there's no dummy entry to reach them anyway.) Just exit passively in hearts (or spades, now that declarer has pitched two of them) and wait to get two diamond tricks at the end.

By cashing a trick early, a defender often blows a trick. It will happen about four times for every one time it saves a trick, yet many players remember that one time they "lost an ace" and resolve never to let it happen again.

Matchpoints, Both vul.

167

♠ J 4 3   ♡ 7 5 4   ◇ A K J 6   ♣ K 4 2

WEST	NORTH	EAST	SOUTH
	pass	pass	?

After the 1-point deduction for a square hand, your hand counts as 11 HCP. Pass. Bidding 1◇ is wrong (but not terrible, thanks to the strength of the four-card diamond suit). Not vulnerable, 1◇ would be acceptable, since down one doubled, or down two not doubled, would not be a disaster.

168

Matchpoints, Both vul.

♠ J 4 3   ♡ 7 5 4   ◇ A K J 6   ♣ K 4 2

WEST	NORTH	EAST	SOUTH
	pass	pass	1◇
2♣	dbl[1]	pass	?

1. Negative double

You should discuss with each of your partners what a non-jump 2NT rebid by opener shows. Some play that it shows a hand that is too weak for a (strong) 1NT opening; others play that it shows substantial extra values (the treatment I favor).

Regardless of what this sequence means

WEST	NORTH	EAST	SOUTH
			1◇
pass	2♣	pass	2NT

recognize that bidding 2NT on the actual auction is radically different. In the above sequence, responder has promised 2-over-1 values. In the actual auction, responder has promised significantly less, perhaps only 1-over-1 values.

Having opened your cheesy hand because of the strength of its four-card diamond suit, you do best to rebid 2◇. A bid of 2NT is not only too encouraging (partner may raise to 3NT) but is almost sure to go down if partner passes.

Another merit of 2◇: with 5-4 in the majors, partner might bid 2♡ or 2♠ and reach a superior contract.

169

Matchpoints, E-W vul.

♠ J 10 3   ♡ A Q 7   ◇ K Q 9 8   ♣ J 6 5

WEST	NORTH	EAST	SOUTH
	pass	pass	?

Open 1◇. You have a 13-HCP hand and you have a good four-card diamond suit in which you would welcome an opening lead. Compare this to the previous deal, where South was vulnerable with a slightly weaker hand and thus risked a matchpoint poison -200. Here you are not vulnerable and you risk a smaller minus.

♠ A K 8 7 6   ♡ 7 4 3   ◇ A Q 8 2   ♣ A

WEST	NORTH	EAST	SOUTH
		1♣	?

It's close between 1♠ and double. Choose 1♠. Your hand isn't too strong for 1♠. Here's one way to look at it: would you worry about missing game if you overcalled 1♠ and three passes followed? You shouldn't, but you should worry about this (hypothetical) problem:

WEST	NORTH	EAST	SOUTH
		1♣	dbl
3♣	pass	pass	?

Would you bid 3♠? Far too dangerous! Would you double again? Care to guess what will happen if you double a second time? The suit partner is most likely to bid is your shortest, and you should act on the assumption that he will. Then you might face:

WEST	NORTH	EAST	SOUTH
		1♣	dbl
3♣	pass	pass	dbl
pass	3♡	pass	?

What would you expect partner to do with

♠ Q 9 3 2   ♡ K 9 5 2   ◇ 7 5   ♣ 9 6 4

or similar? Wouldn't you much rather face the following problem:

WEST	NORTH	EAST	SOUTH
		1♣	1♠
2♣[1]	pass	pass	?

Now you can double without qualms, knowing partner will prefer supporting spades with three to bidding a red suit with four.

1. Or 3♣ if played as weak.

Overcalling and then making a takeout double on the second round after responder raises is one of the most neglected strategies in bridge. Employ it when you have takeout-double values with a strong preference for one of the three unbid suits.

171

Matchpoints, Neither vul.

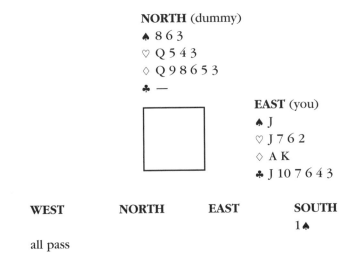

NORTH (dummy)
♠ 8 6 3
♡ Q 5 4 3
♢ Q 9 8 6 5 3
♣ —

EAST (you)
♠ J
♡ J 7 6 2
♢ A K
♣ J 10 7 6 4 3

WEST	NORTH	EAST	SOUTH
			1♠

all pass

Partner leads the ♢J; dummy plays low and you take the ♢K. What now?

    Lead your ♠J to cut down on dummy's ruffs. Do not try to cash the ♢A, as that would set up dummy's ♢Q (and perhaps more).

172

Matchpoints, N-S vul.

♠ Q 9 3 ♡ J 9 8 4 ♢ 8 2 ♣ Q 9 7 2

WEST	NORTH	EAST	SOUTH
	1♢	pass	?

In general, you needn't figure out partner's hand to discover the right call. The right technique is to compare your actual hand with what partner can expect from your previous calls. Here you have no pleasant surprises for partner in spades — you have one spade fewer than you might have had, for example, were your black-suit holdings reversed. You do, however, have a pleasant surprise for partner in diamonds — a second diamond when you might have had only one.

Pass. Bidding a weak four-card suit on this cheese begs for a minus almost regardless of partner's hand. If you pass 1♢, even if it's about to go down two, West will probably save you by balancing. (Today's opponents almost always do, especially if they've been told that it's right to balance with 1NT on as little as 10 HCP.) If West balances with a double and East makes a penalty pass, you can redouble for rescue and get out cheaply in another suit.

    However, you decide to "keep it open" and soon face this problem:

WEST	NORTH	EAST	SOUTH
	1♢	pass	1♡ (!)
pass	1♠	pass	pass
2♣	2♢	pass	?

Pass. When you passed 1♠, you already showed a preference for spades versus diamonds. You need at least two more spades than diamonds to return to 2♠. When you passed 1♠, partner expected you to have a weak hand (though not quite as weak as the one you had) with one or two diamonds and three or four spades. Under the circumstances, he'd be crazy to bid 2◊ with an ordinary five-card suit. His sequence shows four spades and five strong (more likely six) diamonds.

Matchpoints, N-S vul.

♠ J   ♡ K 3   ◊ A J 9 8 6 2   ♣ K Q 8 4

WEST	NORTH	EAST	SOUTH
pass	1◊	1♠	?

You and your present partner play splinters. Bid 3♠, a splinter slam try. This is the hand for which that bid was designed.

    Suppose, however, that you and your partner had agreed to play 3♡ and 3♠ responses to minor-suit openings as natural preempts (a reasonable treatment even for those who use splinter double-jump responses to major-suit openings). What should you bid with this hand in that case?

    You should still bid 3♠. Partner will interpret 3♠ as a splinter because you can't have a natural preempt in overcaller's suit.

Matchpoints, Neither vul.

♠ J 9 8 6 2   ♡ A 5 3 2   ◊ J 7 6   ♣ 3

WEST	NORTH	EAST	SOUTH	
			pass	
pass	1NT[1]	pass	2♣[2]	1. 15-17 HCP.
pass	2♠	pass	?	2. Stayman.

You have a close choice between 3♠ and passing. Don't even think about bidding game yourself. Had partner replied 2◊ to Stayman, you would have bid 2♠ (a signoff in your partnership methods). Does knowledge of partner's fourth spade make your hand two tricks better? No, only one. If he has a 15-HCP minimum, he'll need a miracle to make 4♠. If he has a good 16-HCP or 17-HCP maximum, he'll bid 4♠ over an invitational raise to 3♠.

Anyone who bids 4♠ with this hand is looking through rose-colored glasses.

175

Matchpoints, Neither vul.

WEST (you)
♠ A 9 5 2   ♡ 10 6 4   ◇ J 4 3   ♣ 10 7 3

WEST	NORTH	EAST	SOUTH
	pass	1♣	1◇
pass	2◇	all pass	

Leading an honor from honor-third is right only when you expect declarer to be short in the suit and dummy to have three or four cards to a higher honor in partner's suit. Then you should lead your honor in hopes of retaining the lead.

What should you lead?

Lead the suit your partner opened, clubs. The normal lead from a 1073 suit is the three. No reason to deviate here.

You lead the ♣7, however, and see this dummy:

NORTH (dummy)
♠ K 7 6 4
♡ Q 9
◇ 8 6 5
♣ A Q 6 4

WEST (you)
♠ A 9 5 2
♡ 10 6 4
◇ J 4 3
♣ 10 7 3

Declarer, who is not very gifted, plays the ♣Q from dummy. Partner takes the ♣K, declarer following with the ♣8. Partner then returns the ♣2 to declarer's ♣J, as you follow small. Declarer cashes three top diamonds; on the third diamond, partner discards the ♡5. Next comes the ♠10, which you duck. Dummy's ♠K wins and declarer discards a low spade on dummy's ♣Q. He then ruffs dummy's last club as you discard a spade. A low heart goes to dummy's ♡Q and partner's ♡K. Partner returns the ♠Q, which declarer trumps. What should you play in this end position when declarer leads another low heart towards dummy?

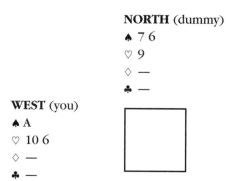

NORTH (dummy)
♠ 7 6
♡ 9
♢ —
♣ —

WEST (you)
♠ A
♡ 10 6
♢ —
♣ —

You have a complete count on the hand. Declarer is heart flush. Partner is marked with a 3-4-2-4 pattern and has one spade and two hearts left. Partner has shown up with the ♣K, the ♠Q, the ♠J and the ♡K thus far. One of his hearts must be the ♡A to give him his opening bid. You must play the ♡10, else dummy's ♡9 may force partner's ♡A, letting declarer's ♡J take a trick at the end.

Matchpoints, N-S vul.

176

♠ A Q 7 6   ♡ 8 5 4   ♢ Q 8 6 3   ♣ A 10

WEST	NORTH	EAST	SOUTH
		pass	1♢
1♡	2♡[1]	pass	?

1. Limit raise or better (by partnership agreement).

Bid 2♠ "on the way" to 3♢. Partner may have a strong hand with four spades and four or five diamonds.

Contrast that with this deal, in which the major suits are reversed:
Matchpoints, N-S vul.

♠ 8 5 4   ♡ A Q 7 6   ♢ Q 8 6 3   ♣ A 10

WEST	NORTH	EAST	SOUTH
		pass	1♢
1♠	2♠[1]	pass	?

1. Limit raise or better (by partnership agreement).

Bid 3♢. You can't bid 3♡ "on the way" to 3♢, as that would take you beyond 3♢. Level governs.

Matchpoints, N-S vul.

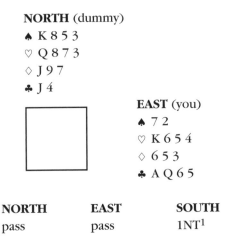

NORTH (dummy)
♠ K 8 5 3
♡ Q 8 7 3
◇ J 9 7
♣ J 4

EAST (you)
♠ 7 2
♡ K 6 5 4
◇ 6 5 3
♣ A Q 6 5

WEST	NORTH	EAST	SOUTH
	pass	pass	1NT[1]
all pass			

1. 15-17 HCP.

Count signals normally apply when declarer breaks a suit in which one partner has to decide whether to hold up an ace or king.

Partner leads the ◇K. Declarer takes the ◇A and plays the ♡A followed by the ♡J. Partner follows "up the line" with the ♡2 and then the ♡9. Should you take the ♡K or duck?

Declarer has ♡AJ. If he had ♡AJ10, he would have led towards dummy's ♠K or ◇J to finesse hearts through you, and partner would have played high-low from ♡92 to help you go right.

If you take the ♡K, partner's ♡10 will fall when declarer enters dummy to cash the ♡Q, and declarer will know that dummy's ♡8 is high. If you duck and declarer crosses to dummy, he may not know that partner's ♡10 can be smothered by the ♡Q, so he may abandon hearts and take only two heart tricks instead of three. Besides, declarer will have to use a second dummy entry even if he guesses the hearts. You have a sure club entry and can always cash the ♡K later if necessary. So you should duck.

However, you take the ♡K. What should you return?

Surely partner led from ◇KQ10x (he doesn't rate to have a fifth diamond, for that would mean South opened 1NT with 2-2 in the red suits). You should return a diamond to set up a second diamond trick for your side.

Some tips about unblocking:

First, don't unblock if you are in any doubt that you need to. It's especially disastrous for both defenders to unblock on the same trick. The second defender who unblocks on the trick is always to blame.

Instead, however, you return a heart to dummy's ♡Q as partner's ♡10 falls and declarer discards a low spade. On the fourth heart, declarer and partner both discard diamonds. A low spade goes to declarer's ♠Q and partner's ace. Partner shifts to the ♣10, covered by dummy's ♣J. What now?

Take the ♣A and return the ♣5 through declarer's ♣K. Partner is known to have the ♣9, his club shift presumably being from ♣109x, but you don't know the size of his third club. If he has led from ♣1097, a low club return is necessary to finesse against declarer's ♣8.

Instead of this, however, you play the ♣Q and declarer takes the ♣K. He continues with a diamond to partner's ◇Q and partner continues with the ♣9. What now?

Partner surely doesn't have ♣1098xx, which would give him a 1-3-4-5 pattern. Not only would he have led the ♣10 from that holding, but that would mean declarer had six spades and a 1♠ opening. If partner has ♣1098x, it doesn't matter whether you overtake his ♣9 or not; if he has any other club holding, however, overtaking blows a trick. You have no reason to assume that he has the ♣8 at all. You are marked with your side's club length and it is partner who must unblock. Partner, with ♣1092, had to continue with the ♣9 because a ♣2 continuation would block the suit when you had ♣AQ8x.

Second, don't unblock unless you are sure that your partner has greater length in the suit than you do.

Third, don't unblock when partner may be squeezed out of his high card in the suit.

Fourth, don't unblock if partner may need to get you in with a high card to lead some other suit through declarer's or dummy's strength.

Fifth, don't unblock when you still have two or more low cards in the suit: wait until the time when the alternative to unblocking is to relinquish your *last small card* in the suit.

Sixth, there's no such thing as unblocking with equivalent cards: both of them block the suit equally.

Matchpoints, E-W vul.

178

NORTH (dummy)
♠ 10 9 4 3
♡ A
◇ A J 9 5 4
♣ J 6 5

EAST (you)
♠ Q
♡ 10 9 6 5 4 3
◇ Q 10 3
♣ Q 10 4

WEST	NORTH	EAST	SOUTH
1♣	1◇	1♡	1NT
all pass			

Partner leads the ♡2 to dummy's ♡A and you follow with the ♡3. You cover dummy's ♠10 with the ♠Q, and declarer takes the ♠A. A low spade goes to dummy's ♠9 and you discard a heart. You follow small to dummy's low club and declarer's ♣8 fetches partner's ♣A. Partner shifts to the ◇2 and you take dummy's ◇9 with the ◇10. You return the ♡10 to declarer's ♡J and partner's ♡K, dummy discarding a diamond. Partner continues with the ◇K to dummy's ◇A. This is the position when declarer calls for dummy's low club:

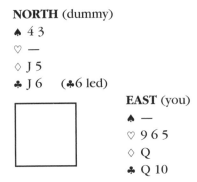

NORTH (dummy)
♠ 4 3
♡ —
◇ J 5
♣ J 6   (♣6 led)

EAST (you)
♠ —
♡ 9 6 5
◇ Q
♣ Q 10

Your ♣Q and ♣10 are equivalent for "blocking" purposes, but not equivalent for beating dummy's ♣J. You must save the ♣Q to beat the ♣J. If by some chance partner started with ♣AKxx (which would give him a balanced 16 HCP and a 1NT opening) and has falsecarded by winning with the ♣A earlier, your last club, whether the ♣Q or the ♣10, will fall beneath his king anyway.

179

Matchpoints, E-W vul.

NORTH (dummy)
♡ Q J 9 8

EAST (you)
♡ K 10 5 3

You are defending against a notrump contract (though the following applies equally to defending against suit contracts) and you find yourself second to play when, in the middle of the hand, declarer calls for dummy's ♡Q. Your partner, who has had to discard once on clubs, has discarded the ♡7. Which heart should you play?

You cannot gain by covering with the ♡K. If declarer has the ♡A, it makes no difference, but if partner has the ♡A, you've just blown a trick. If partner has another heart remaining with his ♡A, you want to keep a ♡K10 tenace behind dummy to score both your honors and avoid setting up dummy's ♡J. If partner, having been forced to keep his diamonds and spades to keep declarer's diamonds and spades from scoring, has only the ♡A left, there will be a loud thud as top honors collide and fall.

180

NORTH (dummy)
- ♠ 10 9 5 4
- ♡ 7 4 3
- ◇ A Q 5
- ♣ 6 5 3

EAST (you)
- ♠ J 8 6 3
- ♡ A K 6
- ◇ 10 9 6 3
- ♣ Q 7

WEST	NORTH	EAST	SOUTH	
pass	pass	pass	1NT[1]	1. 15-17 HCP.
all pass				

Partner leads the ♣J. Which club should you play?

Play the ♣7. You cannot afford to "unblock" the ♣Q. Suppose partner has led from ♣KJ102. In that case, by "unblocking" the ♣Q, you've just set up a second club trick for declarer's ♣A984. But what if partner has led from ♣KJ1084 or ♣KJ109? Then you still don't have to unblock. Whether declarer ducks or takes the ♣A, partner will know that you have the ♣Q. He can always overtake your ♣Q on the second round if he has ♣KJ1084 or ♣KJ109, but if he has ♣KJ102, he'll play the ♣2 on the second round to preserve your side's tricks and prevent declarer from scoring his intermediate club spot cards.

Matchpoints, Neither vul.

181

♠ Q J   ♡ 6   ◇ K J 10 6 5   ♣ K Q 9 8 4

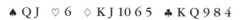

WEST	NORTH	EAST	SOUTH	
	pass	1NT[1]	?	1. 13-16 HCP.

You and your partner play that a 2NT overcall of an opposing 1NT opening shows both minors. Is this a good time to bid 2NT?

I don't know. If your clubs or diamonds were significantly weaker, I would say no. If you were vulnerable, I would say no. However, this time you "have" your Unusual 2NT if you choose to bid it. That's unusual in itself.

Matchpoints, Neither vul.

♠ Q J ♡ 6 ◇ K J 10 6 5 ♣ K Q 9 8 4

	WEST	NORTH	EAST	SOUTH
1. 15-17 HCP		pass	1NT[1]	?

You and your partner play that a 2NT overcall of an opposing 1NT opening shows both minors. Is this a good time to bid 2NT?

Certainly, even if you have some doubts. It's a good idea to stick with the field unless you're confident that you can do better. The field is going to bid 2NT and the field won't be wrong.

By now, you may be wondering, "Is Danny crazy? He presents the same problem twice in a row. The first time he says he doesn't know. The second time he's certain about what to do."

If that's what you think, go back at look at the two problems more closely. They're not really the same. Do you see the difference?

Now that I've told you there is a difference, of course you see it. And now you may be certain that I'm crazy:

"Against the lower-range notrump opening, Danny doesn't know whether it's right to bid an Unusual Two-Notrump, but against the higher-range notrump opening, he's sure that it's right. He's got things backwards."

Matchpoints, Neither vul.

♠ Q J ♡ 6 ◇ K J 10 6 5 ♣ K Q 9 8 4

	WEST	NORTH	EAST	SOUTH
1. 13-16 HCP.		pass	1NT[1]	2NT[2]
2. Unusual Notrump.	dbl	3◇	pass	pass
	3♡	pass	4♡	all pass

This is the first board of the next-to-last round. You and your partner defend perfectly. West, a declarer of average skill, makes 4♡. When you look at the traveling scoresheet you see that, except for this result and one other, the board is completely flat. At ten other tables, West played 4♡ and went down one. Only at one other table did West play 4♡ and make.

What did you do to earn a tie for bottom?

You painted a picture of your distribution for West, who was able to play 4♡ one trick better than any other declarer but one. At ten of the eleven other tables, East, playing 15-17 notrumps (or perhaps 16-

18 at one or two), opened 1♣ on a 2-3-3-5 14-HCP hand. South bid 1◊ and West had little clue about South's distribution.

Here are two more questions.

(1) When a player opens a 13-16 notrump, what is the probability that a player at another table will also open 1NT with his hand?

I make the odds about 5-to-3 against making an identical 1NT opening. More than 62% of hands in the 13-16 HCP range are 13- or 14-HCP hands, which the field doesn't open 1NT (at least in most club games in the United States).

(2) When a player at another table doesn't open 1NT and a player at your table opened a 13-16 notrump, what do you think the other player will open?

He will most likely open 1♣ or 1◊, especially if he's a five-card majorite.

So, returning to the original bidding problem, you really can't tell whether 2NT is the "field" action. More likely than not, it won't be, for the field will more likely than not be confronted with a 1♣ or 1◊ opening and either overcall in the other minor or pass.

If you play Unusual 2NT Overcalls, you should be aware that you're worse off for having used them when your opponents buy the contract, as they usually will when you fight majors with minors.

Matchpoints, E-W vul.

182

NORTH (dummy)
♠ 10 6 5 3 2
♡ 10 2
◊ Q 6
♣ K Q 10 4

SOUTH (you)
♠ —
♡ A K J 9 8
◊ A 8 5 3 2
♣ 6 5 2

WEST	NORTH	EAST	SOUTH
			1♡
pass	1♠	pass	2◊
pass	2♡	all pass	

West leads the ♣J. East tops dummy's ♣Q with the ♣A, returning the ♣3 to West's ♣9 and dummy's ♣10. How should you continue?

Don't take a heart finesse that will let the defenders draw dummy's last trump — a trump that you may need to ruff a diamond.

One good line is to ruff a spade to your hand at Trick 3 and then lead towards dummy's ◇Q in the hope that West has the ◇K. Suppose East has the ◇K, however, and beats dummy's ◇Q with it, returning a low trump. You should take the ♡A, cash the ◇A, ruff a diamond with dummy's ♡10 and ruff a second spade. By the time you reach this ending, you'll have scored one club trick, one diamond trick, one heart trick and three ruffs (a diamond ruff in dummy, two spade ruffs in hand).

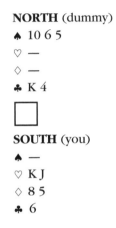

NORTH (dummy)
♠ 10 6 5
♡ —
◇ —
♣ K 4

SOUTH (you)
♠ —
♡ K J
◇ 8 5
♣ 6

Now, when you lead your last club towards dummy, West must ruff. He's out of both minor suits and can exit only in hearts or spades. Either way, you'll score your ♡J to make your contract.

Another good line:

How would you play if dummy had ◇J7 instead of ◇Q7? You would duck a diamond at Trick 3. Say West wins and shifts to a spade to tap you. You ruff, cash the ◇A, ruff a diamond with dummy's ♡10, draw two top hearts and then continue diamonds. The defenders, who have two hearts left, can score both by ruffing, but you lose only those two tricks plus the diamond and the club already lost, making an overtrick!

The presence of the ◇Q in dummy can distract you from your main task, which is to ruff a diamond in dummy and set up your fourth and fifth diamonds.

Matchpoints, N-S vul.

♠ Q 10 3   ♡ A 6   ◇ A K Q J 3   ♣ Q 7 4

WEST	NORTH	EAST	SOUTH
	pass	pass	1◇
1♡	1♠[1]	pass	?

1. In light of negative doubles, at least five spades.

A "good 15 to 18" 1NT opening would have avoided any problems, but your agreed notrump range is 15-17 and you're right to stick to it.

Now your best bet is to jump to 3♠. Such a jump ordinarily requires four-card support, but it's permissible on three when partner has shown a five-bagger. Even though you have a stopper, your hearts aren't really right for a jump to 2NT.

Instead, you cuebid:

WEST	NORTH	EAST	SOUTH
	pass	pass	1◇
1♡	1♠[1]	pass	2♡
3♡	pass	pass	?

1. In light of negative doubles, at least five spades.

Your 2♡ cuebid already forced to game (and was a slight overbid). No need to jump to 4♠ now. Instead, you must discourage slam. Bid a quiet 3♠. If partner cuebids 4♣, try to dampen his enthusiasm by retreating to 4♠. The danger in jumping to 4♠ is that partner may play you for a better hand and try for slam, perhaps reaching 5♠ down one.

Matchpoints, Both vul.

♠ K   ♡ K J 8 6 4 3 2   ◇ Q 7 5 4   ♣ 3

WEST	NORTH	EAST	SOUTH
		pass	?

Pass. Your hearts are too weak for a vulnerable 3♡ and second-seat preempts, more than first-seat preempts, should be classic, based on full values. Opening 3♡ would be wrong, though only a small mistake.

Wisely, you pass. Then:

WEST	NORTH	EAST	SOUTH
		pass	pass
1♣	pass	1♠	?

If 3♡ would be a small mistake at your first turn, it's a big mistake now. An opening 3♡ can't be doubled for penalties, but a 3♡ sandwich can. An opening 3♡ keeps the opponents from bidding spades below the three-level or clubs below the four-level, whereas bidding 3♡ now comes after they've been allowed to bid both black suits at the one-level.

Dare you bid 2♡? It depends. Are your opponents playing Support Doubles? (Did you look at, or ask to see, their convention card?) If they are, 2♡ is much safer than if they aren't, since North, who may have been planning to reverse into 2♡, can't double and will be stuck for a bid.

Matchpoints, Neither vul.

♠ J 8 7 5 4 3   ♡ J 10 4 2   ◇ 2   ♣ A 5

WEST	NORTH	EAST	SOUTH
			pass
pass	1♣	1◇	1♠
3◇	pass	pass	?

The ACBL has changed its regulations to transfer the burden of disclosure from the players that use special conventions and treatments to their opponents. The theory is that only "unusual" calls must be alerted, not conventions and treatments that have become commonplace. To know what your opponents' bids mean, you must look at their convention card, or inquire of the bidder's partner, at almost every turn.

When you look at your opponents' convention card, you see that it is marked for "invitational" jump raises of overcalls. However, even if West's 3◇ were weak, you should pass. You have a weak hand without any assurance of a fit.

NORTH (dummy)
♠ 2
♡ A Q 7 5
◇ K 8
♣ K 10 9 6 4 3

☐

SOUTH (you)
♠ J 8 7 5 4 3
♡ J 10 4 2
◇ 2
♣ A 5

You should you look at your opponents' convention card even if you have no intention of bidding. If you pass without looking, that gives information to all three of the other players. This information is unauthorized to partner, but authorized to the opponents.

WEST	NORTH	EAST	SOUTH
			pass
pass	1♣	1◇	1♠
3◇[1]	pass	pass	3♡ (!)
all pass			

1. Invitational.

You overbid and are lucky enough to catch a fit. You receive a diamond lead and dummy's ◇K falls to East's ◇A. East continues with a diamond to tap you. What now?

Having been tapped in your own hand, you should play to make dummy the master hand by setting up clubs. Cash the ♣A and lead to the ♣K. When no surprises occur in the club suit, lead the ♣10 from dummy. If East discards or ruffs low, trump or overruff. If East follows with the missing club honor, ruff with the ♡10 (West may be unable to overruff). If West can overruff, the defenders may shift to spades to tap dummy. In that case, after ruffing the second spade in dummy, you may be able to draw trumps and run the rest of dummy's clubs. If West does not overruff in clubs, try to draw trumps anyway (if West started with only two clubs, you may get some clue as to where the ♡K is from his tempo).

Suppose instead you play to set up your spades. On the second round, East's ♠Q appears; on the third round, West plays the ♠K. Well, what do you think? Did East start with ♠Qx or ♠AQx?

It doesn't matter as far as your play is concerned. Dummy's hearts are down to ♡AQ7. If you ruff with the ♡Q and East discards, East will be able to overruff dummy's low trump on the fourth round of spades. If you ruff small and East overruffs the third spade, you'll be ruffing with dummy's ♡Q on the fourth round, and it will hold whenever West has the ♡K. So ruffing small won't cost when East is out of spades. However, ruffing with the ♡Q will cost whenever East started with ♠AQx. You must ruff with dummy's ♡7.

IMPs, Neither vul.

186

♠ Q 8 3   ♡ A K J 7 6   ◇ K 5   ♣ K 6 3

WEST	NORTH	EAST	SOUTH
			1♡
pass	2◇	pass	?

Have you discussed with your partner what a 2NT rebid would show?

Few pairs have. Standard American treats it as showing substantial extra values. I endorse this treatment, with the qualifying clause that it should show a hand more suit-oriented than notrump oriented,

$$\spadesuit A83 \quad \heartsuit KQJ76 \quad \diamondsuit 85 \quad \clubsuit AK6$$

or similar. You can bid 2NT now — if your partner understands that this shows extras.

Many, however, play opener's non-jump 2NT rebid as showing a minimum opening. If that is your agreement, you must rebid 2♡. In the absence of any partnership agreement, you can rebid 2♡ as a "safety bid" that partner won't pass. A 2-over-1 response promises a rebid, with rare exceptions, and this is not one of the exceptions.

You should have opened 1NT despite your good five-card major. To see why, ask yourself what you would do after

WEST	NORTH	EAST	SOUTH
			1♡
pass	2♣	pass	?

Have you discussed with your partner what a 3♣ raise would show? Some play that it shows extras, an old-fashioned treatment. If you and your partner have this agreement, you can bid 3♣. It makes more sense, however, to have single raises show minimum hands, as sometimes you may hold

$$\spadesuit 3 \quad \heartsuit A9762 \quad \diamondsuit A53 \quad \clubsuit A863$$

and have no reasonable alternative to raising partner's minor.

With your actual good hand, you'd rebid 2NT — again, only if your partner will understand that this shows extras. Otherwise, make a "safety" 2♡ rebid.

What would you do after this?

WEST	NORTH	EAST	SOUTH
			1♡
pass	1♠	pass	?

You'd have no adequate rebid, which is the main reason I favor opening 1NT. You have too much in high cards to rebid 1NT or raise to 2♠. Bidding 2♡ requires a sixth heart: although opener's rebid of his first suit doesn't generally show six, it shows six when responder makes the cheapest response. Your best bet would to improvise with 2♣, hoping that partner won't pass, reserving an over-strength 2♠ raise as a close second choice.

IMPs, Neither vul.

♠ J 7   ♡ K Q   ◇ A 9 8 5 4   ♣ A Q 10 3

WEST	NORTH	EAST	SOUTH
		pass	?

Your agreed notrump range is 15-17 HCP. You should open 1◇, not a slightly off-shape 1NT. You have a five-card suit and a convenient 2♣ rebid. Although a weak doubleton like your ♠J7 should not preclude a 1NT opening, it should inspire you to look for an alternative.

In contrast:

IMPs, Neither vul.

♠ J 7   ♡ K Q   ◇ A Q 10 3   ♣ A 9 8 5 4

WEST	NORTH	EAST	SOUTH
		pass	?

With this hand, you can still open 1◇ and rebid 2♣; many would do exactly that, thinking it the normal way to bid with four diamonds and five clubs, but this time it would wrong. Open a slightly off-shape 1NT, else you may face:

WEST	NORTH	EAST	SOUTH
		pass	1◇
pass	1♡	pass	2♣
pass	2◇	pass	?

Two diamonds is probably not your best contract, yet you can do nothing but pass. If you bid 3♣, you may be overboard and partner will think you have a fifth diamond.

If your diamonds were weaker, 1NT would be clearer still.

188

IMPs, E-W vul.

♠ K 9 4 3 ♡ A K J 4 3 ◊ 5 3 ♣ 4 3

WEST	NORTH	EAST	SOUTH
			1♡
pass	2♣	2♡[1]	dbl
pass	pass	2♠	?

1. Spades and diamonds.

Double. Partner is not required to pass and should pull with a single-ton spade. If partner has a hand like

♠ 5 ♡ 7 6 ♡ — ◊ K 6 2 ♣ A K Q 10 8 7 2

doubling may be the only way to get him to bid 3NT. Note that from your side, 3NT is a bad contract, doomed to failure on the lead of any diamond higher than the six.

189

IMPs, Neither vul.

NORTH (dummy)
♠ J 10 4
♡ 7 5 4
◊ A 8 4 3 2
♣ Q 7

WEST (you)
♠ 9
♡ A Q 10 9 8 3
◊ J 9
♣ A K 8 6

WEST	NORTH	EAST	SOUTH
	pass	pass	1♠
2♡	2♠	pass	3♣[1]
dbl	3◊	dbl	3♠
all pass			

1. Weak Suit Game Try (not alerted).

You lead the ◊J. Dummy's ◊A wins and the ♠J holds. When declarer calls for a low club from dummy, partner plays the ♣5 and you take declarer's ♣10 with your ♣K. Declarer ruffs your ◊9 continuation and leads the ♣3; you take the ♣A, and partner completes an echo with the

♣2. You exit with the ♣6, which dummy ruffs. When declarer calls for a heart from dummy, partner discards the ♣J. How do you continue after winning a cheap heart trick?

At this point, you have a complete count on the hand: partner is 4-0-5-4 and declarer is 5-4-1-3. Just exit with a low heart for partner to ruff. He can lead another trump to remove dummy's last one (the ♠10) and you'll sit with your ♡AQ over declarer's remaining ♡KJ to get two more tricks.

Cashing the ♡A before giving partner his ruff is costly: it destroys the finessing position you retain by keeping your heart tenace.

Late tricks count just as much as early tricks.

IMPs, Neither vul.

190

♠ J 7 ♡ A 9 8 5 ◇ Q J 10 7 5 ♣ J 8

WEST	NORTH	EAST	SOUTH
			pass
pass	1♣	pass	?

There is no reason to avoid bidding up the line here: five diamonds to three honors versus four hearts to one honor. Respond 1◇. Partner can still bid hearts with four, and this is not a deal where you'd like to play in hearts on a 4-3 fit (if partner has a ruffing value, it will be in diamonds, opposite your secondary strength).

A 1♣ opening is not Stayman. Whoever told you that it is your "duty" to bid a four-card major in response to 1♣ was dead wrong. Your first priority is to find a good fit. Then, if game is on the horizon, your next priority is the find the best game: at matchpoints, usually the highest-scoring; at IMPs, the game with the best chances of making; at either form of contest, it is often (but not always) four of a major or 3NT.

IMPs, Both vul.

191

♠ 9 6 ♡ 10 8 7 3 ◇ Q 5 ♣ K J 7 5 3

WEST	NORTH	EAST	SOUTH
	1♡	2◇	?

You and your partner have agreed to play weak single jump raises. Should you make one here?

No. Bid 2♡. You still need playing strength to bid at the three-level, distributional playing strength rather than high cards when you play weak jump raises.

♠ 9 6 5 2 ♡ K 8 7 3 ◇ 5 ♣ K 7 5 3

would qualify for 3♡, but your actual hand does not.

I dislike weak jump raises. I believe single jumps are effective preempts on weak hands when the opponents have not yet bid a suit (for example, 1♡-double-3♡) but ineffective after they have bid a suit. (Weak jump raises often goad good opponents into bidding more than they would otherwise, and then help them make what they bid.)

IMPs, Neither vul.

♠ A K J 4   ♡ K 10 9 8   ◇ J 9 4 3   ♣ A

WEST	NORTH	EAST	SOUTH
		pass	?

Rank these opening bids in order from best to worst: 1◇, 1♡, 1♠, 1NT.

My order: 1♠, 1♡, 1NT, 1◇. I hate jack-high suits. I love three-honor suits headed by the ace or king. I treat suits as if they were longer or shorter accordingly. Remember, sometimes you wind up playing in the suit you open, either because partner passes or because the opponents intervene and partner raises at the three- or four-level. At other times, your LHO overcalls, or becomes declarer after your RHO enters, and your partner, with no better clues, leads the suit you have bid. It's nice to have bid a strong suit.

You choose the worst of four plausible opening bids, and face:

WEST	NORTH	EAST	SOUTH
		pass	1◇ (!)
1♡	4♣	pass	?

You and your partner have agreed to play splinters. Is this 4♣ a splinter?

No. Preemption takes precedence over splintering in competitive auctions. Once the opponents have shown suits, the only splinters should be in those suits. Partner's 4♣ is natural, based on fear of hearts and perhaps spades. Little can he know that you, a 1◇ opener, are long and strong in both majors.

Of course, if there were any doubt, you could tell by looking at your own hand. If partner's 4♣ were a splinter, then the opponents would have eleven or twelve clubs, which is implausible on the auction. East's failure to open 3♣ as dealer marks him as likely to have no more than six (and some "modern" players routinely open 3♣ with six). If West had as many as five clubs, he might have overcalled an "Unusual 2NT" for the two lowest unbid suits.

♠ 9   ♡ A 4 3   ◇ 5 4 3   ♣ A Q 7 4 3 2

WEST	NORTH	EAST	SOUTH
			pass
1NT	2♡[1]	pass	?

1. Spades.

What would you do if had partner overcalled a natural 2♠? Would you "correct" to 3♣?

I don't think you should. You might catch partner with a singleton club and play in a 6-1 fit at the three-level instead of the two-level. Partner might be entryless except for the ◇A, which the opponents could dislodge early, and his spades might go to waste entirely. Playing in spades, you have a couple of useful tricks to contribute and all of partner's spades will be useful for taking tricks.

Playing transfer overcalls of opposing 1NT openings makes your decision easier still. You have several things going for you that you wouldn't have otherwise.

(1) West, the stronger and more defined hand, will be on opening lead against 2♠. This is usually an advantage. West knows less about the combined East-West assets than East does, and may be endplayed on opening lead.

(2) Your hand, the less defined hand, will be the concealed hand, making it harder for the opponents to know how to defend.

(3) When you bid 2♠, the auction isn't over. Partner may have a surprisingly strong hand or a good playing hand with a second suit and bid again.

Bid 2♠. It's even clearer than passing a natural 2♠ overcall.

Among the many Notrump Defenses available to you are some that utilize transfers. You can see the advantages here. However, there are also some disadvantages: responder can get into the act by doubling or by cuebidding the suit that intervener shows and can show different kinds of hands by passing first and then bidding or doubling.

Because transfer overcalls offer fewer advantages in the passout seat, it is reasonable to revert to natural overcalls when *balancing* against an opposing 1NT, and thus to have two different Notrump Defenses.

Matchpoints, Both vul.

194

♠ 8 5 4   ♡ 9   ◇ K Q 9 7 2   ♣ K 10 7 5

WEST	NORTH	EAST	SOUTH
	pass	1♣	?

You should pass.

The 1◇ overcall is in a class by itself. Not only is it in a minor, but it shuts out nothing that responder might want to bid (except 1◇

itself) and puts another tool in responder's toolkit: a negative double to show both majors at once. Think of it as the opposite of preemptive. Especially when vulnerable and especially when playing Weak Jump Overcalls, a 1◇ overcall should be based on an excellent hand.

However, you bid 1◇ and the auction continues. The deal has been reoriented to make South declarer.

WEST	NORTH	EAST	SOUTH
		pass	1♣
1◇	dbl[1]	pass	2♣
pass	3♡	pass	3NT
all pass			

You are in the West seat, defending against 3NT. What should you lead?

Lead the ◇K. The king, not fourth-highest, is usually best from a suit headed by KQ9. Leading low often lets declarer take a trick with the jack when otherwise partner may have the ten and be able to lead it through declarer on the next round.

You lead the ◇7.

NORTH (dummy)
♠ J 10 3
♡ A K 7 6 4 3
◇ A 8 6 5
♣ —

WEST (you)
♠ 8 5 4
♡ 9
◇ K Q 9 7 2
♣ K 10 7 5

Partner discards the ♣3 as dummy's ◇8 wins the first trick. Declarer follows to dummy's ♡A with the ♡10. On dummy's ♡K, declarer discards the ♣2 — and you?

You need to save all your spades; discard the ◇2. The failure to alert North's double kept partner from bidding 1♠ (he thought North's double promised four spades, as a standard negative double would), but it's clear from the auction and the play thus far that partner is 5-5-0-3.

After you discard the ♠4, declarer leads the ◇5 to his ◇10; partner discards the ♣4. You take the ◇Q and shift correctly to the ♠8. Partner covers dummy's ♠10 with the ♠Q, and declarer (a world-class concealer of his partnership agreements but not a good bridge player) takes the ♠A. By now, declarer's hand should be an open book:

$$♠ A x \quad ♡ 10 \quad ◊ J 10 4 3 \quad ♣ A Q J x x x$$

Declarer leads a "crafty" ♣J. What should you do?

You should grab your ♣K and continue spades so partner can take three hearts and four spades for down five. It's a shame to let this pair escape for any less when South, who apparently plays Negative Free Bids, failed to alert North's double and North didn't announce that there had been a failure to alert and summon the director (as the rules require).

You should summon the director now, if not to demand an adjusted score (a spade lead might have made the defense easier), then at least to inform him so he can impose a procedural penalty on this pair.

Matchpoints, N-S vul.

195

NORTH (dummy)
♠ 10
♡ K 8 6 3
◊ A K J 9 5
♣ J 7 6

WEST (you)
♠ A K Q 7 6
♡ A 10
◊ 6 2
♣ Q 10 5 4

WEST	NORTH	EAST	SOUTH
1♠	2◊	pass	3NT
all pass			

You lead the ♠Q. When you see dummy, what do you expect partner to have?

Expect partner to have a yarborough.

On the first trick, partner plays the ♠4 and declarer plays the ♠5. When you continue with the ♠K, partner follows with the ♠8 as dummy discards the ♣6. Despite partner's low-high signal, you persist with the ♠A. Oops. After dummy discards the ♣7, partner discards the ♣2, as dummy discards low clubs. When you exit with the ◇6, partner plays the ◇3 and declarer wins with the ◇7. Here comes the ♡Q: win or duck?

In general, winning figures to be right; partner may have the ♡J and you can't snare anything better than the ♡Q with your ♡A.

Here, however, it's even easier than that, for you can count declarer's tricks. Partner's ♣2 discard told you not to anticipate catching him with a club that could beat dummy's ♣J, and the first diamond trick tells you that partner has nothing in diamonds either. So, declarer has two established spades, two top clubs and five diamond tricks. The ♡Q, if you let it hold, is declarer's tenth trick. You must take the ♡A to stop the overtrick.

Counting declarer's tricks is basic to defense.

196

Matchpoints, E-W vul.

NORTH (dummy)
♠ 4
♡ A J 8 2
◇ K Q 7
♣ Q 10 7 6 4

EAST (you)
♠ Q J 3 2
♡ 10 7 3
◇ 5 3 2
♣ A K 8

WEST	NORTH	EAST	SOUTH
		pass	1◇
pass	1♡	pass	1NT
pass	3NT	all pass	

Partner leads the ♠10, which holds, as declarer follows with the ♠5. Partner continues with the ♠8, which declarer takes with the ♠A. What significance do you ascribe to partner's ♠8?

Key point: when a defender has a choice of spot cards to lead to the second round of a suit, the most informative card is his original fourth highest. Therefore, you can tell that partner has led from ♠K1098x(x).

Declarer runs five diamond tricks. What should you discard?

You can afford to discard a low club. You can also afford to discard a spade, for you know that partner's spades are ready to roll. You cannot spare a heart, because that makes it too easy for declarer to risk a finesse against the ♡Q (you're unlikely to be discarding from ♡Qxx).

Matchpoints, Both vul.

♠ A Q 8 4   ♡ 8 6 3   ◇ Q 4   ♣ Q 8 5 2

WEST	NORTH	EAST	SOUTH
			pass
pass	1♡	pass	?

Bid 2♡. You are in the single-raise range, not the "three-card limit raise" range (for which 1♠ followed by 3♡ would be appropriate). The dividing line is 10 Support Points: a good 10 puts you in the "limit raise" range, a bad 10 puts you only in the single-raise range.

Why choose the conservative action here?

(a) Queens, especially stray queens (without other honors in the suit), are overrated.

(b) You cannot count a doubleton queen as both a high-card value and a ruffing value.

(c) Weak trumps should induce conservatism (a key point). Though ♡863 is acceptable support, it is not normal support, which you should think of as ♡Q32, ♡5432 or better.

If you respond 1♠ and partner rebids 1NT, 2♣ or 2◇, you do best merely to give preference with 2♡, even though it's a slight underbid. That's why, with your fair-to-middling hand, you should raise to 2♡ directly, which is less discouraging than taking a preference on the second round.

Matchpoints, Neither vul.

NORTH (dummy)
♠ J 10 9
♡ Q J 3
◇ K J 6
♣ K 8 6 3

EAST (you)
♠ 8 4
♡ A 10 8 7 6
◇ Q 8 5
♣ A Q J

WEST	NORTH	EAST	SOUTH
			1♠
pass	3♠[1]	all pass	

1. Limit raise (supposedly).

Partner leads the ♠5. Dummy's ♠9 wins the first trick and declarer continues with the ♠10 to his ♠K and partner's ♠3. How many spades do you think partner has?

A trump high-low shows three. Standard count signals in the trump suit are the reverse of other count signals. Partner has led from ♠753 (surely not from ♠Q53).

Next comes the ♡K. Partner follows with the ♡4, a count card. Can you tell how many hearts partner has?

Not precisely. He can have either two or three. His ♡4 won't be a singleton, else he'd have led it instead of leading a trump. However, it could be the start of a high-low from ♡42 or the start of a low-high from ♡954. It cannot be the start of a high-low from four, however, for with ♡9542, partner would have played the ♡9 or ♡5.

You duck the first heart, win the second heart when partner follows up the line, confirming three, and exit safely with a third heart (on which declarer discards a low diamond). Declarer comes off dummy with the ◇J. Should you cover?

A defender's start of a high-low is generally readable if his partner can see that there are at least *two* lower cards missing.

If you're counting declarer's hand (high-card strength as well as suit lengths), you know the answer is yes. He's already shown up with ♠AKQxx ♡K2. With the ◇A also, he surely wouldn't have passed 3♠. So partner must have the ◇A: your ◇Q is sure to win.

Matchpoints, E-W vul.

♠ A J 3   ♡ 8 4 2   ♢ A J 9 7 3   ♣ 9 5

WEST	NORTH	EAST	SOUTH
	pass	pass	pass
1♣	1♠	dbl[1]	?

1. Negative double.

Should you cuebid 2♣ to show a three-card limit raise?
  Absolutely not, for three reasons.

(1) The best way to interpret a negative double of a 1♠ overcall
    is as a 1♡ response. You have the "death holding" (three low)
    in North's heart suit, so you should lean towards conser-
    vatism.

(2) The best way to interpret a cuebid is as a strong invitation to
    game (or better). Surely that is not what your hand is worth.
    Even if partner were not a passed hand, you would have only
    mild game hopes (enough to raise, and then accept any game
    try that partner might make).

It's pointless to issue a game invitation that you know partner will decline.

(3) A cuebid makes it much easier for opponents to compete than
    a simple raise does. If you bid 2♣, South can bid 2♡ or double.
    If you bid 2♠, South must bid at the three-level, 3♡ or 3♣, to
    compete (and may not be able to do so). Bid 2♠.

If you have but one bid to make, a raise is the bid that will prove most helpful to part-ner. If a single raise is among your choic-es, make it.

Matchpoints, E-W vul.

♠ Q J 10 5   ♡ 10 8 2   ♢ A Q J 7 2   ♣ 6

WEST	NORTH	EAST	SOUTH
	1♣	pass	?

A surprising number of modern players would bypass diamonds here
and bid 1♠. It is foolish to bid a four-card spade suit when you have
four or five perfectly good diamonds. Nowadays, so much foolishness
is taught in the name of "system"! Bid 1♢.

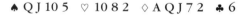

Matchpoints, N-S vul.

NORTH (dummy)
♠ K Q 6 3
♡ Q 10 8 7 4 3
◇ 5 3
♣ 7

SOUTH (you)
♠ A J 9
♡ A J 9 2
◇ Q 2
♣ J 10 3 2

1. Negative double.

WEST	NORTH	EAST	SOUTH
			1♣
1♠	dbl[1]	2♣	2♡
pass	4♡	all pass	

West leads the ♣K; East overtakes and returns the ♠7, which you win with the ♠J. You'd do better to win with the ♠A: do you know why? When you win with the jack, East will know you have the ace (else West would have taken it). If you win with the ace, East won't know who has the jack. How should you continue?

When West didn't lead a top diamond, you were able to infer that he doesn't have both the ◇A and the ◇K. To account for his 1♠ over-call on ♠108542, he must have the ♡K. Even if he has ♡Kx or ♡Kxx, so that you have a sure trump loser, you cannot afford to lose to the ♡K now, lest the defenders cash two diamonds. So lay down the ♡A. If the ♡K doesn't fall singleton, East will have no more hearts with which to ruff when you run spades to discard a diamond.

Matchpoints, E-W vul.

♠ J 7 6 5 3 2 ♡ — ◇ 10 8 6 ♣ A 9 8 7

WEST	NORTH	EAST	SOUTH
pass	1◇	1♠	pass
2♡	dbl	pass	?

What kind of hand do you think partner should have for his double?

He looks to have a strong hand with five diamonds and four hearts. If the opponents had been silent and you had responded 1♠, partner had intended reversing with a 2♡ rebid.

Low-level penalty doubles are often pullable. With three-card support for your partner's suit and a void in the doubled suit where the opponents have a nine-card fit, you should pull to 3◇.

Matchpoints, E-W vul.

NORTH (dummy)
♠ 9 8 4 2
♡ 10
◇ Q J 5
♣ K 10 9 8 5

EAST (you)
♠ K Q 7 6
♡ A 9
◇ 10 7 4
♣ J 7 4 3

WEST	NORTH	EAST	SOUTH
1◇	pass	1♠	4♡
4♠	pass	pass	5♡
pass	pass	dbl	all pass

Partner leads the ♠A and continues with the ♠3. Declarer ruffs the second spade and leads the ♡K, on which partner discards the ◇9. What now?

You know eleven of declarer's thirteen cards: his ten hearts and his singleton ♠10. You can infer that a twelfth card is either the ◇A or the ◇K, for if partner had both, he'd have led one of them. You also know that partner has the ♣A, for without it, he wouldn't have an opening bid, much less a raise to 4♠ (vulnerable!). You know much more about the deal than partner does at this point.

Whether you win the first heart or the second, you should shift to clubs. When declarer is 1-10-1-1, partner will take the ♣A for the setting trick — and then the ◇A if he has it. When declarer is 1-10-2-0, partner won't get his ♣A, but he'll know he can afford to discard it, so when declarer runs off the rest of his trumps, partner will keep his guarded ◇K to beat the contract.

Many bridge books teach defense against squeezes, which is extremely difficult. This book teaches defense against pseudo-squeezes, which is easier and pays higher dividends.

Matchpoints, Both vul.

NORTH (dummy)
♠ —
♡ Q 10 7 2
◊ Q J 9 6 5 2
♣ K 9 3

WEST (you)
♡ J 3 2
♡ A K J 8 4 3
◊ —
♣ J 7 5 2

WEST	NORTH	EAST	SOUTH
	pass	pass	1♠
2♡	pass	2NT	3◊
pass	4◊	all pass	

You lead the ♡A (playing "A from AKx… opening leads"). Partner plays the ♡9 and declarer the ♡5. You win with the ♡K. What now?

Partner's ♡9 would be ambiguous (singleton or top of a doubleton) but for the bidding: partner's 2NT suggests a doubleton heart and declarer's 3◊ suggests a singleton heart. So a heart continuation is clearly wrong. Shift to clubs now before declarer can discard two or three of dummy's clubs on his spades. To cater for partner's possible ♣AQ10, lead the ♣J (not the ♣2).

Matchpoints, Neither vul.

♠ A K J 10 6 5   ♡ 10 4 3   ◊ 8 7   ♣ Q 6

WEST	NORTH	EAST	SOUTH
		1◊	1♠
2◊	2♠	dbl	pass
3◊	pass	pass	?

You must pass. Balanced hands defend. You have neither a side suit to develop nor a singleton. You have no more than could reasonably be expected for your 1♠ overcall, and playing Weak Jump Overcalls, you might even have chosen to bid 2♠ initially. You have only one trick on defense against 4♦ (you can't expect both top spades to live) and can hardly expect partner to contribute more than two tricks. Bidding 3♠ would give the opponents a "Fielder's Choice": bidding 4♦ (in which case a 3♠ bid breaks even), or doubling and beating 3♠ two (which makes your 3♠ bid quite costly).

Matchpoints, E-W vul.

♠ 10 5 3   ♡ K 6   ◇ Q 9 5 4 2   ♣ A Q 6

WEST	NORTH	EAST	SOUTH
		pass	pass
1♡	pass	pass	?

Pass. Do not balance. Your hand, which was just under minimum opening strength initially, has fallen in value because its ♡K is worth substantially less after West opens 1♡. Moreover, you have three very weak spades, not the four spades partner will expect for a double of 1♡. If you push the opponents higher, partner may figure that spades is the one suit you definitely have and may blow a trick with an opening spade lead.

   You don't figure to beat the opponents in what they might bid because the cards are placed favorably for them (the ♡K is onside) and their suits are probably splitting well for them (you have no singleton). Balanced hands defend.

Matchpoints, Neither vul.

♠ 7   ♡ J 9 5 3   ◇ A Q 8 4   ♣ A 9 7 2

WEST	NORTH	EAST	SOUTH
			pass
1♠	2◇	2♠	?

You might well have opened 1◇. Your hand is far too good for 3◇, and easily good enough for 4◇ (assuming you don't play weak jump raises of overcalls, a currently popular treatment). Perhaps it's too good even for 4◇. Your best call is a 3♠ cuebid. That gives partner a chance to bid 3NT if he has

♠ K 9 3   ♡ A 4   ◇ K J 10 5 3 2   ♣ Q 6

or similar, and encourages him to bid 5◇ if he has some other sound 2◇ overcall.

Matchpoints, Both vul.

♠ Q J 7   ♡ 8 6 5 3   ◇ K J 3   ♣ A Q 4

WEST	NORTH	EAST	SOUTH
1♡	pass	1♠	?

Pass. Doubling is out of the question as it promises four- or five-card support for each minor. Would you really want to ask partner to bid 2♣ or 2◇ when you have a balanced hand with only three-card support?

A takeout double is just what the name implies, a request for partner to take it out. It is not a vainglorious show of high card points. When both opponents bid different suits, your partner is unlikely to have the strength you need for your side to be able to buy the contract and make it.

The most important question to ask yourself in competitive auctions is not "How good is my hand?" but "For what is my hand good, offense or defense?" When you have a balanced hand, the answer is almost always, for defense.

Matchpoints, Neither vul.

♠ A K Q 5   ♡ A K 3   ◇ Q 8   ♣ 7 6 4 3

WEST	NORTH	EAST	SOUTH
	pass	1◇	dbl
pass	1♡	2◇	?

Hallelujah, a sound takeout double! But what should you do now?

If you remember that your takeout double was tantamount to a simultaneous 1♡, 1♠ and 2♣ overcall, you'll interpret partner's 1♡ correctly as saying, "If you have minimum opening-bid strength with hearts, spades and clubs, I prefer hearts, but I don't have values enough even to want to 'raise' your hearts to two."

With a fourth heart, you would happily bid 2♡ anyway, for you do have extra strength for your takeout double. With only three hearts, however, you're stretching it a bit to raise. Raising partner's reply to a takeout double shows primary support (at least four trumps) as well as extra values. Bidding 2♡ isn't horrible, but you'd do better to pass.

You bid 2♡ anyway, leading to

WEST	NORTH	EAST	SOUTH
	pass	1♢	dbl
pass	1♡	2♢	2♡
pass	pass	3♢	?

You've shot your wad and must pass. Any further competition must come from your partner (who may be well prepared to double 3♢).

Key point: it's seldom right to raise partner in a competitive auction and then raise again later, uninvited. In competitive auctions, limit bidding applies. You should almost always "raise to the hilt" immediately. Clearly, you weren't strong enough for 3♡ last turn and you're not strong enough now.

Matchpoints, E-W vul.

♠ A 8 7 4 2   ♡ 4   ◇ K Q 10 4 3   ♣ 5 2

WEST	NORTH	EAST	SOUTH
	1♡	1NT[1]	?

1. Four spades, longer minor.

Do you know which minor East has? If he has diamonds, you'll be happy to double the runout to 2◇ or 2♠. If East has clubs and partner can double, you'll also be happy to defend (the hand will be a misfit for both sides).

If you bid 2◇ now, you'll be taking the opponents off the hook. It's better to pass, and better still to double 1NT. Doubling authorizes partner to double 2♣ and creates a one-round force if he doesn't. Suppose you double and West bids 2♣, partner passing. You'll know they have a fit so you can bid 2◊. But perhaps West will pass and East will remove to 2◊. Wouldn't you love to be able to double that?

211

Matchpoints, Neither vul.

NORTH (dummy)
♠ 10 9 3 2
♡ K J 10 2
◊ Q 7 3
♣ A Q

EAST (you)
♠ A J 5 2
♡ 8 4 3
◊ A J 4
♣ 10 8 2

WEST	NORTH	EAST	SOUTH
			pass
pass	1♡	pass	1NT
all pass			

Partner leads the ◊2 and your ◊J wins, as declarer follows with the ◊6. How should you continue?

The play to Trick 1 marks you with the ◊A, which is an entry. Partner has ◊Kxxx, so your side has four diamond tricks, but there is no need to take them now. Use your lead to set up three possible spade tricks for your side, and to dislodge what may be a precious spade entry to declarer's hand. Shift to the ♠2, the only way to ensure three spade tricks if partner has ♠Kx or ♠Qx.

212

Matchpoints, N-S vul.

♠ K 10 7 4   ♡ Q 7 4 2   ◊ Q 7   ♣ J 4 2

WEST	NORTH	EAST	SOUTH
pass	1♣	1◊	dbl[1]
2◊	2♡	pass	?

1. Negative double.

Suppose you did not have negative doubles available. What would you have done at your first turn? You'd have bid 1♡, wouldn't you? The roughly equivalent problem is:

Matchpoints, N-S vul.

♠ K 10 7 4   ♡ Q 7 4 2   ◇ Q 7   ♣ J 4 2

WEST	NORTH	EAST	SOUTH
pass	1♣	1◇	1♡
2◇	2♡[1]	pass	?

Now you recognize that you have an easy, automatic pass. You should also pass in the original problem. Partner's 2♡ bid is, in effect, a raise of your hearts.

To become a good bidder, I recommend starting out without conventions. Then, when you learn conventions, you will be able to compare your conventional auctions with the roughly equivalent natural auctions.

1. Promising four hearts (by partnership agreement).

Matchpoints, N-S vul.

213

♠ J 4 3   ♡ K Q   ◇ J 10 6 4   ♣ K 8 6 4

WEST	NORTH	EAST	SOUTH
1♠	2♡	pass	?

You have an easy, automatic raise to 3♡. Even king-small is normal support for a two-level overcall (and in a pinch, for a one-level overcall as well). How many tricks do you think it's worth to have ♡KQ instead of two small?

On this deal, it happens to be worth three tricks. Partner has overcalled with ♡AJ982, and East has ♡10763 behind him. Your ♡KQ lets partner pick up trumps without loss, whereas if you had ♡54 (for example) and East had ♡ KQ107, partner would have three trump losers.

Matchpoints, Both vul.

214

♠ A J   ♡ Q 10 7   ◇ K 9 8   ♣ Q J 7 3 2

WEST	NORTH	EAST	SOUTH
pass	pass	1♠	?

Despite your "13 points" you must pass. You should not double. Look at the situation:

   (a) Your points are junk points (two queens and two jacks among them).

(b) You have a balanced hand (balanced hands should usually defend).

(c) A double requires partner to bid at the two-level rather than the one-level.

(d) A double of a major normally delivers four cards in the unbid major. Though this rule is not absolute, you should not violate it without truly sound values.

Bidding 2♣ would also be terribly wrong. You have little playing strength, a short, weak suit, little prospect of game facing a passed partner, and little hope of winning a "battle for the partscore" with clubs (the lowest-ranking suit) against spades (the highest-ranking).

Matchpoints, N-S vul.

♠ K 10 7   ♡ Q J 10 7 3   ◇ Q   ♣ K 5 4 3

WEST	NORTH	EAST	SOUTH
		pass	pass
pass	1♠	pass	?

Jump to 3♡. A standard jump shift by a passed hand (sometimes called a "Flower Bid") shows a hand that has improved, which can only happen if responder has a fit for opener's suit. It's right to bid 3♡ rather than 3♠ or 4♠, because you may belong in hearts rather than spades — for example, if partner has

♠ A 8 6 4 3   ♡ K 9 6 2   ◇ K J 5   ♣ A

Matchpoints, Both vul.

♠ A 5 3   ♡ J 10 5 3   ◇ Q 4 2   ♣ Q 6 5

	WEST	NORTH	EAST	SOUTH
				1NT
1. Stayman.	pass	2♣[1]	pass	2◇
	pass	3NT	all pass	

What should you lead?

Lead the ♡3, your best shot for developing tricks. You are not enthusiastic about leading a heart, but everything else is worse. A spade lead from the ace is poor and would be less desirable than a heart lead even if you had four cards in each, e.g.

♠ A 5 3 2   ♡ J 10 5 3   ◊ Q 4   ♣ Q 6 5

Leads from lower honors usually develop tricks for your side; leads from aces usually develop tricks for declarer.

Matchpoints, N-S vul.

217

♠ J 10 7   ♡ 9 4 3   ◊ K J 6   ♣ Q 9 5 2

WEST	NORTH	EAST	SOUTH
		pass	2NT
pass	3NT	all pass	

What should you lead?

There's not much of a discrepancy among your suits. With four weak clubs, your chance of developing club tricks is substantially less than the danger of blowing a trick by leading the ♣2. Combine relative safety with a chance of developing tricks by leading the ♠J.

When it's close, prefer a major-suit lead to a minor-suit lead after responder raises a notrump opening directly without using a Jacoby Transfer or Stayman.

Matchpoints, Neither vul.

218

♠ K Q 7   ♡ A 8   ◊ K Q   ♣ A K 10 7 6 2

WEST	NORTH	EAST	SOUTH
	pass	pass	2♣[1]
pass	2◊[2]	pass	3♣[3]
pass	4♣[4]	pass	4◊[5]
pass	4♠[6]	pass	4NT[7]
pass	5♡[8]	pass	?

You were a bit light for your 3♣ rebid — 2NT would have been better. However, partner has shown an ace, club support and presumably the ♡K. What more do you need for 6NT? Just bid it.

1. Artificial force to 2NT or game (never primary diamonds).
2. Neutral response.
3. Natural, game force.
4. Positive with support.
5. Roman Keycard for clubs.
6. 1-keycard reply.
7. Attempted signoff.
8. Rejecting the signoff.

Matchpoints, E-W vul.

NORTH (dummy)
♠ A K Q 7
♡ J 7 2
◇ K Q 8 7 3
♣ Q

WEST (you)
♠ 9 2
♡ A 9 5 4 3
◇ A J 6 2
♣ 9 4

WEST	NORTH	EAST	SOUTH
			pass
pass	1◇	pass	1♠
pass	3♠	all pass	

S.J. Simon wrote in *Why You Lose at Bridge,* "Never win a trick until you have made up your mind what card you are going to play next." To this I'll add:

Start making up your mind as soon as dummy appears. You don't want to do your thinking at a time when hesitating will reveal information about your hand.

You lead the ♣9 to partner's ♣K. Partner shifts to a low spade. Declarer draws trumps in three rounds, ending in his hand with the ♠J. Then he leads the ◇9. Should you take the ◇A or duck?

Duck. You have nothing to lose and something to gain.

If you are inclined to take the ace because you fear that declarer has a singleton, well, suppose he does have a singleton. If you take the ◇A, dummy will have two diamond tricks, whereas if you duck, dummy will have only one.

Or suppose declarer has a doubleton. Then if you duck, dummy's ◇Q will win, but declarer will need to get to his hand to lead another. If he has ♡Kx, he won't be able to reach his hand at all; if he has ♡K10, he'll face a guess whether to play you for the ♡A or the ♡Q.

Good things can happen if you duck. Bad things can happens if you take your ◇A on the first round. One of those bad things is that you must find a safe exit, and you don't have one.

NORTH (dummy)
♠ J 9 7 2
♡ Q 9 7
◇ A 9 5 3
♣ A 4

EAST (you)
♠ K 10 6
♡ 8 6 2
◇ 8 7 6
♣ J 9 7 2

WEST	NORTH	EAST	SOUTH
			1NT
pass	2♣¹	pass	2◇
pass	3NT	all pass	

1. Stayman.

Partner leads the ♠3 and dummy plays the ♠2. What should you play?

Play the ♠6. From the auction, you can place partner with four hearts. When he leads a spade (other than from a sequence), you can infer that he has four spades too, because a lead from honor-third would be a bad lead.

If partner has ♠A8xx, then your ♠6 will force declarer's ♠Q. A subsequent spade lead will come to your ♠10 and eventually the defense will take three spade tricks to declarer's one. If partner has ♠Q8xx, then your ♠6 will force declarer's ♠A, and again the defense will take three spade tricks to declarer's one. But you can never get three spade tricks by playing the ♠10 (or ♠K) at Trick 1. And if declarer has either ♠A8 or ♠Q8, it doesn't matter whether you play the ♠6 or the ♠10 at Trick 1; declarer will always make two spade tricks.

It would be wrong and show a lack of partnership confidence for you to play partner to have led from ♠Qxx (bad) or ♠Axx (worse).

A key to good defense is for third hand to trust the opening leader to have made a reasonable lead.

Matchpoints, E-W vul.

♠ J 6 3   ♡ J 9 4   ◇ A 9 3   ♣ K 8 6 2

	WEST	NORTH	EAST	SOUTH
		pass	pass	pass
1. Michaels Cuebid.	1◇	2◇[1]	2♡	?

East's 2♡ wasn't alerted and should therefore be presumed natural. It looks like East has five hearts facing West's void. In that case, defending against 2♡ (not doubled) will produce a nice penalty. Pass, hoping for just that.

If you bid 2♠, you'll take East out of his presumed 5-0 fit and give him a second chance to support diamonds with his not-unlikely 1-5-4-3 pattern. Why take the opponents out of their worst spot and give them an opportunity to find their best?

Matchpoints, E-W vul.

♠ Q 6 5   ♡ K 10 5 3   ◇ A 5 2   ♣ 8 5 4

WEST	NORTH	EAST	SOUTH
pass	pass	1♣	pass
1♡	pass	1♠	pass
2♠	pass	4♠	all pass

What should you lead?

Don't lead clubs. Even when you do not have an attractive lead in any other suit, you should almost never lead declarer's first-bid. If you do lead clubs, the right card is the ♣8 ("top of nothing"), not the ♣4: a low club suggests either a singleton or an honor in the suit. However, top-of-nothing leads are generally poor anyway.

Your only reasonable leads are the ♡3 and a diamond (preferably the ◇A). Undesirable as ace-leads (and underleads) are, this auction suggests one. East has shown a very good hand, but he's probably distributional, for he neither opened in notrump nor jumped to 2NT over West's 1♡ response. If dummy is 4-5-2-2 (not unlikely on the auction), declarer may be able to discard dummy's diamonds on the third and fourth round of clubs.

Matchpoints, E-W vul.

♠ A 3   ♡ K 6   ◇ A Q J 10 7 6 3   ♣ Q 9

WEST	NORTH	EAST	SOUTH
			1◇
dbl	pass	1♠	3◇
4♠	dbl	pass	

What should you lead?

Lead the ♠A, planning to continue with the ♠3. Partner's penalty double should tell you that the only way the opponents can take many tricks is by crossruffing. Leading the ◇A may set up a trick for declarer's ◇K.

Matchpoints, Neither vul.

NORTH (dummy)
♠ A 6 2
♡ 7 4
◇ Q 9 5 2
♣ K 6 5 3

EAST (you)
♠ K J 5 3
♡ Q 10 9 6
◇ 6
♣ A 10 7 4

WEST	NORTH	EAST	SOUTH
		pass	1◇
pass	1NT	dbl	pass
2♡	3◇	all pass	

Partner leads the ♠4 to dummy's ♠A as you play the ♠5 and declarer follows with the ♠7. You play low on dummy's ♣3 next, and declarer wins the ♣Q; partner plays the ♣8. What is partner's club holding?

Partner has either a singleton club, a doubleton club or ♣J98. From any other holding, his ♣8 would be a falsecard. A good defender won't falsecard when his partner may need accurate information to

make a play in the suit. Next comes the ♢3 to dummy's ♢Q and the
♣5 from dummy. Are you ready? What do you play?

Playing low (the ♣7) loses only to declarer's original holding of
♣QJ, which would give partner ♣982, from which he wouldn't have
played the ♣8 earlier. So duck again and let partner win or complete
his echo if he started with ♣82.

Suppose, however, you play the ♣A "on air". Declarer follows with
the ♣2 as partner plays the ♣9, confirming that he started with ♣J98.
What now? Time to cash major-suit winners! Come through declarer
with your ♡10.

225

Matchpoints, Both vul.

NORTH (dummy)
♠ J 7 3
♡ 9 4
♢ 7 6 5 2
♣ A K 10 4

EAST (you)
♠ 6 4 2
♡ 10 8 5 2
♢ A 8 3
♣ 7 6 3

WEST	NORTH	EAST	SOUTH
	pass	pass	1♢
dbl	redbl	1♡	3♢
all pass			

Third hand's signal in the suit led ordinarily shows *attitude* (desire for a continuation or shift).

Partner leads the ♠K. How should you signal?

Encourage! Play the ♠6. If partner has the ♠A, you want him to
cash it, for his logical shift (to hearts) will probably blow a trick.
Partner doesn't know that your only high card is the ♢A. On the auction (your 1♡ over the intervening redouble was dubious), he will play
you for the ♡A or the ♡Q instead and lead from his ♡K — unless you
scream as loudly as you can for a spade continuation. A spade continuation cannot blow a trick in the suit: the presence of the ♠J in dummy
tells you that.

Matchpoints, Both vul.

NORTH (dummy)
♠ K J 10 2
♡ 10 5
◇ A Q J 9
♣ Q 6 3

WEST (you)
♠ 9 8 6
♡ A J 8
◇ K 8 7 5 3 2
♣ A

WEST	NORTH	EAST	SOUTH
			pass
1◇	dbl	1♠[1]	2♡
pass[2]	pass	pass	

1. Forcing by agreement.
2. Playing Support Doubles, seldom as many as three spades

You lead the ♠9 and dummy's ♠10 wins. What's going on in the spade suit?

Either partner is holding up with ace-fourth, playing you for a doubleton and thinking to leave you with a spade to lead back to him to get a ruff, or he has queen-fourth and is simply preserving his ♠Q.

The ♡5 goes to declarer's ♡9 and your ♡J. What now?

Unblock the ♣A in order to avoid future endplays and then continue with the ♠8 (down-the-line after leading top of three, unless seeking deliberately to deceive partner and declarer). You don't want to have to lead diamonds often — declarer may get a "free finesse" if you do.

Matchpoints, N-S vul.

♠ J 7 4   ♡ A K J 6 3   ◇ A Q J   ♣ 8 6

WEST	NORTH	EAST	SOUTH
pass	pass	pass	1♡
pass	1♠	pass	?

There's a case for opening 1NT, which simplifies the auction greatly. However, you don't have a notrumpish hand. You have two unstopped suits, nearly all your strength concentrated in the other two suits and a good five-card heart suit. For these reasons, opening 1♡ is better if you do so with the plan of rebidding 2◇. Bid 2◇ as planned. You will right-side 3NT when partner has

♠ K Q 8 6   ♡ 10 8   ◇ 9 6 5   ♣ A Q 7 3

or something similar.

228

Matchpoints, Both vul.

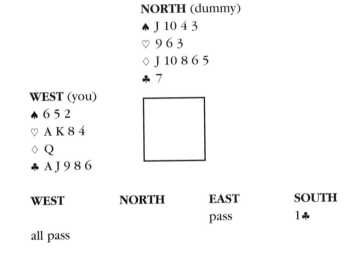

NORTH (dummy)
♠ J 10 4 3
♡ 9 6 3
◇ J 10 8 6 5
♣ 7

WEST (you)
♠ 6 5 2
♡ A K 8 4
◇ Q
♣ A J 9 8 6

WEST	NORTH	EAST	SOUTH
		pass	1♣

all pass

You lead the ♡K. Partner plays the ♡5 and declarer plays the ♡2. What next?

This is a difficult defense and your main concerns should be twofold: to keep yourself from getting endplayed and to keep dummy off lead to prevent declarer from finessing in spades.

Shifting to the ◇Q is a good first move. Partner plays the ◇4 and declarer wins with the ◇A. When declarer leads the ◇7, you discard the ♠2. Dummy's ◇10 wins as partner completes an echo with the ◇2, showing four. Partner covers dummy's ♠J with the ♠K, and declarer takes the ♠A. What do you know about declarer's hand at this point?

I hope you looked at declarer's convention card to see his notrump ranges. If you did, you know that his 1NT shows 15-17 HCP and his 2NT shows 20-21 HCP.

Partner's ♠K is doubleton, for with more than two spades he would wait to cover dummy's last honor, the ♠10. Therefore, declarer has ♠AQxx. Partner's count signal shows ◇xxxx, so declarer has ◇AKx. Declarer has fewer than four hearts, for he would not open 1♣ with a 4-4-3-2 pattern. Partner does not have the ♡Q and probably does not have four hearts, else he'd have encouraged hearts at Trick 1. Declarer has one of these hands (you cannot yet tell which):

♠ A Q x x   ♡ Q J x   ◇ A K x   ♣ K x x

♠ A Q x x   ♡ Q 10 x   ◇ A K x   ♣ K x x

♠ A Q x x   ♡ Q x x   ◇ A K x   ♣ K x x

♠ A Q x x   ♡ Q J x   ◇ A K x   ♣ Q x x

an 18- or 19-HCP hand, in between his 1NT and 2NT ranges.

Declarer continues with the ♠Q, catching the ♠8 from partner, and then leads the ♠9 from his hand. What should you play?

Discard a heart, so partner can ruff and lead clubs through declarer's likely king-third. Then you won't have to break clubs yourself and you'll beat 1♣ two for the matchpoint magic +200. If you ruff and break clubs, declarer will score his king and hold the set to down one.

Matchpoints, E-W vul.

229

NORTH (dummy)
♠ —
♡ A K J 7 6 3
◇ Q
♣ Q 9 8 7 6 2

EAST (you)
♠ A 9 7 4
♡ Q 10 5 2
◇ 7 6 4
♣ A 4

WEST	NORTH	EAST	SOUTH
pass	2♡[1]	pass	3◇
pass	4♣	pass	4NT[2]
pass	5◇	all pass	

1. Weak 2-bid (supposedly).
2. Blackwood (vanilla).

Partner leads the ♠2. Dummy discards the ♣2, so you take your ♠A. Declarer follows with the ♠5. What should you return?

This deal is a curiosity. Many years ago, I read *Journalist Leads* by Larry Rosler and Jeff Rubens. Their technical analyses impressed me very favorably, and with some partners I've played the "third from even, low from odd" spot card leads that they recommended as theoretically correct. However, the authors used constructed (or carefully selected) deals to make their points. Though in theory insoluble problems stemming from fourth-best leads may arise, in real life fourth-best leads have never given me problems. Here fourth-best leads are crucial. Playing "third and low" leads, partner would have led the ♠3 from his ♠J632, and you'd probably have judged that declarer had the deuce and partner had led low from five. Then you wouldn't know to cash the ♣A.

When you play fourth-best leads, deuces are wonderfully informative cards. They are often more valuable than higher spot cards (for example, fives).

Think about the entire deal. (a) What suit were you expecting partner to lead? (b) Did anything about his actual opening lead surprise you?

(a) You should have expected a lead in spades, the unbid suit in an auction in which the opponents bid game in a minor without making any attempt to reach 3NT.

(b) Partner's deuce surely can't be his fourth highest spade. It an "Alarm Clock" lead to induce you to give him a ruff in some other suit?

If partner is void in clubs, then the opponents have missed their 6-5 fit and a cold 6♣. If partner is void in hearts, they have missed their 6-3 major-suit fit and you'll get a fine score anyway (-400 instead of -420). So assume that partner has not made an "Alarm Clock" lead, meaning that declarer has five spades and a likely 5-1-6-1 pattern. You should therefore cash the ♣A before shifting to a trump.

230

When considering whether to make a minimum bid or a stronger bid, compare your actual hand to the hand you might have for the minimum bid. See how much stronger it is and bid accordingly.

Matchpoints, E-W vul.

♠ 10 7 4 2   ♡ K 5   ◊ K Q J 8 3   ♣ 6 2

WEST	NORTH	EAST	SOUTH
	1♡	1♠	pass
pass	dbl	2♣	?

You were almost strong enough to bid 2◊ last turn, but having passed, you are far too strong to bid only 2◊ now. You would bid 2◊ with

♠ 10 7 4 2   ♡ 7 5   ◊ K J 10 8 3   ♣ 6 2

wouldn't you? With your much better actual hand, you should jump to 3◊.

♠ A K 6 5 2   ♡ 10 4   ◇ Q 7 6 2   ♣ J 3

WEST	NORTH	EAST	SOUTH
	pass	1♡	1♠
2♣	4♠	6♣	pass
6♡	pass	pass	?

Pass. Partner preempted, making the opponents guess, and you don't
know whether they've guessed right or wrong. Maybe they're going
down in six. Maybe they've missed seven. You mustn't give them a
chance to correct their misguess, which they might do either by doubling 6♠, or by making a forcing pass and then bidding a cold grand
slam. If they've guessed right, they'll get a good score — even if you
have a profitable save in 6♠ doubled — for the field may not reach
slam at all.

A secret of matchpoint tactics: after you've
made the opponents guess (or in this case,
after your partner has made the opponents
guess), your best bet is simply to hope
they've guessed wrong.

    You have the wrong hand to be thinking of sacrificing anyway: a
balanced hand with little playing strength.

♠ A K 8 4   ♡ 10 6   ◇ A K 9 7   ♣ A 8 2

WEST	NORTH	EAST	SOUTH
			?

Whether the top of your range is 17 HCP or 18, this hand is much too
strong for a strong 1NT opening. Bid 1◇.

    However, you may be able to profit from a 1NT underbid, as your
Notrump Engine includes some fancy responses.

WEST	NORTH	EAST	SOUTH
			1NT (!)
pass	3♣[1]	pass	3◇
pass	3♠[2]	pass	?

1. Game force with five diamonds and
four clubs.
2. Presumably 3-1-5-4.

Jump to 6◇. There is no way for you to describe your hand after having underbid grossly at your first turn. Partner will never believe that
you have five prime cards.

The alternative is to bid 4♠ in the hope that partner will pass, play in a 4-3 major-suit fit and score better than anyone who reaches 5◊ (making, perhaps with an overtrick) or 3NT (going down).

233

Matchpoints, E-W vul.

♠ 9 4   ♡ J 9 6 4 2   ◊ A 9 7 4   ♣ J 8

WEST	NORTH	EAST	SOUTH
			pass
1◊	1♠	1NT	pass
2♣	2♡	3♣	?

Partner has shown a good hand, bidding twice when you've shown no sign of strength or a fit and East has shown at least some spade strength behind him. The hand probably belongs to your side. You have three plausible calls: 4♡ (insisting on game), 3◊ (clear game try) and 3♡ (competitive, but not a "bar-bid").

Bidding 4♡ is overoptimistic; partner has limited his hand by not starting with either with a takeout double (as he would with a slightly stronger hand) or a Michaels Cuebid (strong variety, with intention of bidding again). Even 3◊ is slightly aggressive (with ♡Q9642 instead of ♡J9642, you would do well to bid 3◊). Bidding 3♡ is just about right.

If you had a singleton club instead of a doubleton, 4♡ would be right. You'd be willing to bid it over an anticipated 4♣ by an opponent, forcing the opponents to guess at the five-level.

The auction isn't over. Is your work done?

WEST	NORTH	EAST	SOUTH
			pass
1♠	1♠	1NT	pass
2♣	2♡	3♣	3♡
pass	pass	4♣	?

Mission accomplished! You bid 3♡ competitively, and you've succeeded in pushing the opponents up one higher than they wanted to bid. Pass and take your plus. Second choice, a greedy matchpoint double hoping for the magic +200 against vulnerable opponents. Bidding 4♡ figures to produce a minus.

NORTH (dummy)
♠ A 6 3 2
♡ A 4
◇ A 7 6
♣ K J 6 4

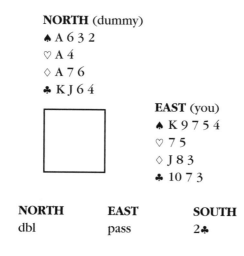

EAST (you)
♠ K 9 7 5 4
♡ 7 5
◇ J 8 3
♣ 10 7 3

WEST	NORTH	EAST	SOUTH
1♡	dbl	pass	2♣
all pass			

Partner leads the ♡K and dummy's ♡A wins the first trick. Declarer cashes the ace and queen of clubs: your partner follows to the first club and discards the ♡3 on the second. Now declarer leads the ♡9 from his hand; partner wins with the ♡J, and shifts to the ◇K. Declarer takes this trick in dummy and calls for another diamond. Partner overtakes your ◇8 to play a third diamond, which declarer ruffs. Now comes the ♡6: partner covers with the ♡8 and dummy ruffs with the ♣J as you discard a spade, leaving:

NORTH (dummy)
♠ A 6 3 2
♡ —
◇ —
♣ K

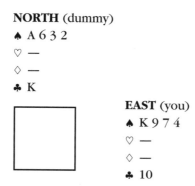

EAST (you)
♠ K 9 7 4
♡ —
◇ —
♣ 10

Now declarer leads a low spade off dummy. What do you know about the two unseen hands, and what should you play?

You know that partner is 2-5-5-1 and declarer is 2-4-2-5. Both have doubleton spades. Partner's other three cards are the ♡Q and two diamonds. Declarer's other three cards are the ♡10 and two low trumps.

If you duck, declarer may score the ♠Q. Then he can either draw your last trump with dummy's ♣K and lose only a heart, or ruff the ♡10 with dummy's ♣K, cash dummy's ♠A, and lose only a trump trick to your ♣10.

If you take the ♠K and exit with the ♣10, declarer must lose a second trick, either to partner's ♡Q or your ♠9.

235

Matchpoints, Neither vul.

♠ K J ♡ K J 9 6 4 3 ◇ Q 7 4 ♣ 93

WEST	NORTH	EAST	SOUTH
			?

You and your partner play Weak Two-bids. Should you open 2♡?

Everything depends on your standards for Weak Twos. My standards include a suit at least as good as AKxxxx, KJ10xxx or KQ98xx, but I favor highly disciplined Weak Twos. You and your partner may have other standards. Regardless, you should discuss standards for Weak Twos with each of your partners and adhere to whatever standards you adopt.

Perhaps because you require "either two of the top three, or three of the top five" honors in your suit (a frequently quoted standard) for a Weak Two, you pass.

WEST	NORTH	EAST	SOUTH
			pass
pass	1♣	pass	?

A jump shift by a passed hand doesn't show a "maximum pass with a long suit," it shows a hand that has improved to opening-bid strength by virtue of a good fit and mesh for partner's suit. With anything less, you shouldn't mind being dropped in a simple non-jump response, since when partner passes, you won't have a game anyway.

Bid 1♡. Don't worry about being dropped there. That should seldom happen. With heart support, partner should almost always raise (knowledge of his support may enable you to promote your hand and bid game). Without heart support he can't afford to pass lest you have only four and belong in some other strain.

Soon you find yourself in game:

NORTH (dummy)
♠ A 9 4 3
♡ A 7 2
◊ 9 8
♣ A Q 7 6

SOUTH (you)
♠ K J
♡ K J 9 6 4 3
◊ Q 7 4
♣ 9 3

WEST	NORTH	EAST	SOUTH
			pass
pass	1♣	pass	2♡ (!)
pass	2♠	pass	2NT
pass	4♡	all pass	

West leads the ♠6. How should you play?

After winning the spade lead, cash your other spade honor and exit in diamonds. Your plan should be to ruff your third diamond in dummy and discard a club on dummy's ♠A.

Suppose instead that you go wrong, starting trumps at Trick 2 by leading the ♡K and catching the ♡10 from West. Then you cash your other spade honor and lead to dummy's ♡A, but West shows out on the second heart. What should you discard from your hand on dummy's ♠A?

Discard a diamond, not a club, else you'll be forced to let the defenders in to cash three diamonds and the ♡Q, and you'll have no chance to try the club finesse. If West has the ♣K, you can make 4♡ despite having gone wrong in hearts.

Matchpoints, Both vul.

♠ Q 7   ♡ A Q J 10 3   ◊ J 6 4   ♣ J 10 9

WEST	NORTH	EAST	SOUTH
		1♣	?

Pass. Do not overcall 1♡. You have a balanced hand. You're vulnerable but you don't have five playing tricks. You have a poor holding in the suit bid to your right: three cards without an honor is poison, and three headed by a jack is almost as bad.

However, you do bid 1♡ and wind up declaring a heart partscore.

NORTH (dummy)
♠ 6 5 4
♡ 8 6 2
◇ A K 7 3
♣ K 8 5

☐

SOUTH (you)
♠ Q 7
♡ A Q J 10 3
◇ J 6 4
♣ J 10 9

WEST	NORTH	EAST	SOUTH
pass	pass	1♣	1♡
1♠	2♡	all pass	

West starts with the the ♣A and shifts to the ♠3, which is won by East's ♠A. East continues with the ♠J to your ♠Q and West's ♠K. West plays back the ♠10, East following as you ruff. What now?

Play a diamond to dummy, a heart to the ♡Q (the bidding marks East with the ♡K) as West follows small, a diamond to dummy and a heart to the ♡J as West follows small again. Then cash the ♡A, dropping East's ♡K and leaving this end position:

NORTH (dummy)
♠ —
♡ —
◇ 7 3
♣ K 8

☐

SOUTH (you)
♠ —
♡ 10
◇ J
♣ J 10

Now if East has the expected 3-3-3-4 hand with both minor-suit queens, the ◇J puts him in to lead from his remaining ♣Qxx. Dummy's ◇7 is high, but East is endplayed anyway. So you wind up losing only to the ♣A, the ♠A, the ♠K and the ◇Q — making an overtrick, courtesy of West's failure to continue clubs.

Matchpoints, Both vul.

(237)

♠ 8 7 5   ♡ Q   ◇ K Q 9 7 4 3   ♣ Q 8 3

WEST	NORTH	EAST	SOUTH
			?

You play Weak Two-bids. Should you open 2◇?

No. Even if the suit meets your standards for Weak Twos (it doesn't quite meet mine), your hand is not strong enough for a vulnerable Weak 2◇ bid.

Matchpoints, E-W vul.

(238)

NORTH (dummy)
♠ K Q J 10 5
♡ 7 5
◇ 5
♣ 10 8 7 5 3

EAST (you)
♠ 7 3 2
♡ K J 3
◇ K 6 3
♣ Q J 9 2

WEST	NORTH	EAST	SOUTH
		pass	1◇
pass	1♠	pass	1NT
pass	pass (!)	pass	

Partner leads the ♡2 to your ♡K, which holds. So does your ♡J. When you lead your last heart, partner tops declarer's ♡9 with the ♡10. Then partner shifts to the ◇Q. Which diamond should you play?

You must encourage with the ◊6. You can't afford to overtake with the ◊K, a card you may need to win a trick later.

239

Matchpoints, E-W vul.

♠ A J 7 6 2   ♡ 10   ◊ 7 6   ♣ A K 8 4 2

WEST	NORTH	EAST	SOUTH
	pass	pass	?

Open 1♣, not 1♠. Contrary to what most modern bidding manuals teach, the normal order of bidding with 5-5 in the black suits is clubs and then spades. There are exceptions — hands with much stronger spades than clubs and hands that are good enough for a "high-reverse" (1♠-2♡; 3♣) but not for a jump-shift (1♣-1♡; 2♠) — but this is not one of them.

Sometime in the 1960s, bidding manuals began teaching, "With two five-card suits, open in the higher-ranking." How did that become dogma? Perhaps those who said it were unaware of the exceptions. Or perhaps, aware of the exceptions, they were willing to sacrifice technical superiority for the sake of simplicity. Simplicity, however, is highly elusive. Here's my 'simple' rule for choosing which of two five-card suits to open: Anticipate the course of the auction and bid accordingly.

Consider this pattern: 5-0-5-3. Your normal opening, unless the spades are much stronger, should be in diamonds. You anticipate bidding spades over hearts next, but if partner responds 2♣, your hand becomes enormous and qualifies easily for a 2♠ reverse.

Similarly, with 3-5-0-5, your normal opening, unless the hearts are much stronger, should be in clubs. You anticipate bidding hearts over diamonds next, but if partner responds 1♠, you can reverse into 2♡ because the fit for spades gives you substantial extra values.

> Anticipate that partner will bid the suit in which you have substantially fewer cards than any other; after all, there are more cards available for him to hold in it. If instead he bids a suit in which you have three or more cards, your fit for his suit will enable you to avoid trouble.

240

Matchpoints, Neither vul.

♠ 8   ♡ A K Q 8 7 3   ◊ 7 6 3   ♣ Q 10 5

WEST	NORTH	EAST	SOUTH
			?

Open 1♡, even if you play Weak Two-bids with a wide "5 to 11 HCP" range. You have too good a hand for a Weak 2♡. Weak Twos are not "point-count" bids, despite the ACBL Convention Card's silly blanks to fill in ranges of high card points..

Hands with 6331 distribution are significantly better than 6322 hands. Let this influence you one way or the other in close cases. With a slightly different hand

♠ 8 7   ♡ A K Q 8 7 3   ◊ 6 3   ♣ Q 10 5

you could open a Weak 2♡ without qualms.

Weak Two-bids have far too wide a range. The difference between the best and worst hand for an opening 2♠ is 6 points and there is no known fit (responder may have one or no spades). I think the range for Weak Twos should be narrowed to 8-11 HCP.

Matchpoints, Neither vul.

(241)

♠ 10 6   ♡ J 10 5 4 2   ◊ 8 5 4   ♣ 8 6 3

WEST	NORTH	EAST	SOUTH
	2♡[1]	dbl	?

1. Weak Two-bid.

Bid 4♡. Take away West's possible 3♡ (or 4♡) cuebid. Take away West's jumps. Psyching some other suit is very dangerous, not only because it leaves your opponents lots of bidding space but also because it may fetch a costly lead in that suit from partner. (How embarrassing if you psych a suit and partner's lead in that suit blows a trick!)

Preemption may work. Deception will work far less often and will boomerang at least as often as it works. A psych might work in a not-yet-contested auction, as LHO's double will be for takeout, but after RHO has intervened, LHO's double will be for penalties, making it easier, not harder, for your opponents to find their fit in the suit you psyched.

Matchpoints, N-S vul.

(242)

♠ Q J 10 7 6 5 2   ♡ J   ◊ A   ♣ A K Q 3

WEST	NORTH	EAST	SOUTH
			1♠
2♡	pass	pass	?

Bid 4♠. You have enough playing strength to do so (though the ♠9 and ♠8 would have provided nice protection against very bad breaks). If you bid anything less, partner won't know to bid 4♠ with

♠ 4 3   ♡ 10 8 7 5 2   ◇ Q 5 4   ♣ J 7 6

or a similar, perhaps even weaker, hand that will nevertheless let you make 4♠.

By the way, you did well not to open the Omnibus 2♣ that goes with Weak Two-bids; an Omnibus 2♣ requires much more high-card strength.

243

Matchpoints, Both vul.

NORTH (dummy)
♠ J 10 6 4
♡ J 10
◇ J 10 5
♣ A Q 9 6

□

SOUTH (you)
♠ A K Q 7 3
♡ Q 7 6 4
◇ A 9 3
♣ 5

WEST	NORTH	EAST	SOUTH
			1♠
pass	2♠	pass	3♡
pass	4♠	all pass	

West leads the ♡A and continues with the ♡3 to East's ♡K. East shifts to the ◇4. What now?

You don't yet know how any of the suits are divided. You have five sure spades tricks, one club, one diamond, one heart and you can get a heart ruff in dummy. However, you may not be able to discard a diamond from dummy on the queen of hearts (a defender may ruff), so you cannot rely on getting a second ruff in dummy for your tenth trick.

Your best bet is to duck the diamond (you must lose a diamond trick in any case). Suppose West wins with an honor and shifts to a club. Then you can rise with the ♣A and play two top trumps. If trumps split 2-2, you can discard one of dummy's diamonds on the ♡Q and ruff one heart and one diamond in dummy. If they split otherwise, you have a choice of plays.

You can ruff one heart in dummy and finesse East for the other missing diamond honor. This will work whenever the diamond honors are split. Although the odds are usually 2-to-1 that East will have been dealt the other honor, given that West has been dealt at least one, the odds in this case are overwhelming. Why? Because you have further information: West led an ace, and an ace in a suit you'd bid at that. Do you think he'd have done that if he had king-queen in an unbid suit?

Alternatively, you can try to cash the ♡Q to discard a diamond from dummy and then crossruff. This will work when hearts split 4-3 (about a 62% chance).

Which line is better?

The answer depends on which opponent shows out on the second spade. If West shows out, the first line is better. If East shows out, the second line is better, because if West, the defender with the third trump, ruffs the ♡Q, you can overruff in dummy and fall back on the diamond finesse.

Matchpoints, Both vul.

244

♠ 6   ♡ A K 10 9 4   ◇ K J 8 3   ♣ 10 7 6

WEST	NORTH	EAST	SOUTH
		2♠[1]	?

1. Weak Two-bid.

Pass. You don't have three-level values. East's Weak 2♠ Bid doesn't make your hand any stronger. Even under pressure of preemption you can't quite afford to stretch with this hand.

Suppose, however, that by some quirk you were barred from passing. What should you do then?

Double. Doubling gives you four possible harbors: 3♣, 3◇, 3♡ and partner may be able to pass for penalties. That's safer than bidding 3♡, which gives you only one harbor.

It is a myth that doubling shows a better hand than overcalling. The difference between overcalls and takeout doubles is one of *suits* and *shape*. The myth may stem from a fact about takeout doubles: because they are virtually forcing, they may be based on hands with enormous strength (the doubler plans to bid again to show his great strength). That fact, however, affects only the *upper* end of the "range" for a takeout double (there is none); it does not alter the lower end (which is not higher than for a simple overcall).

245

Matchpoints, Neither vul.

♠ 9 7 6 4 2　♡ J 10　◇ Q 6 4　♣ J 9 5

WEST	NORTH	EAST	SOUTH
	pass	1NT	pass
3NT	all pass		

You decide to lead a spade: which spade should you lead?

It's a close decision between the ♠4 (fourth-highest) and the ♠7 (hoping that partner will read it as denying a spade honor). The ♠4 is slightly better because you have no suit to which you'd particularly like partner to shift. With slightly stronger diamonds, e.g.

♠ 9 7 6 4 2　♡ J 10　◇ Q 10 6　♣ J 9 5

the ♠7 would be a slightly better lead.

Is it clear to lead spades at all? No. The ♡J is a reasonable alternative, for it might strike partner's long suit, and you do have two useful touching lower honors. However, I prefer a spade lead, because more often than most bridge players think, both declarer and dummy will have only two spades. Also, more often than most bridge players think, declarer will have five hearts. Even when declarer has four hearts, partner won't know it and may go wrong by continuing hearts under the impression that you have four. That's often the trouble with short-suit leads.

246

Matchpoints, Neither vul.

♠ Q 3　♡ K 6 4 3　◇ Q 5　♣ Q J 7 3 2

WEST	NORTH	EAST	SOUTH
			pass
pass	1◇	pass	1♡
pass	2♡	pass	2NT
pass	3♡	pass	?

Pass. Your 2NT was already an overbid with this queen-laden hand. You invited game and partner declined, showing a minimum opening with four hearts. You mustn't bid 3NT now. If you weren't willing to play in hearts facing four-card support, you should never have bid the suit. Your instinct to bid notrump was right: a hand with three or four queens is very notrumpish. It would have been reasonable (though "against the field") to bypass a thin four-card major to respond 1NT initially. In this auction, however, 3NT is not a possible bid: it's inconsistent with all three of your previous calls.

Matchpoints, N-S vul.

♠ A J 8   ♡ J 7 4   ◇ A K Q 10 6   ♣ 9 3

WEST	NORTH	EAST	SOUTH
pass	1NT	pass	?

You have enough, but only barely, to think of slam. You might bid 4NT. However, if your Notrump Engine permits, you do better to transfer to diamonds and then bid 4NT, so that if partner has diamond support and a ruffing value, e.g.

♠ K Q x   ♡ K Q 10 x   ◇ J 9 x x   ♣ A Q
or
♠ K x   ♡ A K Q x   ◇ J x x x   ♣ K J x

you can reach the safer 6◇ slam right-sided.

With no agreements, your best bid is 4NT, inviting partner to bid 6NT with a maximum. Bidding 4◇ does not show a stronger diamond hand than 3◇. Four diamonds is undefined in standard methods, though many pairs use it as "Texas Transfer" showing long hearts, and a few use it as a "South African Transfer" showing long spades (slightly better). You have no agreement with your present partner to use either four-level transfer scheme, so 4◇ is an idle, meaningless bid. Partner, left to guess what it means, is likely to interpret it as a Texas Transfer, since that's the most popular treatment among those who use this 4◇ jump to mean anything at all.

Perhaps because you have not discussed your responses to notrump openings in detail, you make a bid that partner cannot be expected to understand, leading to this:

WEST	NORTH	EAST	SOUTH
pass	1NT[1]	pass	4◇[2]
pass	4♡	pass	?

In slammish minor-suit auctions, 4NT should not be used to ask for keycards. If you *must* have a keycard ask, arrange with your partners to use some other bid.

1. 15-17 HCP.
2. Undefined.

You lucked out! Somehow partner didn't pass you in 4◇. Instead he interpreted 4◇ as a Texas Transfer. Now you'd better just bid 6NT before further confusion sets in. If you bid 4NT, intending to invite partner to a notrump slam, he may (and should) interpret it as Roman Keycard Blackwood for hearts. That's one use of four-level transfers over 1NT: to set trumps and activate keycard asks next.

---

(248)

Matchpoints, E-W vul.

♠ K J 8 6 3   ♡ K 7   ◇ K J 6 5 2   ♣ Q

WEST	NORTH	EAST	SOUTH
		pass	?

It's very questionable whether you should open. You are aceless. You have only 1 1/2 Honor Tricks with some plus values. Your singleton ♣Q isn't worth very much. You have no "stuffing" in your suits (tens and nines would be helpful). Pass. You decide to open, however, and face this auction:

WEST	NORTH	EAST	SOUTH
		pass	1♠ (!)
2♡	pass	3♡	?

Most of the bids that are called "gambling" bids by the perpetrators aren't gambles at all. They are certain to lose, even when partner turns up with the undisclosed golden cards that will suffice to let the bid make. For then partner will bid more — much more — and you'll go down two, often doubled.

You've more than shot your wad already. Your doubleton king of hearts, worth half a trick at the time you opened, when you still could hope that partner had a decent hand, is worth much less now that West has bid 2♡, vulnerable, behind you. There's nothing to indicate that partner has anything better than a balanced yarborough.

Pass. To bid 4◇ exposes you to a monstrous penalty. If your pipedreams come true and partner has enough for you to make 4◇, you'll be a loser for bidding it: -300 in 6◇ doubled, for in light of your very strong bidding, partner will surely bid slam.

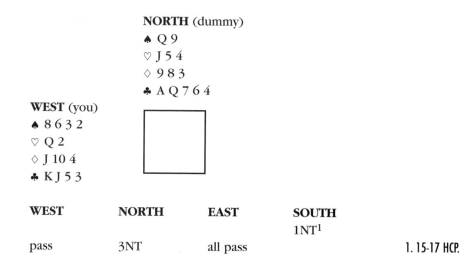

NORTH (dummy)
♠ Q 9
♡ J 5 4
◇ 9 8 3
♣ A Q 7 6 4

WEST (you)
♠ 8 6 3 2
♡ Q 2
◇ J 10 4
♣ K J 5 3

WEST	NORTH	EAST	SOUTH
			1NT[1]
pass	3NT	all pass	

1. 15-17 HCP.

You lead the ◇J; partner plays the ◇7 and declarer takes the ◇A. What do you think the diamond situation is?

There are three unseen diamonds that are lower than partner's ◇7. Two or more unseen lower spot cards are a reliable sign that partner's card is encouraging. Of course, partner might have a doubleton, ◇Q7, so you can't be sure. Declarer's fast play of the ◇A is a big indication that he also has the ◇K; without it, he would very likely duck the first diamond.

Declarer continues with a low club to dummy's queen and then leads dummy's ♠Q. Partner covers with the ♠K, and declarer takes the ♠A. Declarer leads a second club to dummy's ace and partner follows with the ♣10. When declarer leads a third club to drive out one of your honors, partner discards the ♡3 and declarer the ◇5. What should you do after winning the trick with the ♣K?

By the way, you can't fool anyone when you win with the ♣K rather than the ♣J: declarer and partner both know that the other honor is still out and that you have it. Your choice of which honor to win with can only be a suit-preference play, since all other meanings have been eliminated. When you won with the ♣K, you cannot have done so to preserve your tricks (first priority), nor to tell partner your attitude toward the suit led (second priority), nor to show your holding (usually count) in the suit led (third priority). Thus the ♣K suggests that you have useful values in the higher-ranking of the two suits in which your strength is unknown (i.e. spades).

Spades is declarer's suit. Declarer has shown up with nothing in clubs, the ace and king in diamonds and the ace and jack in spades (probably also the ♠10, as he wouldn't try to set up dummy's clubs unless he thought dummy had an entry, which can only be the ♠9). For his 1NT opening, he must have either the king or ace in hearts to come to 15 or 16 HCP, but he cannot have both (as that would give him a splendid 19 HCP).

That should tell you what to do. Continue with the ◇10 to drive out declarer's ◇K and set up a diamond trick or two for your side.

250

Matchpoints, E-W vul.

♠ 8 5   ♡ A K J 10 7 3   ◇ K 6 4   ♣ K 3

WEST	NORTH	EAST	SOUTH
		pass	1♡
1♠	pass	2♠	?

Pass. You don't have three-level values. Your hand figures to take about six tricks in a heart contract. If partner supplies one trick (and you have no reason to think he'll supply two), you can be doubled and set two, for -300.

Won't the opponents be able to make 4♠ if partner supplies only one trick?

Not often. Partner's hand may be worth much more on defense against spades than as dummy in a heart contract. For example, partner may have

♠ J 10 3   ♡ 2   ◇ J 8 7 5 3   ♣ J 9 8 2

a hand that is totally useless on offense, but can provide enough defense to keep the opponents from making 4♠.

When you bid again, you succeed only in pushing the opponents into a game they might not otherwise reach.

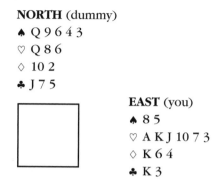

NORTH (dummy)
♠ Q 9 6 4 3
♡ Q 8 6
♢ 10 2
♣ J 7 5

EAST (you)
♠ 8 5
♡ A K J 10 7 3
♢ K 6 4
♣ K 3

WEST	NORTH	EAST	SOUTH
	pass	1♡	1♠
pass	2♠	3♡[1]	3♠
4♡	4♠	all pass	

1. By partnership agreement, merely competitive.

Partner leads a "top-of-nothing" ♡5 and your ♡10 wins, as declarer follows with the ♡9. What now? At IMPs, you would lead a desperation ♣K, hoping for a ruff if you catch partner with the ♣A.

At matchpoints, that's unlikely. With three hearts, a singleton or void in spades and an ace, partner would probably have been more active in the auction. Odds are that partner has a queen and a jack. A typical hand would be

♠ 7   ♡ 5 4 2   ♢ J 9 8 7 3   ♣ Q 10 8 2

and if partner has it, shifting to the ♣K will blow a trick. Even if partner has only ♣9842, a ♣K shift can hurt you. Left to his own devices, declarer may start clubs by leading dummy's ♣J (a small technical error, but not an unusual one). Don't make it easy for your opponents: give them a chance to err. Return a passive ♡K instead of breaking a new suit.

Matchpoints, N-S vul.

♠ K J 10 6 3   ♡ 7 6   ◇ J   ♣ Q 7 5 4 3

WEST	NORTH	EAST	SOUTH
			pass
pass	pass	1♣	?

Pass. Entering the auction with such a weak hand when vulnerable begs for trouble (-200 or worse). If you were not vulnerable, you might risk a marginal 1♠ overcall for its moderate "nuisance value" and more substantial lead-directing value. Nonetheless, you choose to overcall anyway and catch partner with surprisingly good support:

NORTH (dummy)
♠ A 9 5 4
♡ K 8 4 3
◇ 9 8 7 5 3
♣ —

SOUTH (you)
♠ K J 10 6 3
♡ 7 6
◇ J
♣ Q 7 5 4 3

WEST	NORTH	EAST	SOUTH
			pass
pass	pass	1♣	1♠
1NT[1]	3♠	all pass	

1. East and West play negative doubles.

West leads the ◇K and East encourages with the ◇10. How are the major suits splitting?

West has ♠Qxx (possibly ♠Q872) and East has a singleton (possibly a void). West has three hearts (he didn't make a negative double) and East has four.

Where are your tricks coming from? You're not likely to find them in hearts, as East is a favorite to hold the ♡A.

West continues with the ◇2 to East's ◇A, and you ruff. How should you continue?

You can make your trumps separately if you can ruff four times in each hand. Assuming that West is 3-3-4-3, you can ruff only three diamonds in your hand without getting overruffed. Therefore your fourth ruff must be a heart ruff. Prepare to ruff a heart by leading one now, even though you expect East to have the ♡A. However, East might have an unlikely

$$\spadesuit x \quad \heartsuit Q J x x \quad \diamond A 10 x \quad \clubsuit A K J x x,$$

more than enough to open 1♣ even without the ♡A.

Suppose, however, that you lead a heart and East takes dummy's ♡K with the ♡A, cashes the ♡Q and continues with the ♡J. Now you can crossruff clubs and diamonds for nine tricks. If West has the ♡A, you'll make 3♠ even if the defenders shift to trumps (you get one heart and eight trump tricks) and you'll make an overtrick if they don't.

Matchpoints, Both vul.

252

NORTH (dummy)
- ♠ 7
- ♡ K Q 5 4 3
- ◇ K 6 5 4 2
- ♣ K 5

WEST (you)
- ♠ A K 6 5
- ♡ A J 9
- ◇ 7
- ♣ Q 10 8 7 6

WEST	NORTH	EAST	SOUTH
	pass	pass	1♠
pass	2♡	pass	2♠
pass	3◇	pass	3NT
all pass			

Against an unskilled declarer you lead the ♣7. The ♣5 arrives from dummy, the ♣9 from partner and the ♣J from declarer. Declarer plays the ◇A, the ◇Q and the ◇3 to dummy, partner playing the ◇8, the ◇10 and the ◇J in that order. You have two discards to make: what should you discard?

The less capable a declarer is, the more important it becomes for defenders to give count religiously, for they can't draw many inferences from declarer's plays. Giving count won't help a poor declarer as it will a good declarer, for a poor declarer doesn't even look at the defenders' spot cards.

Do not discard any clubs, which have the potential to become winners soon. Discard the ♠6 and then the ♠5, losers both, signaling control of the suit.

On the fourth diamond, which declarer wins in hand, partner discards the ♣2. What's going on in the club suit, and what do you think declarer's hand pattern is?

Partner's ♣2 is a count card. He started with ♣9432. With only three clubs, ♣932 or ♣942, he'd have played down the line in clubs: the ♣3 or the ♣4, not the ♣2. That's key: a defender's second card in a suit, whether as a return of the suit led or as a discard, should give count unless an unblocking play is necessary.

So declarer is almost surely 6-1-4-2. With a 5-2-4-2 hand and top-less spades, he'd undoubtedly have bid 2NT instead of 2♠. Declarer's ♣A is now singleton and dummy is dead thanks to declarer's failure to lead a heart towards dummy early, his blocking of the diamond suit and his winning of the first trick with the ♣J instead of the ♣A.

Discarding even one club would be costly. If you keep all your clubs, you can beat 3NT two by rising with the ♡A on the first lead.

253

Matchpoints, N-S vul.

NORTH (dummy)
♠ 10 7 3
♡ Q J 7 6 4
◇ —
♣ Q 9 5 4 3

EAST (you)
♠ K J 9 8 4
♡ 5 2
◇ Q 8 4
♣ 10 6 2

WEST	NORTH	EAST	SOUTH
		pass	1◇
pass	1♡	pass	3◇
all pass			

Partner leads the ◇2. What are your thoughts as dummy appears?

You should think, "How surprising! This auction doesn't call for a trump lead: there is no indication that dummy can ruff anything. Why isn't partner leading one of the unbid suits, clubs or spades?"

Now answer your own question: partner must have bad black-suit holdings from which to lead. Probably he has something like the ace (without the king) or the king or queen in a short suit holding.

While you are thinking those thoughts, however, you should play your ♢Q. Don't let declarer take a trick with a low diamond. If partner's trump lead blew a trick, that trick cannot be recovered, but by playing low you will blow a trick if partner's lead was from ♢Jxx or ♢109xx.

Matchpoints, E-W vul.

(254)

♠ 10 6 3 2   ♡ Q 10 3   ♢ 10 7   ♣ J 7 6 4

WEST	NORTH	EAST	SOUTH
	1♡	pass	pass
dbl	pass	1♠	?

Pass. Nothing that has happened since you passed last turn has improved your hand. You didn't have a good enough hand then to raise to 2♡, and you don't have one now. Which would be the worse mistake: to have bid 2♡ last turn or to bid 2♡ now?

Here are some facts: you decide.

Bidding 2♡ last turn might have shut West out. All you know is that he thought he had enough to make a balancing double at the one-level; you don't know that he would have made a direct double at the two-level. Even if he would have, an opposing double would have been for takeout. A 2♡ bid now, however, comes too late to shut your opponents out; each has already made a call that conveys information to the other. If you bid 2♡ now, an opponent can double for penalties.

Passing at your first turn doesn't make your hand any stronger at your second turn. Partner will know you have limited strength (thus averting one of the usual dangers your overbid might incur) but the opponents will know also (thus exacerbating the dangers).

Matchpoints, Both vul.

(255)

♠ Q 9 5 4   ♡ 8 6 5 3   ♢ A J 6   ♣ A Q

WEST	NORTH	EAST	SOUTH
		pass	1♢
1♠	dbl[1]	2♠	?

1. Negative double.

Your short club honors are a defect. Likewise it's a defect to have opened in a three-card minor (or a four-card major). Your hand was the barest of minimum opening bids last turn. Now your ♠Q appears to be facing shortness and is worth almost nothing on offense. Your bare-minimum opening has become a sub-minimum. However, your spades will prove pesky on defense. Pass.

To bid 3♡, you would need

♠ 7 5 4   ♡ K Q 8 3   ◇ A Q 9 6 2   ♣ 3

a minimum opening hand, to be sure, but one with pure, prime values.

256

Matchpoints, N-S vul.

♠ 5   ♡ K 7 3   ◇ A K Q J 10 6 2   ♣ 6 3

WEST	NORTH	EAST	SOUTH
pass	1♠	pass	?

Bid 2◇. You have a good hand, but it is not quite good enough for a jump to 3◇. In Chapter 4 of The Secrets of Winning Bridge, a fine book, author Jeff Rubens cites "Culbertson's Rule": Invite a slam if a perfect minimum holding for partner will make it laydown.

A jump shift invites slam. Use Culbertson's Rule. Would a 5-3-2-3 hand that included all three missing aces be a perfect minimum? Partner will certainly think so, but you can't make a slam with it. Actually, a perfect (but unexpected) minimum such as

♠ J 10 9 7 2   ♡ A Q J 5   ◇ 8   ♣ A 7 4

would make slam laydown. However, you have no way to discover whether partner has that hand. When you have a singleton in partner's first suit, you should assume that he has some wasted strength there.

For a 3◇ jump shift that is based on a solid suit, you need either an outside ace or two outside kings. You may make an exception when you only have one outside king, but you should do so only if that king is in partner's suit.

♠ K 7 3   ♡ 5   ◇ A K Q J 10 6 2   ♣ 6 3

would qualify (slam is laydown facing

♠ A Q J 7 2　♡ J 8 4　◇ 8　♣ A 7 4 2

— a "perfect minimum").

IMPs, E-W vul.

NORTH (dummy)
♠ Q J 8 5 2
♡ Q
◇ Q 3 2
♣ J 7 5 4

WEST (you)
♠ 3
♡ 10 7 6 4 3
◇ 9 8 5 4
♣ K 9 2

WEST	NORTH	EAST	SOUTH
			1◇
pass	1♠	pass	1NT[1]
pass	2♠	pass	2NT
all pass			

1. 15-17 HCP (North and South play weak notrumps).

You lead the ♡4. Partner's ♡K wins, as declarer plays the ♡2. Partner continues with the ♡J. Declarer takes the ♡A and discards dummy's ♠2. Then he leads the ◇6 to dummy's ◇Q and partner's ◇K. Partner returns the ♡5. You top declarer's ♡8 with your ♡10, as dummy discards a club. You return a heart to declarer's ♡9; dummy discards the a diamond and partner discards the ♣6. Declarer cashes the ◇A, on which partner's ◇10 falls, and then leads the ♣3. What should you play?

Partner wouldn't discard from a useful club holding. Better to take the ♣K now lest you are forced to lead from it later. You duck, however, and dummy's ♣J wins. Unaccountably, declarer "finesses" the ♣Q. You take the ♣K and the ♡7. Dummy discards another club; partner discards the ♠10 and declarer discards the ♠4, leaving:

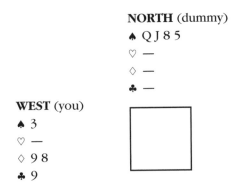

NORTH (dummy)

♠ Q J 8 5
♡ —
◇ —
♣ —

WEST (you)

♠ 3
♡ —
◇ 9 8
♣ 9

Amazingly, four-card endings are the hardest. With what card should you exit?

By now, you should know the entire deal. Declarer has shown up with a good 15 HCP and a 2-4-4-3 pattern:

$$♠ ? 4 \quad ♡ A 9 8 2 \quad ◇ A J 7 6 \quad ♣ A Q 3.$$

His remaining spade cannot be the ♠K or the ♠A, for then he'd have a good 18 or 19 HCP. Partner's ♠10 discard was undoubtedly from ♠AK109x (else he could not spare the ♠10). So lead the ♠3.

Now look at this ending from partner's point of view (only spades visible):

NORTH (dummy)

♠ Q J 8 5

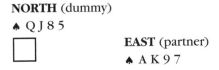

EAST (partner)

♠ A K 9 7

When you lead the ♠3, declarer must put up an honor from dummy to keep partner's ♠9 from taking a trick. Did partner err by discarding the ♠10? Had he discarded the ♠7 instead, he could take the ♠K and the ♠A, and then exit with the ♠10, scoring the ♠9 at the end.

No, partner did not err. He can simply duck dummy's ♠J or ♠Q and take the last three tricks with his ♠AK9. For that matter, he can take the ♠K and exit with a low spade.

Matchpoints, Both vul.

♠ A Q 6 4   ♡ J 5 3   ◇ Q 7 3   ♣ J 10 3

WEST	NORTH	EAST	SOUTH
1♣	pass	1♠	pass
1NT[1]	pass	2◇[2]	pass
2♠	all pass		

1. 12-14 HCP.
2. Artificial one-round force.

What should you lead?

This auction does not call for a trump lead. When West has three spades and didn't raise to 2♠ directly, he is unlikely to have decent trumps with a ruffing value. Lead the ♣J, a passive lead, and the lead least likely to cost a trick. Second choice: the ◇3.

In the absence of any indication to the contrary, you should defend *passively* against suit contracts.

Matchpoints, Neither vul.

NORTH (dummy)
♠ 8 4 3
♡ J 10 5 3
◇ K 7 3
♣ 7 5 4

WEST (you)
♠ Q 10
♡ A K 6
◇ 10 5 4
♣ J 10 9 6 2

WEST	NORTH	EAST	SOUTH
		pass	2NT[1]
pass	3♣[2]	pass	3♠
pass	3NT	all pass	

1. 20-21 HCP.
2. Stayman.

You lead the ♣J, taken by partner's ♣A, as declarer follows small. Partner returns the ♣3 to declarer's ♣K. Declarer cashes the ♠A, overtakes the ◇J with dummy's ◇K, and then leads another spade, losing a finesse of the ♠J to your ♠Q. Partner plays the ♠5, the ◇6 and the ♠7 respectively.

What is declarer's hand, and how should you continue?

Job One for the defenders when declarer has bid notrump naturally is to count declarer's high card points. Take care to examine your opponents' convention cards, or inquire about the exact ranges of their notrump bids. Sometimes that will enable you to place partner with a particular queen or jack.

If you trust partner's carding, declarer has

♠ A K J 6 2   ♡ ? ?   ◇ A Q J   ♣ K Q 8

and if you believe the bidding, declarer cannot have the ♡Q, for that would give him 22 HCP (by his count). So play the ♡K, the ♡A and then the ♡6 to partner's ♡Q before declarer scampers home with nine tricks.

260

IMPs, Neither vul.

♠ K 5   ♡ A K 7 4 3   ◇ 8   ♣ A J 9 6 5

WEST	NORTH	EAST	SOUTH
1♣	1♠	pass	2♣
dbl	pass	pass	?

At your first turn, you cuebid 2♣ to create a force. West, recognizing that your 2♣ did not show clubs, doubled. Why not make him pay? Redouble to suggest playing there. Partner needn't pass (he may be short in clubs), but if he does, you should have little trouble making. Then, even without any overtricks, you'll score +560, a 4-IMP gain if North and South at the other table bid and make game (3NT, 4♡ or 4♠).

261

IMPs, E-W vul.

♠ Q 6   ♡ A 8 5 3 2   ◇ 7 6 3   ♣ K 8 4

WEST	NORTH	EAST	SOUTH
			pass
pass	1♣	pass	1♡
pass	1♠	pass	?

The pedestrian bid is 2♣, but I prefer 3♣ with three working cards: the ♡A, the ♣K and the ♠Q.

When partner bids two or three suits, promote face cards in those suits and demote face cards in the suits he doesn't bid (they may duplicate his shortness).

♠ 7 6   ♡ K 8 5 3 2   ◇ Q 6 3   ♣ A 8 4

wouldn't be nearly as good (only one card known to be working).

NORTH (dummy)
- ♠ Q 9 7 4
- ♡ K Q 5 4
- ◇ K 10 7 4
- ♣ 6

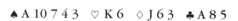

SOUTH (you)
- ♠ A
- ♡ A J 6 3
- ◇ 8 3
- ♣ A Q J 10 5 2

WEST	NORTH	EAST	SOUTH
	pass	pass	1♣
1◇	dbl[1]	pass	3♡
pass	4♡	all pass	

1. Negative double.

West leads the ◇A and continues with the ◇Q. You play the ◇K from dummy and East follows to the second diamond. What next?

Set up your hand. Play the ♡A and then play low to the ♡K. When West discards on the second heart, lead to the ♣A and continue with the ♣Q. If West has ♣Kx (unlikely), or ♣Kxx, or plays the ♣K from ♣Kxxx, you'll make two overtricks; otherwise you'll make one overtrick.

IMPs, Both vul.

♠ A 10 7 4 3   ♡ K 6   ◇ J 6 3   ♣ A 8 5

WEST	NORTH	EAST	SOUTH
			pass
1♣	pass	1◇	pass
1NT	pass	pass	?

You could have opened 1♠, but now you must pass. Your hand is too balanced and your suit is too thin to enter the bidding, especially at the two-level, and especially when vulnerable.

Which is the better spade bid? At the one-level when you can't be doubled for penalties very easily, or at the two-level when you can? If you decided, questionably but not unreasonably, to pass initially, then you must pass later also.

Here's one way to look at it. Your opposite number will probably open 1♠ (rightly or wrongly). There are two cases to consider.

Case (1). You made a "losing decision" not to open 1♠. This could happen, for example, if at the other table a 1♠ opening got your opposite numbers to some making partscore even with North having only one or two spades. If so, you can't recover by bidding 2♠ now.

Case (2). You made a "winning decision" not to open 1♠. This could happen if at the other table a 1♠ opening got your opposite numbers too high, down two in an undoubled partscore. If you bid 2♠ now, you're taking a "won" board and turning it into a loss, perhaps down two doubled in 2♠.

This bears repeating: if you've made a dubious call earlier, don't try to catch up later. You seldom can. Instead, assume that your dubious call has worked, and stick with it. Even truly bad calls sometimes work. Don't throw away a board you may already have won by a "lucky" decision earlier.

IMPs, Neither vul.

♠ K 5   ♡ A K 7 4 3   ◇ 8   ♣ A J 9 6 5

WEST	NORTH	EAST	SOUTH
1♣	1♠	pass	2♣
dbl	pass	pass	2♡
pass	3♡	pass	?

Don't rebid a suit without extra length if you have any reasonable alternative.

You mustn't bid 4♡, for you've already shown at least five hearts and partner may have had nothing better to do than raise on a doubleton queen. Bid 3♠ to show your modest spade support and offer a choice of games. Second choice: 4♣.

IMPs, E-W vul.

♠ K   ♡ 8 3   ◇ K J 10 7 6 2   ♣ K J 8 6

WEST	NORTH	EAST	SOUTH
			pass (!)
pass	pass	1NT[1]	?

1. 15-17 HCP.

You made a dubious decision to pass initially instead of opening a Weak 2◇. Assuming that it was a winning decision, what should you do now?

Let's think how passing could have been a winning decision. Perhaps your teammates reached a making 3NT after South at the other table opened 2◇. Perhaps East at the other table, with a 4-4-2-3 pattern, doubled for takeout and caught West with either a diamond stack and a profitable penalty pass or a four-card heart suit that produced a superior partscore contract.

If you know that your opposite number plays Weak 2◇ Bids, you should pass now. However, nowadays so many pairs use specialized 2◇ openings (such as Flannery) that you are unlikely to know. So this is one situation in which you may be able to "catch up" to the South at the other table by overcalling a natural 2◇, if your Notrump Defense permits. You may even be ahead of the game by overcalling 2◇, for your opposite number may play a conventional defense to 1NT that keeps him from overcalling 2◇. If he must double ("BROZEL") or bid 2♣ (Hamilton) with a diamond one-suiter, your 2◇ overcall will be more effective than his intervention. It's a guess, but you can gamble 2◇ now.

Matchpoints, E-W vul.

266

♠ A J 9 6 4 3   ♡ J 9 5   ◇ A K   ♣ 10 3

WEST	NORTH	EAST	SOUTH
			1♠
pass	2♣	2♡	2♠
pass	3◇	pass	3♡
pass	5♣	pass	?

A jump in an already game-forcing auction like this shows an extra-good suit. Partner's 5♣ here shows a solid suit. You have two known working cards that will be a pleasant surprise for partner.

Use the Hand Comparison Technique. Compare your actual hand with the normal minimum hand that your partner might expect you to have for your bidding. That might be

(a) ♠ A K J 9 3   ♡ J 9 5   ◇ A 6 4   ♣ 103

or

(b) ♠ K Q J 6 4 3   ♡ J 9 5   ◇ A K   ♣ 10 3

Which do you think is the most valuable? Hand (a) with the ♠K instead of the ◊K? Hand (b) with its possibly worthless spade picture cards? Or your actual hand? Which hand is partner playing you for when he jumps to 5♣?

Your actual hand is distinctly more useful than any hand partner could reasonably expect. Bid 6♣.

267

Matchpoints, Neither vul.

♠ 8 5   ♡ J 8 7 4 3   ◊ K Q 9 4   ♣ Q 9

WEST	NORTH	EAST	SOUTH
pass	1♠	dbl	pass
2♡	2♠	3♡	dbl
pass	3♠	pass	?

The Hand Comparison Technique is more powerful here than in the previous problem. For your double of 3♡, you might have had

♠ 8   ♡ K Q 9 4   ◊ J 8 7 4 3   ♣ Q 9 5

Compare your actual hand to that one. See how much better yours is? You have a second spade and two useful diamond honors instead of strength largely wasted in hearts. You have an easy raise to 4♠.

268

Matchpoints, E-W vul.

NORTH (dummy)
♠ K J 9 3 2
♡ A K 7 2
◊ 8
♣ J 7 6

EAST (you)
♠ 5
♡ J 10 4 3
◊ Q 9 7 5 2
♣ K 9 3

WEST	NORTH	EAST	SOUTH
			1♣
pass	1♠	pass	1NT[1]
pass	2◊[2]	pass	2NT[3]
pass	3NT	all pass	

1. 12-14 HCP.
2. "New Minor Forcing."
3. Neither three spades nor four hearts.

Partner leads the ◊J. You play the ◊9 to encourage and declarer takes the ◊A. Who has the ◊K?

Unless declarer has opened 1♣ with a balanced hand and ◊AKxx (most players would open 1◊ with such a hand), partner has the ◊K. If partner had been dealt ◊J10xx with neither the ◊9 nor the ◊8 (which you see in your own hand and dummy), he would have led fourth-highest, not the ◊J.

Declarer leads the ♡Q, on which partner plays the ♡5 and you play the ♡4, and continues with the ♡6 to dummy's ♡K. On the second heart, partner plays the ♠6, and you complete an echo by following with the ♡3. How many hearts does partner think you have?

Partner is probably very puzzled. Given that South's 2NT denies four hearts, partner will think you have six and wonder why you didn't play the ♡J on the first round from your supposed ♡ J109843.

You should be puzzled too. An alarm clock should ring in your head: "Why is partner discarding from dummy's long suit when he's the one who has length in it?"

Well, why is he?

Partner thinks that he has longer diamonds than you and that he must save them all to take tricks, for now he reads declarer's pattern as 2-2-4-5. He wouldn't think that unless he had five diamonds, for if he had only four, then you would have four too. That should tell you that declarer is 2-4-2-5. You are the captain of the defense at this point, because you are the only defender who is in position to know what's going on.

Next declarer leads the ♠2 to his ♠A, followed by ♠7 to dummy's ♠J. When you pause to consider your discard, declarer asks, "Are you showing out?"

"Yes," you reply.

"Then I'm going down," says declarer.

You are still contemplating your discard. What should you do?

Call the director! Declarer's remark constitutes a concession and play must stop. Else your partner, who already has a false count on the hand, may misdefend. Remember, too, that 'player rulings', such as asking declarer to 'play the hand out' are completely illegal — once a claim has been made, if there is a dispute, you must call a director.

There are players (including some fine experts) who favor "Jack Denies, 10 or 9 shows 0 or 2 higher" opening leads, to clarify the position for the opening leader's partner. Most of the time, however, the opening leader's partner can figure things out without that opening-lead convention, and it gives declarer a great deal of information. Looking for the nine and the eight of the suit led often helps.

269

Matchpoints, Neither vul.

♠ 7　♡ A Q 10 7 2　◇ K J 8 5　♣ J 6 5

WEST	NORTH	EAST	SOUTH
			?

You have a clear 1♡ opening: a good three-honor suit, a convenient rebid in diamonds and enough defensive and high-card strength (though none to spare). You must not pass and let an opponent open in spades. Even if partner opens in spades, your auction won't be smooth.

In the battle of the majors, hearts must speak (spades can wait).

If you swap your hearts and spades, it is still right to open 1♠, but it is no longer urgent to do so. With the "boss" suit (spades), you'll often be able to enter safely later.

270

Matchpoints, Neither vul.

NORTH (dummy)
♣ J 9 5

EAST (you)
♣ Q 8 3 2

WEST	NORTH	EAST	SOUTH
			1NT

all pass

What can be simpler than a one-suit problem? Partner leads the ♣4, and declarer calls for dummy's ♣9. What should you play?

Play the ♣8. Declarer has two clubs; if one of them is the ♣K, withholding your ♣Q saves a trick.

If you trust your partner to be a reasonably good opening leader, you won't play him to have led from ♣AKxx. However, he may have led from ♣10764 or ♣A764 if his only four-card suit is clubs or if leads from other suits are even less appealing. Play the ♣8 rather than a low one to encourage him to play the ♣A next.

NORTH (dummy)
♠ Q 7 5 4
♡ K 8
◊ Q 8 6 3
♣ J 7 4

☐

SOUTH (you)
♠ K J 9 3
♡ 5
◊ J 7
♣ A Q 9 6 5 2

WEST	NORTH	EAST	SOUTH
			1♣
pass	1◊	pass	1♠
pass	2♠	pass	3♠ (!)
all pass			

West leads the ◊K, on which East plays a discouraging ◊2. He then shifts to the ♡4. What should you play from dummy?

The opponents have ten hearts and 21 HCP between them, yet neither entered the auction at the one-level. It's almost certain that the hearts are divided 5-5 and that West, who has already shown the ◊A and ◊K, does not have five hearts headed by the ♡A. However, he may have the ♡Q. Play low from dummy and give East a chance to go wrong by playing the ♡A from ♡AJxxx. The richest source of matchpoints is not your own brilliant play but the errors of opponents.

However, East takes the ♡Q and continues with the ♡A. What should you do?

Trump it. This is not the time for a "loser on loser" discard of the ◊J, for that will let East tap you twice: by returning a diamond now and by returning another diamond after getting in with the ♠A.

Matchpoints, both vul.

NORTH (dummy)
♠ K J 3
♡ Q 10 4
◇ A J 6 4
♣ J 9 5

WEST (you)
♠ A 9
♡ J 8 7 3
◇ 7 5 2
♣ K Q 6 3

WEST	NORTH	EAST	SOUTH
	1◇	pass	1♠
pass	2♠	pass	4♠
all pass			

You lead the ♣K. Partner follows with the ♣2 and declarer takes the ♣A. You follow with the ♠9 as declarer leads the ♠2 to dummy's ♠J, partner playing the ♠4.

Dummy's ♡4 fetches the ♡A from partner and the ♡9 from declarer. Partner returns the ♣10 to your ♣K, and you exit with the ♣3, to which all follow. Declarer crosses to the ♡K, on which partner plays the ♡2. He then leads the ♠6 to your ♠A, partner following with the ♠5. With three tricks home, you are on lead in this ending:

What, if anything, was wrong with your opponents' bidding?

North should not have opened

♠ K J 3 ♡ Q 10 4 ◇ A J 6 4 ♣ J 9 5

— a square, jack-laden hand worth closer to 10 HCP than 12 HCP.

South, who had

♠ Q 7 6 2 ♡ K 9 ◇ K Q 9 3 ♣ A 8 4

should have bid 3NT, not 4♠, over North's 2♠ raise, trusting North to correct to 4♠ with four-card support.

NORTH (dummy)
♠ K
♡ Q
◇ A J 6 4
♣ —

WEST (you)
♠ -
♡ J 7
◇ 7 5 2
♣ 6

What do you think is going on in the spade suit?

Partner is marked with ♠10x remaining. You know this not only from declarer's play (not continuing with the ♠K after taking dummy's

♠J) but also from partner's. With three spades, partner would have played high-low to give you a count.

Lead the thirteenth club. Whether declarer ruffs in hand or in dummy, partner's ♠10x will take a trick.

Matchpoints, Both vul.

273

NORTH (dummy)
♠ K 9
♡ Q 10 8 4 3
♢ A 7 5 4
♣ 10 4

WEST (you)
♠ A 8 7 2
♡ A K 6
♢ Q
♣ Q 8 7 3 2

WEST	NORTH	EAST	SOUTH
			pass
1♣	pass	1♠[1]	2♢
2♠	3♢	pass	pass
3♠	pass	pas	4♢
all pass			

1. Extra length or extra strength.

You lead the ♡K, fetching partner's ♡2 and declarer's ♡7. Now what? Is this a good time to underlead your ♠A, hoping that declarer has ♠Jx or ♠Jxx and will misguess?

No. To underlead the ♠A is to rely on a *parlay*. Look at all the things that have to happen for it to succeed:

A parlay is an action whose success requires that all of several conditions, called legs, be met. Parlays are unreliable; if any "leg" fails, the parlay fails. The more legs in the parlay, the less likely it is to succeed.

(1) Declarer must have exactly two spades. Your special partnership agreement tells you that he can't have three, for your partner's failure to bid again denies extra strength and thus implies extra spade length.

(2) Partner must have the ♠Q.

(3) Declarer must have the ♠J (else there's no guess).

(4) Declarer must misguess.

It's a much better bet that partner has the ♣K; unless he has the ◇K (unlikely in view of South's 2◇ bid), it's the only strength aside from the ♠Q and the ♠J that he can have to justify his 1♠ response. Even if partner has

♠ Q J 6 5 4   ♡ 9 5 2   ◇ K 2   ♣ 9 6 5

or similar, it costs you next to nothing to shift to the ♣3 anyway.

274

Matchpoints, N-S vul.

NORTH (dummy)

♠ A K 9 8 7
♡ A 7 3
◇ A 6
♣ 7 5 4

SOUTH (you)

♠ 4
♡ K Q 9 4 2
◇ Q 7 4
♣ A 8 6 3

WEST	NORTH	EAST	SOUTH
	1♠	pass	2♡
pass	2NT[1]	pass	3NT
pass	4♡	all pass	

1. Substantial extras.

West leads the ♡6. You take East's ♡J with the ♡K, play a diamond to dummy's ace, and another diamond to your queen and West's king. West continues with the ♡8. Take it from there.

    You must play low from dummy. Either you'll win with the ♡9 or East will play the ♡10 to force your ♡Q. Then you'll be in hand to ruff your last diamond with dummy's ♡A and can get back to your hand in clubs to draw the last trump.

    Playing dummy's ♡A needlessly exposes you to two dangers.

(1) You can enter your hand with the ♣A and ruff your last diamond in dummy, but if East started with ♡J10x and a doubleton diamond, he will overruff.

(2) If East does not overruff, you'll need to return to hand to draw the last trump. You can cash dummy's ♠A and ♠K, but when you lead a third spade and trump it, West will overruff if he started with ♡1086 and only two spades.

These dangers aren't large, but why expose yourself to them at all?

Matchpoints, E-W vul.

275

♠ J 10 7 4   ♡ A 8 6   ◇ —   ♣ A J 8 6 5 2

WEST	NORTH	EAST	SOUTH
		pass	?

You have an acceptable 1♣ opening: shape, a good suit, the requisite 2 Quick Tricks for opening distributional hands and a convenient rebid in spades.

You decide to pass, however, and the auction continues:

WEST	NORTH	EAST	SOUTH
		pass	pass
1◇	pass	1♡	?

You should surely enter the auction now with a takeout double.

However, you pass again, but the bidding is not over.

WEST	NORTH	EAST	SOUTH
		pass	pass
1◇	pass	1♡	pass
2♡	pass	pass	?

How lucky can you get? After missing two opportunities to enter the bidding, you have a third. You should double, offering partner a choice of black suits. With equal length, he'll prefer to bid spades, not only because it's a major suit but also because he can bid it one level lower than clubs.

Second choice: 3♣. To balance with 2♠ is out of the question. If you're going to put all your eggs in one basket, why choose the (much) leakier one?

276

Matchpoints, N-S vul.

♠ Q 6   ♡ Q 10 7 5   ◇ Q J 4   ♣ K 9 8 6

WEST	NORTH	EAST	SOUTH
	1♣	1◇	1♡
pass	1♠	pass	?

I formulated the "Rule of the Three Queens" many decades ago, and it almost never fails: When you have three (or four) queens, seek to play in notrump if plausible.

There's no one in the world who favors raising a 1♣ bidder's clubs more vehemently than I do. However, this hand illustrates a rare exception. Your best call by far is 1NT.

The most likely ruff in a club contract is West's ruff of your third-round diamond trick; it won't be partner ruffing anything in his own hand or dummy. The key to the winning action is your very queenish hand. Queens duplicate doubletons and thus are the cards most likely to be ruffed in suit contracts. In notrumps, however, queens come into their own, retaining their full value because they are immune to ruffing.

277

Matchpoints, N-S vul.

♠ J 10 3   ♡ K J 9 7 2   ◇ Q   ♣ 10 7 5 4

WEST	NORTH	EAST	SOUTH
		pass	pass
1◇	pass	1♡	pass
3◇	pass	3NT	all pass

What should you lead?

At IMPs, lead the ♡2 — the fifth-highest card in declarer's suit, because the fourth-highest card often has trick-taking potential. That's your best bet to beat the contract: partner may have ♡A10x, or ♡A8x with dummy having a singleton honor.

At matchpoints, where it is important to stop overtricks against apparently normal contracts, a safe lead that is likely to stop overtricks is better than a risky lead that is a long shot to beat the contract. Lead the ♠J, which does not give up on beating 3NT anyway (it may hit partner's suit).

Matchpoints, Both vul.

♠ K 8 6   ♡ A 8   ◇ A K Q 5   ♣ Q J 7 3

WEST	NORTH	EAST	SOUTH
			1◇
pass	pass	2♣	?

Pass. Other Souths won't be content to pass; they'll double, or bid 2NT, to "show" their extra strength. The doublers will wind up "showing" their extra strength, all right, when they put down their hands as dummy in heart contracts. They are sure to go down. Don't imagine that you can make 2NT either, or any other two-level contract, opposite the woefully weak hand that partner is likely to have. Defending against 2♣ offers you the best chance at a plus score. If, by some miracle, partner does have enough for your side to make a two-level contract, you figure to collect the magic matchpoint +200 defending against East's 2♣.

Defending against vulnerable partscores is the most overlooked source of tops at matchpoints.

Matchpoints, Neither vul.

♠ A 6   ♡ A K 5   ◇ A Q J 8 7 2   ♣ 7 4

WEST	NORTH	EAST	SOUTH
		1♣	?

With your present partner, you play Strong Jump Overcalls. Is this a good hand for 2◇?

It's a bit too good. A Strong Jump Overcall shows 7-8 winners at the two-level, 8-9 winners at the three-level. With anything more, you should start with a takeout double.

When you do, the auction takes a turn that you may not have anticipated:

WEST	NORTH	EAST	SOUTH
		1♣	dbl
pass	3♠	pass	?

A double-jump at the three-level in reply to a takeout double shows a very specific hand: a weak hand (about 3-6 HCP) with a decent (but not strong) six-card suit.

Either ♠Kxxxxx or ♠QJxxxx "and out" should give partner good play for ten tricks. Raise to 4♠. Your great high-card strength compensates for having only doubleton support (an eight-card fit is adequate anyway).

280

Matchpoints, Both vul.

♠ J 7 2   ♡ K 4   ◇ A K Q 6   ♣ 8 7 5 3

WEST	NORTH	EAST	SOUTH
2♡¹	pass	pass	?

1. Weak Two-bid.

Pass or balance?

If you balance, you have two plausible calls: 2NT and double. Balancing with 2NT will protect your ♡K against a lead-through, but only temporarily. West can afford to lead hearts even if it costs him a trick to do so, for he can set up his whole suit. After you score your ♡K, you'll need to take lots of tricks in a hurry. Where do you think they'll be coming from?

If you balance with a double, you also figure to go minus, often -200 or worse. What makes your hand bad for doubling?

   (a) It's a balanced hand.

   (b) The ♡K is poorly placed.

   (c) A balancing double will often fetch a reply in spades, the suit that partner will usually be most willing and able to bid, and you have only weak three-card support.

Pass. You'll often score +200, while all the balancers go minus. Passing is an "anti-field" action (almost everybody nowadays feeling it a duty to balance against low-level contracts indiscriminately), so you'll occasionally get a bottom, but far more often you'll get a top.

Matchpoints, E-W vul.

NORTH (dummy)
♠ A J
♡ A K 6 5
◇ A J 3
♣ 6 5 4 3

EAST (you)
♠ Q
♡ 8 3
◇ 8 7 5 4
♣ A Q J 9 7 2

WEST	NORTH	EAST	SOUTH
			2♠[1]
pass	4♠	all pass	

1. Weak Two-bid.

Partner leads the ♡Q to dummy's ♡K. You follow with the ♡3 and declarer plays the ♡2. Declarer plays dummy's ♠A and ♠J (which holds); you discard the ♣9. Next declarer attacks diamonds, cashing dummy's ◇A and letting the ◇J ride. Partner wins with the ◇Q and exits with the ♡10 to dummy's ♡A, as declarer's ♡9 falls. When declarer leads to his ◇K, partner ruffs with the ♠8. Partner shifts to the ♣K. You overtake with your ♣A and declarer follows with the ♣8.

All right, you have the lead: what are you going to do with it?

At this point you have a complete count on the hand. Declarer has six spades and four diamonds, two hearts and therefore only one club. You'd better let partner ruff your last diamond with his ♠10; if you continue clubs, declarer will ruff and play the ♠K to draw partner's last trump.

Matchpoints, Neither vul.

♠ K J 10 9   ♡ Q J 3   ◇ Q 7   ♣ Q 9 4 2

WEST	NORTH	EAST	SOUTH
		1♠	pass
1NT	2♡	pass	?

Do not bid any number of hearts. Bid 2NT (3NT if you are feeling especially rambunctious). There are both general and specific grounds for preferring notrump to hearts, despite your three-card support for partner with two honors in his suit.

The "Rule of Three Queens" applies. Also, you are well-girded in spades and have some reason to fear ruffs (even a possible club-spade crossruff) in a heart contract.

283

Matchpoints, Both vul.

♠ Q 8   ♡ 6 3 2   ◇ Q 9 6 5 3 2   ♣ Q 9

WEST	NORTH	EAST	SOUTH
1♠	dbl	2♠	?

You have the wrong hand to bid 3◇, even if you have a partnership understanding that it is merely "competitive" rather than constructive. Your ♠Q simply isn't worth "2 points" for offensive purposes.

♠ 8 6   ♡ 6 3 2   ◇ K J 9 5 3 2   ♣ Q 9

(also "6 HCP and a six-card suit") would barely justify 3◇.

284

Matchpoints, E-W vul.

♠ 6 3   ♡ A 10 4 2   ◇ Q 8 6 3   ♣ J 7 2

WEST	NORTH	EAST	SOUTH
		1♠	pass
2◇	pass	2NT	pass
4♠	all pass		

Your opponents play a system in which West's 2◇ response is forcing to game, East's 2NT rebid does not show any extra strength and West's jump to 4♠ topsy-turvily denies slam aspirations.

What should you lead?

Not the ♡A. Ace leads are usually very bad. Best: ♣2. Next best: ♠3.

NORTH (dummy)
♠ 6 5
♡ Q J 9
◇ A K 10 8 2
♣ Q 8 5

☐

SOUTH (you)
♠ A K J 7 4
♡ A K 6
◇ 7 6
♣ K 9 3

WEST	NORTH	EAST	SOUTH
			1♠
pass	2◇	pass	3NT
all pass			

You are declarer in 3NT and West leads the ♡2. You overtake dummy's ♡9 with your ♡K to start diamonds with the ◇7. West follows small. What should you play from dummy?

Certainly don't play a top honor. You may need to surrender two diamond tricks and you have only one sure dummy entry outside the suit. You should lose whatever diamond tricks you have to *early*, while you still have a diamond in your hand to continue the suit.

Should you let the ◇7 ride, therefore, hoping West has the ◇9? You could instead insert dummy's ◇10, planning to play the ace and king on the next two rounds. Let's compare the two lines:

Line A. Let the ◇7 ride:

If the ◇7 wins, you know that West has QJ9x, so playing the ◇10 would also have brought you four diamond tricks. The two lines break even.

If the ◇7 loses to an honor (presumably what you were hoping would happen), you can continue either with another finesse or by playing the ace and king.

(i) Let's say you finesse your ◇6 and cover West's card. This gains (compared to playing the ◇10 in the first place) if East started with Jx or Qx (a total of 6 holdings) or either honor singleton — so in a total of 8 cases.

When in doubt, choose the line that will work on the greater number of holdings. What should you do if there are as many specific holdings favoring one line as another?

In the absence of other information about the defenders' hands, choose the line that succeeds on the more balanced divisions of the missing cards.

(ii) If you play the ace and king now, you gain when East started with a doubleton QJ or QJx — a total of 5 holdings. So this is clearly inferior.

At best, there are 8 cases where it would be better to let the ◊7 ride.

Line B. Insert dummy's ◊10:

Playing the ◊10 on the first round gains when East has QJx (4 holdings) and when East has singleton 9, 9x, or 9xx (7 cases) — for a total of 11 cases.

All in all, there are 8 cases where it would be better to let the ◊7 ride and 11 cases where playing the ◊10 gains. The odds clearly favor playing the ◊10 on the first round.

286

You can afford to make a forcing bid with a weaker suit than you would need for a non-forcing bid, because partner won't pass, nor will he raise without at least modest support.

A 1-over-1 responder must often bid the fourth suit artificially at his second turn in order to create a force in one of the three suits bid previously by the partnership.

Matchpoints, Neither vul.

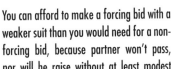

♠ J 10 7 5 3 2   ♡ A J 8   ◊ 9 8   ♣ A Q

WEST	NORTH	EAST	SOUTH
	1◊	pass	1♠
pass	2♣	pass	?

Three spades is non-forcing and overstates the suit while understating the hand. You must bid 2♡, the fourth suit, which is often artificial. If partner bids 2NT next, you'll continue with 3♠, which, in light of your 2♡, *is* forcing. With a doubleton spade, partner will raise to 4♠.

287

Matchpoints, N-S vul.

♠ A Q J 6 2   ♡ 9 8 7   ◊ 6 4 2   ♣ 10 5

WEST	NORTH	EAST	SOUTH
		pass	pass
1♣	pass	1♡	?

Pass. A 1♠ sandwich ("coming between two bidders") would be reasonable if you weren't vulnerable, but it's simply too risky when you are vulnerable.

Matchpoints, E-W vul.

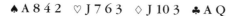

288

♠A 8 4 2 ♡ J 7 6 3 ◇ J 10 3 ♣A Q

WEST	NORTH	EAST	SOUTH
			?

Pass. Your high cards are in the wrong places, and the suit you would have to open is short and weak. With cards in the right places, a good suit to open and a good rebid, e.g.

♠A 8 4 2 ♡ 6 3 ◇ J 10 3 ♣A Q J 7

your hand would be fine for a 1♣ opening.

Matchpoints, N-S vul.

289

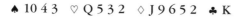

♠ 10 4 3 ♡ Q 5 3 2 ◇ J 9 6 5 2 ♣ K

WEST	NORTH	EAST	SOUTH
		1◇	pass
pass	1♠	2♣	?

Pass. Your ♣K is worth little on offense, but it may be worth a trick on defense where East cannot know it is singleton. He is likely to finesse partner for it. You have only three weak spades and your ♡Q and ◇J are dubious values. Don't raise to 2♠. Avoid that "matchpoint poison" -200.

Matchpoints, N-S vul.

290

♠ 10 4 3 ♡ Q 5 3 2 ◇ J 9 6 5 2 ♣ K

WEST	NORTH	EAST	SOUTH
		1◇	pass
pass	1♠	2♣	2♠
3♣	3♡	4♣	?

If partner's 3♡ is a game try, you must reject it — you didn't even have your 2♠ raise. But suppose 3♡ simply shows four hearts and extra values, offering you a choice of majors? So what? To bid 4♡ here you need not only four hearts but the top of your 2♠ raise, and you don't even have the bottom. Pass and hope to beat 4♣, but don't risk -200.

Matchpoints, E-W vul.

♠ A Q 10 7   ♡ J 9 6 5   ◇ 9   ♣ A 6 5 4

WEST	NORTH	EAST	SOUTH
			?

This hand is easily worth a 1♣ opening. You have two aces, including the ace of the suit you open, and 2½ Quick Tricks. You have a singleton. You have a convenient rebid over a response in your short suit. Bid 1♣. It's not as if you were playing rubber bridge with a partner who would expect more.

However, you pass, and later you face a defensive problem. Slide over to the East seat:

NORTH (dummy)
♠ 8 5 3
♡ K 10
◇ K J 5
♣ K Q 9 8 3

EAST (you)
♠ A Q 10 7
♡ J 9 6 5
◇ 9
♣ A 6 5 4

WEST	NORTH	EAST	SOUTH
		pass	pass
pass	1♣	pass	1◇
pass	2◇	dbl	3◇
all pass			

Partner leads the ♠2. You take the ♠A, continue with the ♠Q (which holds) and lead the ♠7 to partner's ♠K, as declarer's ♠J falls. Partner shifts to the ♡3, and you cover dummy's ♡10 with your ♡J. Declarer takes the ♡Q and leads the ♣10. Partner follows with the ♣2 and you take dummy's ♣Q with your ♣A. What now?

Might partner have underled the ♡A?

Certainly. For all he could tell, you might have had

♠ A Q 10 7   ♡ Q 9 6 5   ◇ A   ♣ 10 6 5 4

(a reasonable initial pass, because the singleton ◇A and the weak club suit you'd have to open dictate that you deduct points). So return the ♡5 lest declarer's remaining hearts go away on dummy's clubs. (As you might infer from partner's failure to lead the ♣2, it is declarer, if anyone, not partner, who has a singleton club.) Then partner can tap dummy with a third heart to protect the ◇Q (if he has it) from a possible finesse.

Matchpoints, E-W vul.

292

♠ K 4 2   ♡ K J 2   ◇ A J 9 7   ♣ Q J 4

WEST	NORTH	EAST	SOUTH
		pass	?

Your 1NT range with your present partner is 15-17 HCP. What do you open?

Open 1◇, not 1NT. This is a 13-HCP hand, not 15, with flat distribution, poor spot cards and 3 of its HCP in jacks.

Matchpoints, Both vul.

293

♠ A Q 7 5 4 2   ♡ 10 5   ◇ J 9   ♣ 9 8 7

WEST	NORTH	EAST	SOUTH
			?

With your present partner, you play Weak Two-bids and the range marked on your convention card is 5 to 11 HCP. Should you bid a Weak 2♠?

No, just pass. The convention card is deficient in not having spaces for at least two ranges of Weak Twos, vulnerable and non-vulnerable. Vulnerable Weak Twos should embrace only the top half of your range and deliver stronger suits.

♠ A Q J 5 4 2   ♡ 10 5   ◇ J 9   ♣ 9 8 7

would barely qualify.

294

Matchpoints, Both vul.

♠ K 8 5   ♡ 7 5 2   ◇ Q 10 4   ♣ A J 9 3

WEST	NORTH	EAST	SOUTH
	pass	pass	pass
1◇	pass	1NT	all pass

What should you lead?

Lead either the ♡7 or the ♠5 (a close choice: neither would be wrong). A 1NT response to 1◇ is usually based on a hand with clubs (no four-card major to respond, no diamond raise). A club lead is seldom right. Also, leads from four-card suits headed by the ace are seldom good even against notrump contracts.

295

Matchpoints, E-W vul.

♠ 8   ♡ K Q 9   ◇ 9 5 2   ♣ K Q 10 5 4 2

1. Weak Two-bid.

WEST	NORTH	EAST	SOUTH
2♠[1]	3♡	4♠	5♡
pass	pass	dbl	pass
5♠	pass	pass	?

Pass. Don't double. Your king and queen of clubs are in your long suit and therefore may not take a defensive trick. Your king and queen of hearts are in partner's long suit and therefore may not take a trick either.

"May not"? I should say "will not", as West's removal of East's penalty double is surely based on shortness. Doubling may be unnecessary. East's bidding suggests that his partner may have gone out on a limb by entering the auction at all — by pushing the opponents to 5♠ you may have "won the board" already. You shouldn't risk a bottom by doubling greedily in hopes of turning a near-top into a clear top.

♠ K 4 3 2 ♡ A K 8 7 5 ◇ 7 ♣ Q 7 6

WEST	NORTH	EAST	SOUTH
pass	pass	1◇	?

Current fashion is to overcall any time you have a five-card major. Current fashion is wrong. With 4-5-1-3, it's usually best to double. With 3-5-1-4, it's usually best to overcall, planning to double if responder raises and it comes back to you. Suit quality is also a consideration, of course, so I say "usually" rather than "always" (though "almost always" may be closer to the mark).

NORTH (dummy)
♠ 7 6 3
♡ 8 5
◇ Q J 7 6 3
♣ J 10 7

EAST (you)
♠ A K 8 5
♡ 10 6 4
◇ A 9 8 5
♣ A 6

WEST	NORTH	EAST	SOUTH
		1◇	1♡
1NT	pass	pass	2♠
pass	pass	dbl	all pass

Partner leads the ◇4 of diamonds. Dummy plays the ◇3. How should you defend?

From what holdings can partner have led the ◇4? The ◇2 is not showing, so the ◇4 can be from one of two holdings: ◇42 or ◇K104. (Partner wouldn't bid 1NT with a singleton ◇4.) In either case, your correct play is the ◇5. Then, when the ◇5 holds, you can return the ◇8, starting to tap declarer. If instead you play the ◇A at Trick 1, declarer can discard and set up dummy's diamonds.

Watch those spots!

298

Matchpoints, N-S vul.

♠ A Q J 8 6　♡ K Q　◇ Q 8　♣ A K 7 3

WEST	NORTH	EAST	SOUTH
		pass	1♠
2♡	pass	pass	?

Some would double, thinking that's the way to show a strong hand. That's wrong. A double will usually draw a 3◇ reply, and you won't like it at all. Bidding 3♣ is much better and shows a hand as strong as this one. The difference between doubling and bidding 3♣ is not one of strength but of pattern — if you double, you should be prepared for any call partner might make, in particular, a bid in your shortest suit.

299

Way back in 1946, before Philadelphia lawyer Charles Goren converted from Honor Tricks to Point-Count, another Philadelphia lawyer named Charles, Charles Solomon, wrote a booklet on *Notrump Bidding.* He taught a 4-3-2-1-½ count. Was the wisdom of Solomon accurate?

Almost, but not quite. On average, the value he assigned to tens was a slight overestimate. Tens, even more than the other low honors (queens and jack), become valuable mainly when they bolster other high cards in the suit. When accompanied by two other honors, or one other honor and a *nine*, they are worth more than half a point; otherwise, they are worth less.

Matchpoints, Neither vul.

♠ J 4 3　♡ A Q 5　◇ K J 6　♣ A 8 5 2

WEST	NORTH	EAST	SOUTH
		pass	?

Do not open 1NT even if your range for 1NT includes bad 15-pointers. This is a *bad* 14-HCP hand (square, no spots, a stray jack). Open 1♣. In contrast

♠ J 10 3　♡ A Q 10　◇ K J 10　♣ A 10 9 2

is worth a full 16 HCP despite its square shape.

Matchpoints, Both vul.

NORTH (dummy)
- ♠ 5 4 2
- ♡ 10
- ♢ A Q J 9 8 7
- ♣ 7 6 2

WEST (you)
- ♠ K Q 6 3
- ♡ 7 6
- ♢ 4
- ♣ A K J 10 5 3

WEST	NORTH	EAST	SOUTH
			1♡
2♣	pass	pass	2♠
pass	3♠	pass	4♠
dbl	all pass		

You lead the ♣K, dropping declarer's ♣Q, and continue with the ♣A. Declarer trumps with the ♠7, cashes the ♡A-K, discarding dummy's last club and leads a low heart for dummy to ruff. You discard the ♢4 (good!). Declarer crosses to the ♠A, under which partner's ♠J falls, and leads another low heart for dummy to ruff. You discard the ♣3 and partner's ♡Q falls. Then declarer tries to cash dummy's ♢A in this position:

NORTH (dummy)
- ♠ —
- ♡ —
- ♢ A Q J 9 8 7   (♢A led)
- ♣ —

WEST (you)
- ♠ K Q 6
- ♡ —
- ♢ —
- ♣ J 10 5

What should you play?

Do not ruff. Declarer's last five cards are ♠1098 and ♡Jx. If you discard the ♣5, he will be stuck in dummy and will get only the current trick (the ♢A) and one more (a ruff of a minor suit). You will have trump control and get four more tricks: down two doubled for +500.

If you ruff, you get the current trick and your two high trumps, only three more tricks: down one doubled for +200.

When playing a "forcing game", look for opportunities to let declarer tap himself out of trumps.

Matchpoints, E-W vul.

♠ Q J 6   ♡ K 4 3   ◇ K 9 8 5   ♣ A 10 8

WEST	NORTH	EAST	SOUTH
		pass	1◇
pass	1♠	dbl	?

Bid 2♠ to keep West from bidding a suit at the two-level. Passing lets West bid cheaply and a pass followed by a "balancing" 2♠ won't shut out anything. Would you like to be playing Support Redoubles, which would let you redouble here to show a "three-card raise"?

No. While Support Doubles have merit, and may even be optimal when used in a regular partnership with the right detailed understandings, Support Redoubles, as played by most users, have far less merit and one big defect: they let the opponents find a fit cheaply. Sometimes the best three-card raise is a *raise*. This time, a raise to 2♠ might not have bought the contract.

NORTH (dummy)
♠ 9 5
♡ A J 9 5
◇ Q 4 3
♣ K 9 7 4

EAST (you)
♠ Q J 6
♡ K 4 3
◇ K 9 8 5
♣ A 10 8

WEST	NORTH	EAST	SOUTH
	pass	1◇	pass
1♠	dbl	pass	2♡
pass	pass	2♠	3♡
all pass			

Partner leads the ♠3. How many spades does he have?

Four or five. Although you won't know with absolute certainty until you see the deuce appear, partner almost certainly has five spades, else South, with four spades including the ace, would probably have doubled 2♠ instead of taking the push to 3♡. So despite some slight theoretical uncertainty, in practice you *know*.

Oops, that would be true with some other partner, but your present partner has insisted on abandoning "fourth-highest" opening leads in favor of playing "third- and fifth-best" opening leads against suit contracts. How many spades do you think he has now?

Four, five or six. If declarer has the ♠2, partner has five spades. If partner has the ♠2, he has either four spades or six. We've already dismissed the possibility that partner has four spades, but the ambiguity remains: five spades or six?

At Trick 1, you play the ♠J and declarer follows with the ♠10. Does this tell you whether partner has five spades or six?

No. Declarer may be falsecarding from ♠A102 or truecarding from ♠A10.

Would any rival lead convention distinguish between five spades and six?

Yes. "Third from even, low from odd" would do so. In that case, declarer's falsecard from ♠A102 wouldn't fool you, because if declarer had ♠A10, partner would have ♠K87432, from which he would have led the ♠7.

Back to the game. How should you continue when your ♠J holds?

You should return the ♠Q, which cannot hurt. Do not break a new suit. Even a trump shift can harm you, for declarer (if he has only two spades) can win, cash the ♠A and the ♡A, and then toss you in with your ♡K, forcing you to break a new suit or give a ruff-and-sluff in spades.

"Third and *low*" is demonstrably better than "third and fifth" opening leads. Nonetheless, the ACBL convention card lists only "3rd/5th Best" as the alternative to "4th Best" (even though nobody, to my knowledge, has ever made a case for "third and fifth").

Matchpoints, N-S vul.

302

♠ — ♡ A Q 7 4 2 ◇ K 10 6 2 ♣ K Q J 8

WEST	NORTH	EAST	SOUTH
			1♡
2◇	2♠	pass	3♣
pass	3♡	pass	?

Bid 4♡. Though your ◇K isn't pulling full weight in front of the diamond bidder and your spade void is a defect facing partner's known five-card suit, you have a full opening bid outside of diamonds. Only if the ◇K were part of your opening bid, as partner may have feared during the auction, would you be right to pass. For instance, 3♡ would be the right contract if you had

♠ —   ♡ A Q 7 4 2   ◇ K 10 6 2   ♣ K 8 4 3

or similar.

303

Matchpoints, E-W vul.

♠ 6   ♡ A K 7 5   ◇ A K 10 4 3   ♣ A J 4

WEST	NORTH	EAST	SOUTH
	pass	pass	1◇
pass	1♠	pass	2♡
pass	2♠	pass	3♣
pass	3◇	pass	?

Bid 3NT. First, however, make sure you understand your sequence. The modern treatment of opener's reverse after a 1-over-1 response is forcing and promising a rebid. Thus, with a weak hand, partner must let you deliver the promised rebid without getting too high. Over 2♡, his possible bids to indicate a weak hand were 2♠ (five spades, perhaps a very strong four), 2NT (stopper in clubs with at least a little bit extra) and 3♣ (perhaps no club stopper).

You have extra values enough to bid 3NT in spite of partner's weak hand. You've already shown five diamonds. However, you mustn't bid 4◇ for two reasons: not only does it bypass 3NT (the most likely contract) but it shows extra length in diamonds (a sixth diamond).

304

Matchpoints, N-S vul.

♠ Q 9 8 3   ♡ A K 6 2   ◇ 5 3 2   ♣ 10 9

	WEST	NORTH	EAST	SOUTH
1. 20-21 HCP.			pass	pass
2. Transfer.	2NT[1]	pass	3♡[2]	?

If you pass, then more often than not, partner will lead a minor suit against the eventual spade or notrump contract. You won't like that at all. Live dangerously: make a lead-directing double. They might redouble and make it, but not doubling will cost more matchpoints on average.

Matchpoints, N-S vul.

♠ K J ♡ K Q J 9 5 ◇ K 8 6 ♣ Q 7 5

WEST	NORTH	EAST	SOUTH
	pass	pass	?

With your present partner, you play 15-17 HCP notrumps. Should you open 1NT?

No. Your hand simply isn't worth 15 HCP; I'd call it a bad 14. Its defects include no aces, no tens, a stray queen and a blank ♠KJ. Prior to the point-count, 1NT was defined as 3½ – 4 Honor Tricks. That usually translates to 16-18 HCP. A "good 15" will contain either 3½ Honor Tricks, or 3 Honor Tricks and a plus-value. With only 2 Honor Tricks, open 1♡.

Matchpoints, Both vul.

NORTH (dummy)
♠ K 8 2
♡ Q
◇ A K 8 5 2
♣ A 10 7 5

EAST (you)
♠ A J 10 7 6 4
♡ J 7
◇ 10
♣ 6 4 3 2

WEST	NORTH	EAST	SOUTH
		pass	1NT
2◇	3NT	all pass	

You and your partner play a 2◇ overcall of an opposing 1NT opening as natural — except against "Kamikaze" 10-12 HCP notrumps, in which case 2◇ shows hearts.

Partner leads the ♡A. What should you do?

Partner's ♡A is a standard lead asking you to drop an honor (if you have one) or give count. But before dropping the ♡J, you should digest the fourteen new pieces of information you have been given — dummy's thirteen cards and your partner's opening lead — and count the HCP that your partner has.

Add your 6 HCP to dummy's 16 and you get 22. Crediting declarer with at least 15, you can count partner for at most 3 HCP. It's impossible for him to have the ace he just led, much less a vulnerable 2◇ overcall in diamonds (where dummy has five good ones). Wake up and call the director!

You will learn that North "announced" South's 10-12 HCP notrump in tones so soft that your partner, whose hearing is acute, could hear but you could not.

307

Matchpoints, Both vul.

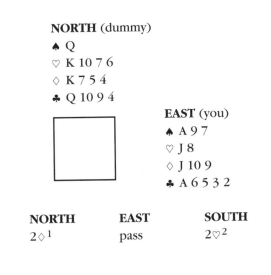

NORTH (dummy)
♠ Q
♡ K 10 7 6
◇ K 7 5 4
♣ Q 10 9 4

EAST (you)
♠ A 9 7
♡ J 8
◇ J 10 9
♣ A 6 5 3 2

WEST	NORTH	EAST	SOUTH
	2◇[1]	pass	2♡[2]
all pass			

1. 10-13 HCP, 4-1-4-4 or 1-4-4-4.
2. "Pass or correct."

Partner leads the ♡3 and dummy plays low. What should you play?

Try the ♡8. If partner has underled from ♡A9x(x), your ♡J may take a trick later. He's unlikely to have led from ♡ AQx(x), the only holding to which playing the ♡J caters, or from any other holding including the ♡Q.

308

NORTH (dummy)
♠ 10 8 3
♡ Q J 10 5
◇ A 3
♣ A Q J 4

WEST (you)
♠ Q J 9 2
♡ K 7 4 3
◇ K J 6
♣ K 6

WEST	NORTH	EAST	SOUTH
			3◇

all pass

You lead the ♠Q, which holds, partner playing the ♠7 and declarer the ♠5. You want partner to win the second spade and shift to hearts. Which spade should you play?

Play the ♠2, original fourth-highest. If partner has ♠AK764, it doesn't matter, as declarer will ruff. If partner has ♠AK7x, however, he'll have a count in spades and appreciate the futility of leading a third one. If partner has ♠AK7, he'll know to cash a third spade before making the obvious shift to hearts.

Matchpoints, N-S vul.

309

♠ A 6   ♡ 5 3 2   ◇ 9 5 4   ♣ A K J 8 2

WEST	NORTH	EAST	SOUTH
	1♡	pass	2♣
pass	2♡	pass	?

Bid 4♡. Except for your weak hearts, you have prime cards and shouldn't want to stop in 3♡ even facing a minimum.

Matchpoints, E-W vul.

♠ 9 3   ♡ 6   ◇ Q 10 7 5 4 2   ♣ A K 10 4

1. Good 15 to 18 HCP.
2. Diamonds

WEST	NORTH	EAST	SOUTH
	1NT[1]	pass	2NT[2]
pass	3◇	pass	?

Most pairs that play a 2NT response to 1NT as showing diamonds use opener's 3♣ rebid of the transfer as a super-accept. You and your partner use it to show a preference for clubs over diamonds, allowing responder to pass and reach the best partscore with a weak minor two-suiter.

Bid 3NT. Transferring to diamonds *en route* to 3NT suggests doubt. If you belong in 5◇ or 6◇, partner will know to continue.

Matchpoints, N-S vul.

♠ Q 9 5 4   ♡ A 9 6 5 3 2   ◇ 7   ♣ K 6

WEST	NORTH	EAST	SOUTH
pass	1◇	pass	1♡
pass	1♠	pass	?

It's a close decision whether to invite game or force to game. The ♣K may not be a working card though, so I'd give the nod to an invitational 3♠. If you want to reach game, shoot it out by jumping to 4♠ directly.

312

Matchpoints, Neither vul.

♠ A 10 7 6 3   ♡ Q 4   ◇ 8 7   ♣ 8 6 5 3

WEST	NORTH	EAST	SOUTH
		pass	pass
pass	1◇	pass	1♠
pass	2NT[1]	pass	?

1. 19-20 HCP.

Your system with your present partner includes an artificial 3♣ "checkback" (for four hearts or three-card spade support). Is this a time to use it?

Yes. If partner has three spades, 4♠ figures to do better than 3NT.

What should you do if you don't have a checkback available in your system?

Bid an old-fashioned 3♠. In reply, partner will retreat to 3NT with only two spades, raise to 4♠ or cuebid an ace with three-card support.

One advantage of playing a notrump range that includes 18-HCP hands is that opener's *jump notrump rebids* promise at least 19 HCP. Then responder can make natural forcing rebids in any suit at the three-level, removing the need for fancy conventions that let the partnership stop in three of any suit (except clubs).

Matchpoints, N-S vul.

313

West (you)

♠ K Q 8 2   ♡ K 8 3   ◇ A 4   ♣ K J 10 3

WEST	NORTH	EAST	SOUTH	
1NT	pass	pass	2♡[1]	1. Majors.
pass	3♡	all pass		

What should you lead?

Lead the ♡3. Here are the indications that call for a trump lead:

(a) You have a balanced hand.

(b) You have values in declarer's other suit.

(c) You can't expect to find partner with help anywhere.

(d) You have no safer lead.

Matchpoints, N-S vul.

314

♠ A 5 4   ♡ 10 8 6 5 3   ◇ A 7 4   ♣ 6 5

WEST	NORTH	EAST	SOUTH
	pass	pass	1♡
pass	1♠	pass	2♣
pass	2◇	pass	3♣
all pass			

What should you lead?

Lead the ♣6. Don't lead (or underlead) either of your aces in dummy's suits. Ace leads are bad enough normally, but even if you had ♠QJ10x or ♠QJ10x, you should seriously consider a trump lead on this auction. That's usually advisable when dummy, after denying four-card support for opener's second suit, chooses to play in it. It's odds-on that dummy has a singleton heart; even if partner can eventually overruff dummy, he may have to burn a trump trick to do so.

315

Matchpoints, N-S vul.

♠ A K 6   ♡ J 10 3   ◇ A J 7 6   ♣ J 8 3

WEST	NORTH	EAST	SOUTH
			1◇
pass	1♡	pass	1NT
pass	2♣	pass	?

What should you open with a minimum 3-2-4-4 hand?

In my view you should open 1♣, not the 1◇ recommended by most "authorities," unless your diamonds are markedly stronger ... or you are so weak in the majors as to be unwilling to raise spades or bid 1NT over a major-suit response. If you open 1♣, you can get to 2◇ when responder has five hearts and four diamonds, but if you open 1◇ and rebid 1NT, you won't get to 2♣ when responder has five hearts and four clubs. Also, when you open 1♣ and partner responds 1♠, you can raise to 2♠ with more confidence that you haven't missed a superior 4-4 fit in the unbid minor than if partner had responded 1♠ to a 1◇ opening.

Since you neither opened 1♣ nor rebid 2♣, and a 1◇ opening followed by a 1NT rebid seldom delivers four clubs, responder should not go looking for a 4-4 club fit. However, responder will often have a hand with a four-card major and longer clubs. If he's too weak to respond 2♣ to a 1◇ opening (which requires a good hand even if you don't play "Two-Over-One Game Force"), he must bid as your partner has bid on this deal. So partner's sequence shows five or more clubs and four or more hearts. Therefore, you should not give preference to 2♡ unless you have a genuine preference (three hearts and two clubs). Here you should simply pass. At matchpoints, with five decent hearts and five clubs, responder should rebid 2♡ and not introduce clubs at all.

For comparison's sake, examine this altered problem with the minor suits switched:

Matchpoints, N-S vul.

♠ A K 6   ♡ J 10 3   ◇ J 8 3   ♣ A J 7 6

WEST	NORTH	EAST	SOUTH
			1♣
pass	1♡	pass	1NT
pass	2◇	pass	?

Bid 2♡ now. This is a radically different auction. Responder shouldn't have four hearts and longer diamonds, for a 1◇ response to 1♣ does not require 2-over-1 values. Responder shows five hearts and four or five diamonds.

NORTH (dummy)
♠ Q J 9 6 5
♡ 3
◇ 10 7 4
♣ A Q 6 4

EAST (you)
♠ K 4
♡ Q 6 5
◇ Q J 6 2
♣ 7 5 3 2

WEST	NORTH	EAST	SOUTH
	pass	pass	1♡
pass	1♠	pass	1NT[1]
all pass			

1. The North-South 1NT *opening* range is 15-17 HCP.

Partner leads the ◇9, covered by the ◇10 and the ◇J, and taken by declarer's ◇A. Partner covers declarer's ♣J with the ♣K and dummy's ♣A wins. Declarer finesses his ♡J, which holds, and leads the ♣9. Again partner covers, and dummy tops partner's ♣10 with the ♣Q. Declarer finesses his ◇8 successfully and cashes the ♣8, on which partner discards the ♠8. Finally, declarer cashes the ♡A and the ♡K and then leads a low heart to partner's ♡10. You must find a discard on partner's heart trick in this ending:

NORTH (dummy)
♠ Q J 9
♡ —
◇ —
♣ 6

EAST (you)
♠ K 4
♡ —
◇ Q 6
♣ 7

Declarer has shown up with

♠ x (?)   ♡ A K J x x   ◇ A K 8 (?)   ♣ J 9 8

Which pattern does he have, (a) 2-5-3-3 or (b) 1-5-4-3?

If you've been counting declarer's high card points, you'll notice that he has already shown up with 16 HCP and 4 Honor Tricks. That appears to be inconsistent with his supposed 12-14 HCP for the 1NT rebid. This is all the clue you should need about declarer's distribution. With

♠ x   ♡ A K J x x   ◇ A K 8 x   ♣ J 9 8

he would have had an easy 2◇ rebid, but with

♠ x x   ♡ A K J x x   ◇ A K 8   ♣ J 9 8

After a 1♠ response to a 1♡ opening, be on the lookout for over-strength 1NT and under-strength 2NT rebids by opener.

he has no good rebid (2◇ is still correct) and has trapped himself into rebidding an over-strength 1NT. That's not unusual for 1♡ bidders who might have opened 1NT if they'd thought about their rebids. Regardless, you know that partner has the ♠A, and that he can count you for the ♠K. So discard a diamond, and keep your ♣7, an established winner, to which your ♠K will be an entry.

317

Matchpoints, Neither vul.

♠ 7 5 4   ♡ 2   ◇ J 10 7 6 5 3 2   ♣ 8 6

WEST	NORTH	EAST	SOUTH
			pass
1♠	dbl	2NT[1]	pass
3♠	pass	4♠	?

1. Limit raise or better.

Pass. To bid 5◇ as a sacrifice is a big gamble. It isn't clear that 4♠ will make: you can get three top tricks and a ruff if partner has

♠ 9   ♡ A K 8 3   ◇ A 9 4   ♣ Q 10 7 3 2

or any number of other classic takeout-doubling hands. Nor is it clear that 5◇ doubled won't go down more than two (partner may have

♠ 9 3 ♡ Q 10 9 3 ◇ K Q 9 ♣ A J 7 4

or

♠ 9 3 ♡ K Q 9 3 ◇ K 9 4 ♣ A J 7 4

and you'll lose two spade tricks and one trick in every other suit). Yes, East *should* have four spades for his jump to 2NT, but you'd be surprised how many responders, given the assurance of at least five spades in opener's hand, will show a "limit raise or better" with only three-card support. In short, for 5◇ to be a successful save requires a three-legged parlay:

(1) 5◇ doubled goes down no more than two.

(2) 4♠ makes.

(3) The "field" reaches 4♠ (if others play 3♠, -300 is a bottom regardless).

Each leg reduces the probability of a parlay, and I haven't even considered the possibility that partner's takeout double of 1♠ is slightly off-shape. Avoid parlays, especially when they have more than two legs.

Most saves, by the way, are parlays. Don't overlook Leg (3).

Matchpoints, Neither vul.

318

♠ 10 3 2   ♡ A 10 6 4   ◇ 10 7 6 3   ♣ 5 4

WEST	NORTH	EAST	SOUTH
		pass	pass
pass	1♠	pass	pass
2♡	2♠	pass	?

You were just short of a 2♠ raise at your first turn. With an ace, three tens (figure that one of them may be useful), three trumps and a doubleton, you owe partner a raise to 3♠. After all, partner bid 2♠ knowing that you might be short in spades and entirely broke.

Matchpoints, E-W vul.

♠ A Q 5   ♡ K J   ◇ K Q J 8   ♣ 10 7 6 3

	WEST	NORTH	EAST	SOUTH
1. Good 15 to 18 HCP.				1NT[1]
2. Transfer.	pass	2◇[2]	pass	2♡
3. Puppet to 2NT.	pass	2♠[3]	pass	2NT
4. Forcing.	pass	3♣[4]	pass	?

Bid 3NT despite your four-card club support. Of your 16 HCP, 12 are in spades and diamonds, the suits partner doesn't have, but these 12 HCP will cover at most two losers (perhaps only one) in a suit contract.

Matchpoints, Neither vul.

♠ 5 4   ♡ A   ◇ K J 10 9 5   ♣ J 7 5 4 2

WEST	NORTH	EAST	SOUTH
	1♠	2♣	pass
pass	2♠	pass	?

Bid 4♠. 3♠ would be reasonable on

♠ 5 4   ♡ A   ◇ J 7 5 4 2   ♣ K J 10 9 5

a hand with likely wasted values in clubs, but 3♠ is a definite underbid when all your cards figure to be working.

Matchpoints, N-S vul.

♠ 10 7   ♡ —   ◇ K Q J 9 8 3   ♣ A Q 9 5 4

	WEST	NORTH	EAST	SOUTH
			4♡	4NT[1]
1. Minors.	5♡	6◇	6♡	?

You are in a "forcing pass" situation. Should you double, bid 7◇ or leave it up to partner to decide?

Double. You must not bid 7◇ on your own, and you shouldn't encourage partner to do so by passing when you don't have the ♠A. A forcing pass shows not only the requisite control in the opponents' suit, but a willingness for partner to bid more. You have your vulnerable-against-not 4NT bid, but just barely, not anything more.

Matchpoints, N-S vul.

322

♠ Q J 9 5 3   ♡ 10   ◇ 8 7 5 4   ♣ J 6 3

WEST	NORTH	EAST	SOUTH
	2♣[1]	pass	2◇[2]
pass	2♡	pass	?

1. Strong and artificial.
2. Neutral response.

With your present partner, you have a "second" (true) negative available: 3♣. Should you use it, or should you make a positive response in spades?

Bid 3♣ (second negative). Here's a good way to look at it: if you would have passed partner's opening one-bid in a suit, you don't have a positive response to his (strong) two-bid in that suit.

When you bid a natural positive 2♠, you create a new problem for yourself, as you've exhausted the messages you want to send:

WEST	NORTH	EAST	SOUTH
	2♣[1]	pass	2◇[2]
pass	2♡	pass	2♠[3]
pass	3♡	pass	?

1. Strong and artificial.
2. Neutral response.
3. Natural positive.

Partner has shown six hearts; normal support requires two, a combined eight cards in a suit being the target for a trump suit. So do not raise to 4♡. You won't be overstating your spades or your hand if you bid 3♠. You have no entry, and your spades will be useful only as tricks if you play in spades, or as stoppers if partner plays in notrump. Bidding 3♠ lets you reach game in any of three strains: hearts, spades or notrump. Bidding 4♡ commits to hearts.

When no bid seems perfect, but two or more bids seem plausible and it's at all close, lean towards the cheapest bid.

Matchpoints, E-W vul.

♠ A K 10 5   ♡ A 8 6 2   ◇ 8 6   ♣ A 10 6

WEST	NORTH	EAST	SOUTH
			1NT[1]
pass	2♠[2]	pass	3♣
pass	3◇[3]	pass	?

1. Good 15 to 18 HCP.

2. Clubs or balanced 8-9 HCP

3. Natural and forcing.

If partner has values in hearts, you may belong in 3NT. Otherwise, you belong in a suit contract: 5♣, perhaps 4♠ if partner has ♠QJx, or perhaps a slam. Don't bid 3NT, which puts a damper on other contracts. Bid 3♠ to show partner where your strength lies.

However, you bid 3NT, which is just where partner would have put you had you bid 3♠:

NORTH (dummy)

♠ 7

♡ K 5 3

◇ K Q J 4

♣ Q 9 8 7 5

☐

SOUTH (you)

♠ A K 10 5

♡ A 8 6 2

◇ 8 6

♣ A 10 6

West leads the ♠4 to East's ♠Q. You take the ♠A and lead a low diamond to dummy's ◇J, which holds. Now what?

You must work on clubs, of course. There is a percentage play in the suit, but that's not the most important thing. East is the danger hand (risk of a spade through you), so you'd do well to lose any club trick to West rather than East, even if it is slightly anti-percentage. Start with dummy's ♣9. If East plays low and West wins, West can't continue spades without blowing a trick.

♠ K Q 5 4 3 ♡ 8 ◇ A K J ♣ 10 6 5 4

WEST	NORTH	EAST	SOUTH
		pass	1♠
2♡	pass	pass	?

Pass. If you're worried about missing a juicy penalty against 2♡ when West has overbid and partner has a stack, stop worrying. If partner has that hand, you'll probably collect +200 for down two *not* doubled, with no game your way, which will be more than others will score at tables where West prudently stays out of the auction. If partner has enough for you to make a game with this hand, he should not have "trap" passed.

When Al Roth popularized negative doubles in 1957, he met with resistance from old-timers who were reluctant to give up penalty doubles of overcalls: "But how can I nail an opponent who steps out?"

The answer that Roth and other negative double advocates gave to their critics was, essentially, "You can still nail opponents who overcall on trash by having partner *balance* with a takeout double. Then you, the frustrated penalty doubler, can make a *penalty pass*." As a result, many teachers of negative doubles talk about opener's "duty to protect" a frustrated penalty doubler by balancing with a take-out double. That indeed will protect responder when he has a trump stack, but a trump stack (with enough other strength to beat a low-level contract facing a minimum opening) is infrequent. Since it is unlikely partner has this hand, and couldn't bid, raise, or make a negative double, opener should in fact be very cautious about reopening with a weak hand.

There's another reason for this: in the current era, most players use Weak Jump Overcalls and very wide-range simple overcalls. The wide range of their overcalls, combined with the ineptitude of many players in advancing overcalls, makes it not at all unlikely your opponents have missed a game. Reopening with minimum values gives them another chance to bid it.

325

Matchpoints, E-W vul.

♠ K 7 6 ♡ 10 8 5 4 ◇ Q 3 ♣ A J 9 4

WEST	NORTH	EAST	SOUTH
	1◇	pass	1♡
pass	2◇	pass	?

Bid 3◇; second choice, 2NT. Do not pass. Your ◇Q3 is golden facing partner's six-bagger and your hand counts to 11 HCP (you should count the ◇Q as 3 HCP). The threshold for responder making a second bid (other than a bid at the one-level, a raise of opener's 1♡ or 1♠ rebid to two or a preference to opener's first suit) is a good 10 HCP. Partner's 2◇ in this auction has a wide range (2♣ would have a wider range still); you owe him another bid.

326

Matchpoints, E-W vul.

♠ J 7 5 3 ♡ K Q 7 6 ◇ K Q 10 2 ♣ 3

WEST	NORTH	EAST	SOUTH
			pass
pass	pass	1♣	dbl
2♣	2♠	3♣	pass
pass	3◇	4♣	?

On a deal where neither you nor your partner could open, you've pushed an opponent who might have passed it out to four of a minor. Good enough? I think so. Conceivably, partner may be able to double. You have as much as partner can expect and there may be a magic matchpoint +200 in your future. Do not compete any further; just pass.

327

Matchpoints, N-S vul.

♠ A K 5 ♡ A Q 7 4 ◇ 7 2 ♣ K Q 10 6

WEST	NORTH	EAST	SOUTH
	1◇	pass	1♡
pass	2◇	pass	?

In minor-suit auctions, 4NT should never be used to *ask* for anything (except values enough to bid slam); it is vital to have a way to suggest slam while permitting the

A keycard ask, if available, won't disclose the information you need to make an intelligent slam decision. A natural 4NT is correct.

partnership to rest in 4NT when slam is not in the offing. If you want to have a keycard ask in minor-suit auctions, *Roman Keycard Gerber* (4♣) is optimal, and using four of the agreed minor to ask for keys is reasonable too.

Matchpoints, Both vul.

328

♠ K 8 3 2   ♡ 9 7 5 2   ◇ A Q 9   ♣ 5 2

WEST	NORTH	EAST	SOUTH
pass	1♣	1♠	?

Suit quality counts for something — more than most modern players think. Though a negative double (if you play negative doubles) would not be bad, 1NT is slightly better. This may be your last chance to make a descriptive bid in notrump, which is likely to be your best strain when opener doesn't have four hearts.

Matchpoints, Both vul.

329

♠ Q 7 5 2   ♡ A 6   ◇ A 10 6 3   ♣ A 9 8

WEST	NORTH	EAST	SOUTH
			1◇
pass	1♠	pass	2♠
pass	3NT	pass	?

Partner's 3NT shows four spades and offers a choice between 3NT and 4♠. Might partner have

♠ K J 10 4   ♡ K 9 3   ◇ K 4   ♣ K Q J 2

or

♠ A K 9 6   ♡ K 9 3   ◇ K 9 4   ♣ K 6 2

or some other hand that could produce a slam facing your four-card support and maximum with prime values?

Yes. Instead of simply taking partner back to 4♠, cater for the chance that slam is on by cuebidding 4♣ "on the way" to 4♠. If partner cooperates by cuebidding 4◇ (he can cuebid the king of your first-bid suit just as if it were an ace), continue with 4♡, another cuebid.

330

Matchpoints, E-W vul.

NORTH (dummy)
♠ Q
♡ K 10 5 3 2
◇ 7 5 4
♣ A 9 7 3

EAST (you)
♠ 10 9 8 4
♡ J 8 7 6
◇ K 8 6 2
♣ 6

WEST	NORTH	EAST	SOUTH
			1♣
pass	1♡	pass	1♠
pass	2♣	all pass	

Partner leads the ◇3 and your ◇K falls to declarer's ◇A. Declarer leads low to the ♣A, and then low to the ♣J. Partner wins the ♣Q and cashes the ♣K, as declarer plays the ♣10. You discard the ◇2 and the ◇6. Now partner exits with a fourth club to dummy's ♣9. What should you discard?

You must keep a diamond to lead through declarer. You can safely discard a heart, however, because declarer is marked with a 4-2-3-4 pattern.

What's that you ask? Might not declarer be 4-3-2-4? Isn't this a situation in which you need the "third from even, low from odd" opening-lead convention to let you know whether partner has three diamonds or four?

Absolutely not. You must learn to milk the opening lead for the vast quantity of information it conveys. If partner had four diamonds, they could only be ◇Q1093, ◇QJ93 or ◇QJ103: all holdings from which he would have led an honor instead. Partner's lead must therefore be from ◇Q93, ◇Q103 or ◇J93.

If you don't keep a diamond, partner will think that you did and he may go wrong later in the defense by playing declarer to be 4-3-2-4. (Partner's knowledge of declarer's pattern is less complete than yours.)

Matchpoints, Both vul.

331

♠ J 9 5 4   ♡ A K 3   ◇ Q 10 6 5   ♣ J 3

WEST	NORTH	EAST	SOUTH
		3◇	pass
pass	dbl	pass	?

Weak 2◇ bids are not nearly as common as Weak 2♡ and 2♠ bids. Many pairs play 2◇ as something else. So what do frustrated would-be weak 2◇ bidders do? They open 3◇!

You have tremendous defense against 3◇. Your ◇Q1065 *behind* the 3◇ bidder figures to be worth two tricks on defense, and your (relatively short) ♡AK3 is likely to take two more. If partner takes three more tricks, that's down three. By making a "penalty pass" of partner's takeout double, you'll score +800, more than what you can make in your own best contract.

Your other options are 4♠, 3NT and a 4◇ cuebid that says, "You pick the suit, partner." Bidding only 3♠ is out of the question; your hand is far too strong.

If the ◇10 were a small card, your decision would be closer (you'd have only one trump trick against 3◇ doubled). A significant deciding factor is the system of the opponents. Playing at a club whose owner condones failing to display convention cards, you should *demand* to see your opponents' convention card. If you do, you may notice that they don't play Weak 2◇ bids. In that case, which is more likely, that East has six diamonds or that he has seven for his 3◇ preempt?

Obviously, six-card suits are more common than seven-card suits, but can you guess how much more common? Nearly five times as common. Given that East has either six or seven diamonds, he'll have six about 82% of the time. That makes passing partner's double much clearer than it would be against pairs that play Weak 2◇ bids.

Matchpoints, Neither vul.

♠ 10 3   ♡ Q J 8 2   ◇ A 10 5 4 3   ♣ K J

WEST	NORTH	EAST	SOUTH
	pass	1♠	?

Pass. You have neither a good enough suit nor a good enough hand for a 2◇ overcall. The opponents are probably destined to play in spades, and with a balanced hand that lacks a source of tricks and a thin five-card suit, you don't want to compete with them in diamonds. If the opponents are headed for notrump from the West side, you want partner to lead his best suit, as you have two honors in both hearts and clubs.

Second choice: double. The downside is that partner may reply in clubs, but your two honors, though not enough to make him a favorite in any club contract he may bid, may be enough to prevent the opponents from doubling. The upside is that you may find a good contract in *hearts* if partner has four.

Matchpoints, N-S vul.

NORTH (dummy)
♠ K 9 6 5 3
♡ K 10 4
◇ 9 7 6 2
♣ A

SOUTH (you)
♠ 4
♡ Q 8
◇ A K J 5 3
♣ K J 7 6 4

WEST	NORTH	EAST	SOUTH
pass	pass	1♣	1◇
pass	1♠	pass	2♣
pass	2◇	pass	pass
2♡	3◇	all pass	

West leads the ♡3. You play low from dummy; East plays the ♡J and you take your ♡Q. What now?

Return your low heart to dummy's ♡10 to set up a second heart trick. That gives the defenders a chance to make a mistake (neglecting to cash the ♠A), so that you can discard your singleton spade on dummy's ♡K.

Matchpoints, E-W vul.

♠ A 4   ♡ 7 4   ◇ J   ♣ A K Q 8 7 6 4 2

WEST	NORTH	EAST	SOUTH
			1♣
1♡	1♠[1]	2♡	?

1. Playing negative doubles, implying five spades.

Cuebid 3♡. If partner has a heart stopper, he'll almost surely bid 3NT, which you'll be happy to pass. If he doesn't, you can still bid 5♣ next turn (a mild overbid, with three fast red-suit losers possible).

A good case can be made for jumping to 4♣, provided you understand that if partner bids 4NT, he is suggesting a final contract, not asking for keycards.

Matchpoints, Neither vul.

♠ J 6   ♡ Q 8 5 3 2   ◇ A 7   ♣ K 8 6 4

WEST	NORTH	EAST	SOUTH
			pass
1◇	1♠	1NT	?

Your suit isn't good enough to bid 2♡, which is non-forcing. Partner may pass with a doubleton, and leave you to play 2♡, so you need a good suit. Points have nothing to do with it. Bridge is still a game of tricks.

♠ J 6   ♡ Q J 10 8 3 2   ◇ A 7   ♣ 8 6 4

has two fewer points than your actual hand but its three-honor six-card suit makes it a normal hand for 2♡ in this auction. With your hand, the choices are to pass and to bid a slightly aggressive 2♠.

However, you bid 2♡. Now move over to the East seat and defend against the 3◇ to which you may have pushed your opponents.

NORTH (dummy)
♠ K 9 3
♡ 10 6 4
◇ Q 9 3
♣ J 10 5 2

EAST (you)
♠ J 6
♡ Q 8 5 3 2
◇ A 7
♣ K 8 6 4

WEST	NORTH	EAST	SOUTH
		pass	1◇
1♠	1NT	2♡ (!)	3◇
all pass			

Partner leads the ♡A and, despite your discouraging ♡2, continues with the ♡J to declarer's ♡K. After cashing the ♣A, declarer leads the ◇10 and lets it ride. What now?

Take the ◇A and cash the ♡Q. Partner's discard will help you figure out what to do next. If he plays the ♠2, a discouraging low card, you'll know not to shift to spades. In that case, your best bet will be to exit with your last trump, *passive* defense being the norm. If declarer has spade losers, dummy has no winners on which to discard them.

Declarer is already known to have three hearts, and figures to have six diamonds (conceivably seven). That leaves four (conceivably three) black cards. What do you think his clubs are?

They can't be ♣AQ or ♣AQx. If he had the ♣Q, he wouldn't cash the ace; he would wait to take a club finesse against your ♣K (dummy's ♠K will surely be an entry).

Suppose that instead of cashing the ♡Q and returning a trump, you shift to the ♠J. Partner takes declarer's ♠Q with the ♠A and returns a low spade; dummy's ♠9 holds. Dummy's ◇Q draws your last trump and partner's, and dummy continues with the ♣5. What should you play?

You can be quite sure that partner has the ♣Q; declarer's ♣A was most likely a singleton. You should duck; declarer is going to ruff anyway, so why squander your ♣K?

♠ A 8 5   ♡ A 7 6 4 3   ◇ J 8 6   ♣ A 3

WEST	NORTH	EAST	SOUTH
1♣	dbl	1♡	?

Here are some typical hand patterns for a takeout double of 1♣: 4-4-4-1, 5-4-3-1, 4-5-3-1, 4-3-5-1, 3-4-5-1, 4-4-3-2, 4-3-4-2, 3-4-4-2.

Facing any of these hand patterns, why would you want to play in notrump? In notrump, the defenders will knock out your ♣A early and run enough club tricks to beat you.

A jump to 2NT would be appropriate with

♠ A 9 4   ♡ J 3   ◇ Q 5 4 2   ♣ K Q 10 6

(11-12 HCP with clubs doubly stopped). With that hand, you don't even need a heart stopper, for by doubling 1♣, partner has in effect bid 1♡ (as well as 1◇ and 1♠). With your actual hand, you should double — a penalty double showing hearts and a decent hand. If the opponents run back to clubs, partner will be able to bid hearts, relying on you to have a decent hand with at least four hearts to go with four hearts of his own, and you can raise. If partner doesn't bid hearts, you can bid hearts at your next turn (because you have a fifth heart).

However, you bid 2NT and the auction continues:

WEST	NORTH	EAST	SOUTH
1♣	dbl	1♡	2NT (!)
pass	3◇	pass	?

There's really no way to recover fully from your failure to double 1♡ earlier. Subsequent bids almost never correct earlier mistakes. To rebid 3NT is to compound your earlier error (it's seldom right to rebid notrump after your partner removes your previous notrump bid to a suit). Partner's message when he bid 3◇ was, "I don't think you can make 2NT." Have you any reason to think he was mistaken? The best you can do now is to raise to 4◇.

A double of an opening suit bid is presumed to be a simultaneous overcall in the other three suits (until shown otherwise).

337

Matchpoints, Neither vul.

♠ Q 5   ♡ A 4   ◇ A 10 6 5 4 3   ♣ 8 5 4

WEST	NORTH	EAST	SOUTH
	pass	pass	?

With your present partner, you play Weak Two-bids. Should you open 2◇?

No. In a way, Weak Two-bids resemble two-level overcalls, though Weak Twos are weaker, being limited to just under opening-bid high card strength. You have more than enough points but the wrong kind of hand for a Weak 2◇ bid: too skinny a suit, and too much of your strength outside it. Pass.

338

Matchpoints, N-S vul.

NORTH (dummy)
♠ K Q 3
♡ A
◇ Q 6
♣ A J 8 7 6 5 2

EAST (you)
♠ 10 7 6 4
♡ Q 7 2
◇ 10 7
♣ K Q 10 3

WEST	NORTH	EAST	SOUTH
pass	1♣	pass	1♡
pass	3♣	pass	3♠
pass	4♠	all pass	

Partner leads the ◇5 and dummy's ◇Q takes the trick, as declarer plays the ◇3. All follow to dummy's ♣A and then declarer leads a low club from dummy, letting your ♣10 hold. Declarer discards the ◇4 and partner discards the ◇2. What now?

Declarer is trying to set up dummy's clubs. Don't help him by continuing clubs. Play your last diamond (which can't hurt).

Matchpoints, Neither vul.

♠ K Q 10 4   ♡ 6 3   ◇ Q 10 7 2   ♣ K 10 3

WEST	NORTH	EAST	SOUTH
	2♣[1]	pass	?

1. Omnibus 2♣.

Bid 2◇, a neutral response. Do not even think of bidding 2NT.

There's virtually no such thing as a 2NT response to an Omnibus 2♣. It shuts out the three most likely rebids that opener had planned (2♡, 2♠ and 2NT). Moreover, it gets the notrump played from the wrong side when notrump is right.

With

♠ A J 7   ♡ K 5   ◇ A K J 4   ♣ A Q J 6

(a hand on which partner planned to rebid 2NT), partner can claim 6NT, but if you declare 3NT, you may go down.

If you ever pick up a balanced responding hand with at least a king in every suit, you could respond 2NT without risk of wrong-siding the contract, but wouldn't you be better off responding 2◇ to leave room for partner to bid 2NT or two of a major (the most common rebids by an Omnibus 2♣ opener)? Until you learn other responses to the Omnibus 2♣, respond 2◇ automatically, making an exception only for decent hands with decent heart suits, on which you can respond a natural positive 2♡ without obstructing partner's intended rebid.

Matchpoints, E-W vul.

♠ A 8 7   ♡ K Q 7 4 3 2   ◇ A 10 6   ♣ 6

WEST	NORTH	EAST	SOUTH
		pass	1♡
dbl	2♣	2♠	?

You must pass. You have a minimum opening bid, your only real extras being your sixth heart. Partner's 2♣ shows a good hand for playing in clubs, but not for anything else. With three-card heart support, partner would have bid 2♡ and you could compete to 3♡. With a doubleton heart, partner might have bid 1NT, so you *might* have been able compete to 3♡ (at least it wouldn't have been a *misfit*). When partner bids 2♣, however, you can expect him to have few hearts, usually only one.

West's double strongly suggests shortness in hearts (also usually one, perhaps two), so East is very likely to have four, perhaps five. You have three or four trump losers in a heart contract. Note that heart spot cards are important when contemplating bidding hearts again if partner may not have support, just as when contemplating a Weak Two-bid. With a suit like ♡KQ10982, you could be confident of losing only two trump tricks (as opposed to three or four) — perhaps only one if the ♡J were to fall singleton or doubleton.

341

Matchpoints, Neither vul.

NORTH (dummy)
♠ Q 7 4
♡ 9 8 4
◇ J 6 5
♣ A K 9 3

SOUTH (you)
♠ —
♡ A Q 6
◇ A K 8 7 4 2
♣ 10 6 4 2

1. Insufficient.
2. Condoning the insufficient bid.

WEST	NORTH	EAST	SOUTH
			1◇
dbl	1NT	2♠	2◇[1]
2♠[2]	3◇	3♠	4◇
all pass			

West leads the ♠A. Plan the play.

Did you look at the your opponents' convention card to see their carding agreements? If so, you will have seen "A from AKx…" and guessed that West might have the ♠K as well.

You ruff, play the ◇A, dropping West's ◇Q, and draw two more rounds of trumps ending in dummy. Now you may as well cash dummy's ♣K before doing anything else. If you do, you'll notice that East's ♣Q falls. (If either missing honor, the ♣Q or the ♣J, falls, it is almost twice as likely to be singleton as from ♣QJ doubleton).

Your best bet now is to lead dummy's ♡9 and let it ride if not covered, or cover an honor if East plays one. West has nearly all of the missing high cards, as his takeout double indicates. He'll win the first heart, but have no safe exit from his hand:

♠ A K x x ♡ K J 10 x ◇ Q ♣ J 8 7 5

Another heart will let your ♡Q score; a low spade will let dummy's ♠Q score; the ♠K will let you ruff and take a trick with dummy's ♠Q later; a low club will let you score your ♣10. Then all that's left is to take the proven finesse against West's remaining ♣J.

Pay attention to the bidding — it can help you read the opponents' cards.

Matchpoints, Neither vul.

NORTH (dummy)
♠ K 4
♡ A 3
◇ A Q 10 9 7 2
♣ K 7 4

SOUTH (you)
♠ A Q 10
♡ Q 9 7 6
◇ J 3
♣ Q J 8 6

WEST	NORTH	EAST	SOUTH
		pass	1♣
pass	2◇	pass	2NT
pass	3NT	all pass	

After opening a slightly under-strength hand and ignoring your weak four-card heart suit, you wind up declaring 3NT. West leads the ♠3. You call for a low card from dummy and East plays the ♠9. With which spade should you take the trick?

Win with the ♠10, not the ♠Q. That way you retain the option of overtaking dummy's ♠K with your ♠A later. Moreover, as declarer, you should not want to reveal to the defenders what assets you hold. Wouldn't you prefer that East think West may have led from spades headed by ♠QJ rather than the ♠J alone?

At Trick 2, you lead the ◇J, which holds. On the next diamond, however, West discards. You play dummy's ◇9 and East takes the ◇K. He returns the ♠7 and you win with dummy's ♠K. What now?

Before you discard all your hearts, you should drive out the ♣A. Play dummy's ♣K, and if it holds, play a low club to your ♣Q. If the defenders take the ♣A on the first or second round, you'll have a club entry to your hand and can cash the ♠A to pitch dummy's low heart. If they duck the ♣A twice, you'll discard dummy's low heart on the ♠A next and make eleven tricks regardless.

You can't afford to discard all four hearts or you'll have no way to score dummy's ♡A after driving out the ♣A. Another successful line of play would be to discard three hearts and one club on dummy's diamonds.

 343

Matchpoints, Neither vul.

NORTH (dummy)
♠ Q J 8
♡ K J 6
◇ J 10 7 4
♣ Q 10 2

☐

SOUTH (you)
♠ K 4
♡ A 9 5 3
◇ A K Q
♣ K 8 6 3

WEST	NORTH	EAST	SOUTH
			2NT[1]
pass	3NT	all pass	

1. 20-21 HCP (supposedly).

West leads the ♠10 to your ♠K. Reasonably enough, you decide to attack hearts. How should you go about it?

Don't begin at Trick 2. First you should unblock diamonds. Remember how, early in this book, I said that AKQ in a suit is worth less than AKQ2? This is one of the reasons: you must sometimes cash your tops in the suit early to avoid blockage.

Something good can happen if you cash your three top diamonds early: a defender may have a doubleton diamond and may guess wrongly in discarding. He's less likely to make a wrong guess later in the play when he has more information about your hand.

Then, supposing diamonds split 3-3 and you get no clues from a defender's discard, you can attack hearts. Your best hope is to find the ♡Q with West, so lead a low heart towards dummy and insert the ♡J when West follows small.

Playing a low heart to dummy's ♡K, followed by dummy's ♡J, figures to gain only when East has ♡Qxx or ♡Q10xx and makes the mistake of failing to cover. That's counting on *two* good things to happen to you (including a defensive error) instead of one. Also, if you start hearts with the ♡K, you burn a scarce dummy entry early and may find yourself unable to get to dummy later to take a second spade trick.

When attacking a suit, always think, "What am I hoping for?"

Matchpoints, E-W vul.

344

♠ J 4   ♡ J 6 2   ◇ 7 6 5 3 2   ♣ 8 7 5

WEST	NORTH	EAST	SOUTH
1♣	dbl	redbl	?

Even though West's redouble relieves you of the obligation to bid, you shouldn't "pass the buck" back to partner unless you are willing to have him remove to his own best suit (probably hearts or spades). Think of partner's takeout double as a "simultaneous overcall in all the unbid suits" and a request to take a preference among them. Bid 1◇: it does not promise strength, only preference. With a hand like

♠ J 4 3   ♡ J 6 2   ◇ 7 6 5 2   ♣ 8 7 5

however, you could pass happily; your preference for diamonds is slight, not marked, and with equal length in two or three suits, partner will remove to the cheapest.

Matchpoints, Both vul.

345

♠ K 9 6   ♡ K Q 9   ◇ A J 8 7   ♣ Q 5 4

WEST	NORTH	EAST	SOUTH
		pass	?

With your present partner, you play 15-17 HCP notrumps. Any reason not to open 1NT here?

Be suspicious of any seeming 15-HCP hand that contains anything less than 3 Honor Tricks and a plus-value. Such a hand "isn't worth its point-count".

1. 15-17 HCP (supposedly).
2. Transfer.

It is worth learning a comprehensive structure for continuing when responder, after using a Jacoby Transfer, bids three of a minor next. I've developed one, and I call it *Meyers*.

Jill Meyers, a world-champion bridge player, is welcome to adopt the *Meyers* convention as her own, but for mnemonic reasons I named it after the Meyers of *Jacoby and Meyers* (a well-known law firm).

With four-card support for responder's major and a slammish hand, jump in his major. With four-card support for responder's minor and three-card support for responder's major, raise his minor so that if he isn't looking for slam, he can retreat to four of his major confidently. With four-card support for responder's minor but only a doubleton in his major, bid three of another suit, so that if he isn't looking for slam, he can retreat to 3NT. With a fit for neither of responder's suits, bid 3NT yourself. Otherwise, take a simple preference to three of responder's major.

Yes. This hand has two defects: a stray queen (the ♣Q) and a flat 4333 distribution. Make sure you subtract for them. This is only a 14-HCP hand (a bit closer to 13 than to 15). Open 1◇.

However, you open 1NT anyway and soon face another bidding problem:

WEST	NORTH	EAST	SOUTH
		pass	1NT[1]
pass	2◇[2]	pass	2♡
pass	3♣	pass	?

Take a simple 3♡ preference. A jump to 4♡ here should show extras in the form of *four-card* heart support.

However, you bid 4♡ and your overbidding orgy inspires partner to put you in 6♡. It's a wonder he didn't bid 7♡.

NORTH (dummy)
♠ A 5
♡ A J 10 8 2
◇ Q 5
♣ A K 8 3

SOUTH (you)
♠ K 9 6
♡ K Q 9
◇ A J 8 7
♣ Q 5 4

West leads the ♠3. How should you play?

First see if you can execute a Dummy Reversal (actually a "reverse" Dummy Reversal, since the transfer bid resulted in the short hand declaring). Here's how you would do it:

Take the ♠A and lead the ◇Q for a finesse. East will play the ◇K and you'll take the ◇A. Cash the ♡K to verify that trumps are not 5-0. Then take the ◇J and ruff a diamond with dummy's ♡A. Lead a low heart to your ♡Q to verify that trumps are not 4-1, and ruff your last diamond. Lead to your ♠K and ruff your last spade with dummy's last trump. Enter your hand with a club to the ♣Q and draw the last trump with your ♡9, discarding dummy's last low club. Dummy's two top clubs take the last two tricks — making an overtrick to beat the pairs that are in 6NT that take only twelve tricks (five hearts, two spades, two diamonds and three clubs).

Suppose, however, that you do not try for a Dummy Reversal. Instead you take dummy's ♠A and draw trumps (which split 3-2) ending in dummy. A defender must discard on the third trump. Are you watching to see what he discards?

Assume that West discards a low club. Now you lead the ◇Q from dummy for a finesse and East covers with the ◇K. Take the ◇A and the ◇J, and ruff the ◇8 in dummy. Then play the ♣Q and enter dummy with the ♣K. When both defenders follow to two rounds of clubs, dummy's clubs run and you have the rest.

But suppose West hasn't discarded a club on the third round of trumps. Now you can't can't tell whether clubs are splitting 3-3 or 4-2. What now?

Cash dummy's ♣A; if both defenders follow, you have the rest. If not, the defender who was short in clubs will have to discard. You will have been watching all the discards, of course. You will be looking to see if a defender has discarded a club (dummy's last club is high), or if the ◇10 and the ◇9 have fallen (your ◇7 is high) or if the ♠Q, the ♠J and the ♠10 have all fallen (your ♠9 will become a trick). If none of these good things happen, you will reach this end position:

NORTH (dummy)

♠ 5
♡ J
◇ —
♣ 8

☐

SOUTH (you)

♠ K9
♡ —
◇ 7
♣ —

Finally, you lead dummy's last trump.

If West has the last club, East will have to discard a diamond or a spade. Suppose the only missing diamond is the ◇10 or the ◇9 and East has it. East must keep it, so he'll discard a spade. If you guess that East has the high diamond (or West has shown out when you ruffed the ◇8), you'll discard the ◇7. East's spade discard will help you guess:

if it's an honor, you'll surmise that he's forced to discard it to guard diamonds. West must then discard a spade to keep dummy's low club from scoring. Now neither defender will have been able to keep more than one spade, so your ♠K will drop the remaining spade honors and your ♠9 will be good for an overtrick.

You'll just have executed a Double Squeeze without knowing it. All you'll know is that you put pressure on the defenders, who had to guard all three plain suits but could only guard two, and whose discards therefore let you score an extra trick with a low card.

 346

Matchpoints, N-S vul.

♠ 7 ♡ A K Q 6 4 ◇ 5 2 ♣ A 8 7 4 2

WEST	NORTH	EAST	SOUTH
		pass	1♡
1♠	2NT	pass	3♣
pass	3♠	pass	?

After an intervening overcall, a 2NT response is invitational (11-12 HCP). Your 3♣ declines the game invitation (partner can pass). However, his 3♠, a cuebid in the opponent's suit, shows that he likes his hand especially well when you bid clubs. In light of his previous non-forcing 2NT previously, he cannot now decide that his hand is worth a game bid (e.g. 3NT or 5♣); he must give you an out. You must choose among 4♣, 5♣ and 3NT. Of these, 4♣ is the weakest, a signoff.

What would you bid with a weaker hand, e.g.

♠ 7 ♡ A Q J 6 4 ◇ 5 2 ♣ A 8 7 4 2

or similar? You'd bid 4♣, wouldn't you? So with your actual hand, you must bid something else: 3NT or 5♣.

♠ A K J 6   ♡ K Q 8 5 4   ◇ K 7 6   ♣ 10

WEST	NORTH	EAST	SOUTH
	pass	pass	1♡
pass	2♡	pass	?

You have enough to invite game. Your best invitation is with 2♠. You might even belong in spades rather than hearts, for partner may have three hearts and four or five spades for his 2♡ raise. If partner bids only 3♡ over your 2♠, you'll pass; if he bids 2NT or 3♣, you'll retreat to 3♡; if he bids 3◇, your hand improves, so you'll bid 4♡.

However, you jump to 4♡. Can you make it facing the "wrong" dummy?

NORTH (dummy)
♠ 10 9
♡ J 7 3
◇ Q 4
♣ K J 9 7 6 4

☐

SOUTH (you)
♠ A K J 6
♡ K Q 8 5 4
◇ K 7 6
♣ 10

West leads the ◇5. East plays the ◇J and you take your ◇K. You lead the ♣10 and West plays the ♣3. Who do you think has the ♣A?

Much depends on your estimate of the defenders. A good defender in the West position may duck the ♣10 in tempo; a poor defender will either hesitate before ducking or rise with the ♣A whenever he has it. If you think East has the ♣A, finesse West for the ♣Q, so the ♣K will be good for a discard.

However, you think West has the ♣A, so you call for dummy's ♣K. Unfortunately, it loses to East's ♣A. East returns the ♡9, which you (properly) let ride to dummy's ♡J. What now?

You have too many potential losers to ruff all of them in dummy. Your best hope is that not all your potential losers are actual losers. In spades, you're missing only the ♠Q. You're desperate for tricks, so play for the ♠Q to be on side. Lead dummy's ♠10 and let it ride if East plays low. When the finesse works, repeat it: play the ♠9 to your ♠J, and discard dummy's ◇Q on your ♠A. Then ruff a diamond, ruff a club, ruff your last diamond with dummy's last trump, and ruff another club (or discard the ♠K if West's ♣Q has fallen on the second round). With one diamond trick, three spade tricks, two ruffs in dummy and four trump tricks one way or another, you'll take ten tricks and make your very iffy 4♡ game.

Matchpoints, Both vul.

♠ A 6   ♡ K 9 7   ◇ K 8 4   ♣ Q 8 7 5 3

WEST	NORTH	EAST	SOUTH
		pass	?

Should you open 1♣ or pass? The right call depends on your notrump range. A minimum opening with a balanced hand should be regarded as 3 HCP below the bottom of your notrump range. Thus: if 1NT requires 16 HCP, then one of a suit requires 13; if 1NT requires a *good* 15, then one of a suit requires a *good* 12; if 1NT requires 15, then one of a suit requires 12. I recommend a range of a *good* 15 to 18; playing that range, you should pass. Playing 15-17 notrumps, you may open 1♣.

When in doubt about leads against "blind" notrump auctions, prefer majors to minors, black suits to reds, the suit in which the highest card is lower, and the suit in which the second highest card is higher; if choosing between four-card suits, prefer the suit in which the fourth highest card is lower, and the suit in which the third highest card is higher. High middle cards and low extreme cards make a lead in a suit desirable.

Matchpoints, Both vul.

♠ J 10 7   ♡ Q 6 5 4   ◇ Q 10   ♣ Q 5 4 2

WEST	NORTH	EAST	SOUTH
pass	pass	1NT	pass
3NT	all pass		

What should you lead?

In the absence of a Stayman or transfer bid by responder, you prefer a major-suit lead to a minor-suit lead. It's close between the ♠J and the ♡4. Either could work well. Lead the ♠J, which is substantially safer than the ♡4, while being only slightly less constructive.

Are these enough tie-breakers for you?

Matchpoints, E-W vul.

♠ 10 9 6 5   ♡ 10 3   ◇ A K 7 4   ♣ A 9 2

WEST	NORTH	EAST	SOUTH
		pass	pass
pass	2♣[1]	pass	2◇[2]
pass	3♣	pass	?

1. Strong, artificial, forcing.
2. The only response you know (waiting).

Partner's Omnibus 2♣ is based on primary clubs, which means he must be prepared to play an eleven-trick game; he can hardly have less than ten tricks in his own hand, or fewer than two aces. It's slam time, baby — grand slam time.

Do you know how to continue from here? Most who tout and teach Weak Two-bids to beginners neglect to teach how the auction should go after an Omnibus 2♣. There are many ways to continue, and each requires partnership agreements. Without such agreements, it's foolish to play the convention.

You dare not bid 4NT. Even if you play Blackwood, this isn't it: *suit agreement* is necessary for 4NT to be ace-asking, and no suit has been agreed. Besides, 4NT is needed as a natural slam-invitational bid, since 3NT is needed for a weak, balanced responding hand like

♠ Q J 5   ♡ J 10 5 3   ◇ J 10 7 4   ♣ 9 2

(you can't pass 3♣, you don't have club support, and you don't have a decent suit to bid). So with a better hand, e.g.

♠ Q J 5   ♡ J 10 5 3   ◇ K J 10 4   ♣ 9 2

you'd have to jump to 4NT to show your values.

Suppose partner were ignorant enough to think 4NT is Blackwood in this auction. Would it then be right for you to bid 4NT?

No. You already know that partner has both missing aces for his strong bidding. And you don't have the second-round controls you need in the unbid suits, hearts and spades. If anyone needs to know how many aces the other has, it is your partner, who is the only one with the kings, queens and jacks that will solidify suits and take tricks.

The simplest solution is to raise 3♣ to 4♣. If you bid notrump at all, your best choice is 7NT, relying on partner to have a ten-trick hand including the two missing aces.

351

Matchpoints, Both vul.

♠ J 9 4　♡ A Q 8 5　◇ K Q 9 8　♣ 10 9

WEST	NORTH	EAST	SOUTH
			1◇
pass	1♠	pass	?

Ordinarily, you should want ♠Qxx, ♠J10x or better to raise in this auction. If you had clubs stopped, or even a 3-3-4-3 hand, a 1NT rebid would be fine. However, with two weak clubs, you should prefer to raise to 2♠.

352

Matchpoints, E-W vul.

♠ K 10 9 6　♡ A 9 7 3 2　◇ 10 8　♣ K J

WEST	NORTH	EAST	SOUTH
pass	pass	1◇	?

Your hearts are too weak to bid 1♡ on marginal values. If West bids notrump, you shouldn't want partner to lead hearts. You should want him to lead his own best suit.

It is reasonable to make a takeout double. Although you are a club shy, your two honors in the suit give you a bit of protection, and with equal length in clubs and a major, partner will ordinarily bid the major. Better still (though not by much) is to pass.

353

Matchpoints, E-W vul.

♠ 10 7 4 3　♡ K J　◇ A K　♣ A K 9 8 5

WEST	NORTH	EAST	SOUTH
1♠	pass		?

It's not unreasonable to bid 4NT, Roman Keycard Blackwood, as this may be your last chance to do so. If you jump shift to 3♣, and partner bids 3♠, he'll (correctly) take your 4NT next turn as asking in clubs, not spades.

However, it's better to tell your story and let partner take control. You can do so if you know how to continue after you jump shift. Recall that a jump shift can be based on three types of hand: (F) Fit, (B) Balanced, or (I) Independent suit, and your rebid should normally clarify which you have.

WEST	NORTH	EAST	SOUTH
	1♠	pass	3♣
pass	3♠	pass	?

With (I), you could bid 4♣, which is forcing because partner can't pass below game. However, you dare not bid 4♠ to show (F) because you have reached game and partner might pass with a minimum like

♠ K Q J 9 8 2   ♡ A 3   ◇ Q 9 8   ♣ 10 4

(cold for 6♠ or 6NT facing your hand). Because 4♣ is forcing and 4♠ is non-forcing, a 4◇ or 4♡ cuebid implies spade support, not independent (0- or 1-loser) clubs.

So bid 4◇, setting spades as trumps. Then 4NT by either partner will be RKCB for spades, and asker will discover that one keycard is missing and settle for a small slam.

Many modern experts play "Soloway Jump Shifts," in which responder's new-suit rebid following his jump shift shows a fit for opener's suit and a singleton in the new suit. I dislike that convention because responder will have a side ace more often than a singleton, and hands with singletons will often be suitable for Roman Keycard Blackwood. On this deal, "Soloway Jump Shifts" would not work at all.

Matchpoints, Neither vul.

354

NORTH (dummy)
♠ A J 10 6 4
♡ Q 2
◇ 7 5
♣ 9 7 6 3

WEST (you)
♠ 9 8 3
♡ A 10 7 3
◇ 6
♣ Q J 10 5 2

WEST	NORTH	EAST	SOUTH
			1◇
pass	1♠	pass	1NT[1]
all pass			

1. 12-14 HCP.

You lead the ♣Q. Partner takes the ♣A and returns a club to declarer's ♣K. Declarer plays the ♠K, and then takes a losing spade finesse. After winning with the ♠Q, partner shifts to the ◊3. Declarer wins with the ◊Q and leads the ♡5 towards dummy. What should you play?

If declarer has the ♡K, you can't keep him from reaching dummy with the ♡Q to run dummy's spades. Suppose you rise with the ♡A to run clubs. The ending will be:

NORTH (dummy)
♠ A J 6
♡ Q
◊ —
♣ —

WEST (you)
♠ 9
♡ 10 7 3
◊ —
♣ —

You'll have to put dummy in to take four tricks anyway. If you duck, dummy takes the same four tricks. Then declarer must surrender the rest. So rising with the ♡A breaks even when declarer has the ♡K.

However, if partner has the ♡K and declarer has the ♡J, rising with the ♡A will cost at least one trick. Instead of getting three heart tricks (partner will top dummy's ♡Q with the ♡K and return a heart to let you score the ♡A and the ♡10), you'll get only two. Once again, playing an ace "on air" blows a trick.

355

Matchpoints, N-S vul.

♠ Q J 6 3   ♡ A K 8 5   ◊ K 3   ♣ K 7 4

WEST	NORTH	EAST	SOUTH
			1NT
2◊[1]	3◊[2]	pass	3♡
3♠	4♡	pass	pass
4♠	5♣	pass	?

1. Diamonds and a major.
2. Stayman without a diamond stopper.

How many hearts has partner shown? How many hearts have you shown?

The answer to both questions is four. So why is partner bidding 5♣ instead of letting 4♠ come around to you, or bidding 5♡ himself?

Because he, like West, has a wildly distributional hand. He thinks eight trumps in the combined hands won't be enough to handle a five-level contract, but that nine or ten will be. If partner has a wildly distributional hand (e.g. singletons in both of West's suits), and has only four hearts, his clubs must be very long indeed. Let him play 5♣ (unless you have a fifth heart).

However, you bid 5♡, leading to this declarer play problem.

NORTH (dummy)
♠ 8
♡ 10 9 6 2
◊ 5
♣ A Q J 10 9 6 5

☐

SOUTH (you)
♠ Q J 6 3
♡ A K 8 5
◊ K 3
♣ K 7 4

WEST	NORTH	EAST	SOUTH
			1NT
2◊ [1]	3◊ [2]	pass	3♡
3♠	4♡	pass	pass
4♠	5♣	pass	5♡
pass	pass	dbl	all pass

1. Diamonds and a major.
2. Stayman without a diamond stopper.

West leads the ◊A and shifts to a low spade. East takes the ♠A and returns a diamond to your ◊K. Now what?

Do you think East would double without what appears to be a trump trick? I don't. Play West for no better than a small singleton (a priori odds favor this by 3-to-2, and East's double makes it very unlikely that West has an honor).

Ruff a spade to reach dummy and lead the ♡10 through East, intending to let it ride if not covered. You'll need to reach dummy a second time to take a second heart finesse, and can reach dummy in clubs after West's lone heart is gone (even if West is 6-1-6-0).

Matchpoints, N-S vul.

♠ K Q 9 4 3 2   ♡ A 8 4   ◇ Q 4   ♣ 8 7

	WEST	NORTH	EAST	SOUTH
			pass	2♠[1]
	pass	2NT[2]	pass	3♡[3]
	pass	3♠	pass	?

1. Weak two-bid.
2. One-round force.
3. Maximum, heart feature.

This is another deal in which Hand Comparison Technique works. When partner makes an invitational bid, compare your actual hand with the minimum hand you might normally have for the calls you have made thus far, and act accordingly. A simple concept, but an important one.

Partner's 2NT was game-invitational or better, and his 3♠ rebid shows that he merely intended to invite game. You have enough to accept. Consider how you'd bid a similar hand with ◇64 instead of ◇Q4. The ◇Q is worth something, isn't it? Facing partner's king, for example, it guarantees that you'll lose only one diamond trick. If instead you had two low diamonds, there'd be about a 50% chance you'd lose two diamond tricks.

You should also consider that many if not most players would open one spade with your hand, and then they would surely reach game. However, you pass.

NORTH (dummy)
♠ J 8
♡ K 9 2
◇ K 8
♣ A K 10 9 3 2

SOUTH (you)
♠ K Q 9 4 3 2
♡ A 8 4
◇ Q 4
♣ 8 7

	WEST	NORTH	EAST	SOUTH
			pass	2♠[1]
	pass	2NT[2]	pass	3♡[3]
	pass	3♠	all pass	

1. Weak two-bid.
2. One-round force.
3. Maximum, heart feature.

West leads the ♣Q, and East plays the ♣4 beneath dummy's ♣K. When you call for dummy's ♠J, East plays the ♠A and returns a diamond to West's ◇A. West continues with the ♣5. What do you think is going on in the club suit?

West is much more likely to have led from ♣QJxx or ♣QJx than from ♣Qx; wouldn't you? East's ♣4, the lowest club except for dummy's visible ♣2 and ♣3, is very likely to be a singleton, so East is about to ruff the second club. If dummy's ♣A gets ruffed, you'll have no way to dispose of a heart loser, but if a low club gets ruffed, dummy's ♣A will give you the heart discard you need. Play low from dummy.

Note that declarers in 4♠ may fail if they receive the same defense and get one of dummy's top clubs ruffed.

Matchpoints, E-W vul.

357

NORTH (dummy)
♠ A J 7 4 2
♡ Q 9 4 3 2
◇ 3
♣ K J

WEST (you)
♠ —
♡ A K 6 5
◇ A J 9 7 5 4
♣ Q 5 2

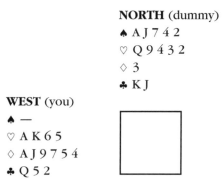

WEST	NORTH	EAST	SOUTH
		pass	2♠[1]
dbl	4♠	dbl	all pass

1. Weak Two-bid.

You lead the ♡K. Partner plays the ♡8 and declarer drops a heart honor. What now?

Partner's ♡8 can be either a singleton or the top of a doubleton. For his double of 4♠, partner must have some defense. He cannot have counted the ♠Kx as a trick, for the Weak 2♠ bidder may have the ♠A behind him. He must have an ace. You know it's the ♣A, but declarer cannot tell whether it's the ♣A or the ◇A. So shift to the ♣2 now, putting declarer to the guess before he can get any clues. If declarer guesses to play dummy's ♣J, partner will take the ♣A. Then, even if he has a singleton heart and cannot return one, his diamond return will put you in to cash the ♡A and lead a third heart for him to ruff.

Cashing the ♡A is unnecessary when you have a sure entry, and cashing the ◇A lets an observant declarer go right in clubs.

358

Matchpoints, Neither vul.

♠ 9 5 2   ♡ K Q 8 7 2   ◇ A 9   ♣ Q 8 2

WEST	NORTH	EAST	SOUTH
			?

Pass. This is an ordinary 11-point hand. Eleven-point hands should be opened only when they have good suits and shape; 5-3-3-2 hands do not. Moreover, you have no decent rebid: what will you do if partner responds 1♠? A hand like

♠ 5   ♡ K Q 8 7 2   ◇ A 9 2   ♣ Q 9 8 2

would be a reasonable 1♡ opening. You can rebid 2♣, or raise two of a minor to three.

359

Matchpoints, Both vul.

NORTH (dummy)
♠ Q 4 3
♡ K
◇ K Q 10 9 8 7
♣ A 5 4

EAST (you)
♠ J 5
♡ 10 9 8 7 6
◇ A 6 4 3
♣ K 7

WEST	NORTH	EAST	SOUTH
	1◇	pass	1♡
pass	2◇	pass	2NT
pass	3NT	all pass	

Partner leads the ♠10, which holds, as all follow small. Partner shifts to the ♣2. You win with the ♣K and return the ♠J. Partner overtakes with the ♠K and returns the ♠6 to dummy's ♠Q; you discard the ♡6. Here come the diamonds, starting with dummy's ◇K. You duck, and declarer follows with the ◇J. You duck the second diamond, and declarer discards the ♡2 as partner completes a high-low with the ◇2 after playing the ♢5 on the previous trick. You win the third diamond with your ♢A. Declarer discards the ♡3 and partner discards the ♣6. You are on lead in this ending:

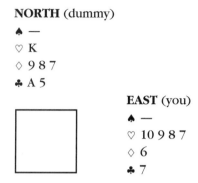

NORTH (dummy)
♠ —
♡ K
♢ 9 8 7
♣ A 5

EAST (you)
♠ —
♡ 10 9 8 7
♢ 6
♣ 7

What now?

Declarer has the ♠A left. If he also has the ♡A, he has the rest of the tricks, because he can overtake dummy's ♡K and cash the ♠A to discard dummy's low club (even if partner has the ♣Q). So you must shift to hearts, as your only other trick can come from partner's ♡A.

Why didn't partner "signal" his ♡A by discarding a high heart instead of a club?

He may not have had a high heart to spare. Neither the ♡4 nor the ♡5 (the heart spot cards that remain unseen) would be readable as a high one. Furthermore, the standard and effective way of discarding is to discard from a suit one does not guard (discarding from a suit one does guard often blows a trick). Finally, you must play him for the ♡A as it is your only chance of taking another trick.

Matchpoints, E-W vul.

360

♠ A K Q 7 4 ♡ Q 8 4 ♢ K J ♣ J 8 2

WEST	NORTH	EAST	SOUTH
pass	1♡	pass	1♠
pass	2NT[1]	pass	?

1. Good 18 to bad 20 HCP.

When opener may have 20 HCP for a jump 2NT rebid, any below-game rebid by responder is forcing. Bidding 6NT is premature. Partner's five-card heart suit is a source of tricks, and so is your five-card spade suit, unless partner has two small spades. A grand slam is possible even if the combined partnership total is only 34-36 HCP. What is your best way to find out?

Bid 3♠. If partner has only two spades, he will rebid 3NT, but if he has three spades, he will raise.

Suppose you bid 3♠ and partner then bids 4◇. What does that mean? Partner's 4◇ is a cuebid that shows the ace while affirming three-card spade support and slammish values. Now that spades are agreed, you can use RKCB. Here's how the bidding might go:

WEST	NORTH	EAST	SOUTH
pass	1♡	pass	1♠
pass	2NT	pass	3♠
pass	4◇	pass	4NT[1]
pass	5♣[2]	pass	5♡[3]
pass	5NT[4]	pass	6♣[5]
pass	6NT[6]	pass	7NT
all pass			

1. RKCB (spades).
2. 0 or 3 keycards (obviously 3).
3. Specific King Ask (one step beyond the Queen Ask, not counting a bid in the trump suit).
4. ♡K (5NT shows the king of the suit used to ask).
5. Authorizes partner to bid beyond six of the agreed suit if he has the ♣K.
6. Showing the ♣K (bidding one step beyond 6♠).

That's 13 tricks if both major suits run — if partner has a jack in either, it almost surely will — plus additional chances if only one major runs. Partner's possible ◇Axx or ♣AK10 gives him a finesse for a thirteenth trick and East's opening lead in a minor may give partner a "free" finesse.

361

Matchpoints, Both vul.

NORTH (dummy)
♠ A Q 5 2
♡ 6 3
◇ A J 9 2
♣ J 7 4

EAST (you)
♠ J 9 8 3
♡ A Q 8 4
◇ K 4
♣ 8 6 3

WEST	NORTH	EAST	SOUTH
	1◇	pass	1NT
all pass			

Partner leads the ♡10. You take the ♡A and return the ♡4. Declarer plays the ♡J on the second heart. Partner takes the ♡K, cashes the ♡10 and continues with the ♡7 to your ♡Q. Dummy discards a diamond and a spade, and declarer discards the ◇3.

You shift correctly to the ♠3 (you can't stop dummy's ♠A and ♠Q from taking tricks anyway). The ♠3 is the right spot card to lead because it tells partner you have a useful honor in the suit. This is, of course, not the ♠K, from which you wouldn't lead at all. Declarer plays the ♠4, and partner's ♠7 dislodges dummy's ♠Q.

Dummy's ♣J rides to partner's ♣Q, and partner leads the ♠K to knock out dummy's ♠A. Declarer runs four club tricks, on which partner discards three diamonds "up-the-line", leaving you to discard behind dummy in this ending:

NORTH (dummy)
♠ —
♡ —
◇ A J
♣ —

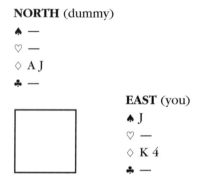

EAST (you)
♠ J
♡ —
◇ K 4
♣ —

Again, what should you keep, and what should you throw, on this, declarer's last club?

Your ♠J is high. When in with the ♣Q, partner could have exited with the ♠10 to drive out dummy's ♠A, but only if he had the ♠10. So he doesn't have it. Declarer does.

You have a complete count on partner's hand regardless. He followed to four rounds of hearts, two rounds of clubs and the first two spades. He then discarded "up-the-line" in diamonds, showing an odd number that can only be five. This confirms that he is 2-4-5-2, so declarer's remaining cards must be the ♠10 and a diamond. If declarer's diamond is the ◇Q, you've been squeezed and can do nothing about it. If declarer's diamond is a low one, however, then partner has ◇Qx remaining and you can afford to discard the ◇4. Discarding your spade winner can only cost, never gain.

It's amazing how many times the simple principle *keep winners, throw losers* works. Even when it doesn't gain directly, it helps partner know what to play you for.

Matchpoints, N-S vul.

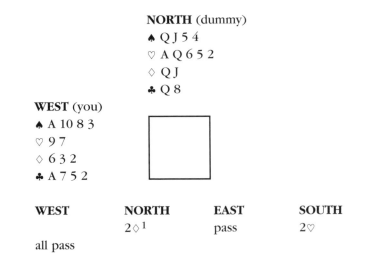

NORTH (dummy)
♠ Q J 5 4
♡ A Q 6 5 2
◇ Q J
♣ Q 8

WEST (you)
♠ A 10 8 3
♡ 9 7
◇ 6 3 2
♣ A 7 5 2

WEST	NORTH	EAST	SOUTH
	2◇[1]	pass	2♡
all pass			

1. Flannery: five hearts, four spades, 11-15 HCP.

You lead the ◇6. Partner takes the ◇A, declarer following small, and shifts to the ♣3. You take the ♣A and return a club, which partner ruffs with the ♡3. Partner returns the ◇7. Declarer takes the ◇K and ◇10 to discard a spade from dummy, and then leads the ♣K to discard another spade. Partner ruffs with the ♡4 and leads the ♠2 to your ♠A. You return the ♠3 to partner's ♠K. Partner then leads the ◇9, to which declarer follows small. You have to play in this five-card ending:

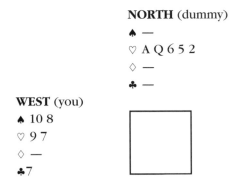

NORTH (dummy)
♠ —
♡ A Q 6 5 2
◇ —
♣ —

WEST (you)
♠ 10 8
♡ 9 7
◇ —
♣ 7

Partner leads the ◇9 and declarer follows small.

Once again, you are the defender who has a complete count on declarer's hand. He has shown up with six clubs, is following to a fourth round of diamonds with the thirteenth diamond, and has followed to two spades. That's twelve cards, and from partner's carding (low spade led from the ♠K) it appears that declarer's thirteenth card

is a singleton heart. So partner remains with three hearts and a low
spade. The hearts that remain are the ♡K, ♡J, ♡10 and ♡8. Uppercut
with the ♡7; doing so can't cost but may gain (especially if partner has
♡J108 left). Discarding your last club can also work, as then you may
be able to uppercut with the ♡9 later when declarer, stuck in hand
with the ♡K or ♡J, has only clubs left and must lead one. Discarding
a spade cannot gain.

Matchpoints, N-S vul.

363

NORTH (dummy)
♠ 2
♡ K J 8 7
◇ K J 9 8
♣ K Q 7 2

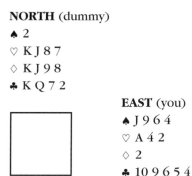

EAST (you)
♠ J 9 6 4
♡ A 4 2
◇ 2
♣ 10 9 6 5 4

WEST	NORTH	EAST	SOUTH
	1◇	pass	1♠
pass	2♣	pass	2◇
pass	2♡	pass	3NT
all pass			

Partner leads the ♣8. Declarer wins with the ♣A and cashes the ♣J.
He then plays ◇A and another. You tilt your hand forward, and
declarer sees that you have no more diamonds, so he "deep finesses"
dummy's ◇8. You discard a heart. Next he cashes dummy's ♣K and
♣Q, on which partner discards the ♡3 and ♡5. Declarer crosses to the
♠A and cashes the ♠K. Partner's ♠Q falls, and dummy discards a heart.
Then declarer leads another diamond to dummy's ◇J and continues
with dummy's ◇K. You must come down to three cards by discarding
twice from ♠J9 ♡A4 ♣10. Which three cards should you keep?

Keep your winners (♡A, ♠J, ♣10) and throw losers (♠9, ♡4). If
you keep ♠J and ♡A4, you can a duck low heart from dummy and survive (provided partner has the guarded ♡Q), but keeping ♡A and ♠J9
gives you no chance at the rest of the tricks, as the ♠9 is a loser.

Matchpoints, N-S vul.

NORTH (dummy)
♠ —
♡ 10 8 7 3
◇ 10 9 8 7 6
♣ J 10 5 2

☐

SOUTH (you)
♠ A Q 10 8 4
♡ A K Q 5
◇ Q 5
♣ K 3

WEST	NORTH	EAST	SOUTH
		pass	1♠
all pass			

West leads the ◇K and shifts to the ♡9. Plan the play.

First you should cover the ♡9 with dummy's ♡10, to ensure no heart losers (except by defenders' ruffs). East will probably play the ♡J. Win with the ♡K. Now you must cash a second heart trick before a defender can discard his remaining hearts when the suit is splitting 3-2. You have two reasonable lines:

Line A. Try to "steal" a third heart trick. Cash the ♡A next and follow with your low heart to dummy's ♡7. If West, who started with ♡9x, thinks that East has the (as yet unseen) ♡Q, he may discard instead of trumping.

Line B. Use the second heart trick to reach dummy by leading low to the ♡7 at Trick 3. Then try to guess the clubs: play low towards your ♣K if you think East has the ♣A and West the ♣Q; play the ♣J from dummy (intending to let it ride if not covered) if you think East has the ♣Q and West has the ♣A.

I prefer Line A. If it works, you'll be in dummy and can try a club play next.

My Queen Guessing Rule (guaranteed to work much more than 50% of the time): If you have nothing else to go on, play LHO for the queen of trumps and RHO for any other missing queen.

NORTH (dummy)
- ♠ K 6 4 3
- ♡ K
- ◇ Q 8 6 5
- ♣ A J 7 3

WEST (you)
- ♠ A Q 9 8 5 2
- ♡ A 10 2
- ◇ 4 2
- ♣ Q 6

WEST	NORTH	EAST	SOUTH
	1♣	1◇	1♡
1♠	pass	pass	2♡
all pass			

You lead the ◇4 and dummy plays low. Partner takes the ◇J and declarer follows with the ◇7. Partner continues with the ◇A and declarer's ◇10 falls. With a choice of ◇A or ◇K to cash, partner's card is suit-preference, so when he shifts to the ♠J you can tell that it's a singleton and partner wants a spade ruff.

Declarer follows with the ♠7 and you take your ♠A. Now what?

Continue with the ♠Q. If dummy plays the ♠K, partner will ruff and declarer's ♠10 will fall, so your ♠9 and ♠8 will be high. If dummy plays low, partner will discard, declarer will follow with the ♠10, and your ♠Q will take the trick, allowing partner to preserve his trumps. Then you can continue with the ♠9 to let partner ruff dummy's ♠K.

Leading the ♠9 before declarer's ♠10 has fallen lets declarer duck in dummy. Dummy's ♠K will then provide him with a trick and a useful discard. You must lead the ♠Q to pin that ♠10!

What would it have meant if you had doubled South's 1♡ response in this auction?

I suggest playing a double of a third-suit response as showing the fourth suit plus modest support for partner's overcall, a convention called Snapdragon that is popular among experts. It makes little sense to play a double of a forcing response as a penalty double.

Save this problem for the leap year. Count yourself lucky if you see one like it once in four years.

Matchpoints, Both vul.

NORTH (dummy)
- ♠ K 9 7 4
- ♡ Q 6 5
- ♢ 9 4
- ♣ K 5 4 2

EAST (you)
- ♠ 6 3 2
- ♡ 10 2
- ♢ A 7 5 3 2
- ♣ 10 9 7

WEST	NORTH	EAST	SOUTH
			2♠[1]
pass	2♢[2]	pass	3NT
pass	6NT[3]	all pass	

1. Strong, artificial and forcing.
2. Artificial positive response.
3. After barring his partner by bidding an insufficient Stayman 3♣.

Partner leads the ♡9. Declarer wins in hand with the ♡A, and plays ♠AQJ, overtaking when West follows to the third spade with the ♠10. Declarer then cashes dummy's ♠9. You discard the ♢2. Declarer discards the ♣3, and West discards the ♡3. Next comes the ♢4. Are you ready?

You play the ♢3 and declarer wins with the ♢K, partner's ♢8 falling. Declarer overtakes the ♡J with dummy's ♡Q to lead the ♢9. Are you ready again?

You play the ♢5, and partner's ♢10 falls beneath declarer's ♢Q. You still have ♢A7, while declarer remains with ♢K6.

Declarer, who started with

♠ A Q J   ♡ A K J   ♢ K Q J 6   ♣ A 8 3

decides that if you didn't want to take a trick with the ♢A on either of the two occasions when he offered it to you, you don't deserve to take it ever. He cashes the ♡K, plays the ♣A and another club to dummy's ♣K, and surrenders a club trick to your partner, who cashes the ♡8 for the setting trick. Down one, a cold top for you.

In *Why You Lose at Bridge*, S.J. Simon wrote, "I have been a confirmed ducker of aces for years; and the number of cases in which it has cost me a contract or even a trick are very few. It will not always yield two tricks in return, but at any rate the ducked trick almost invariably comes back. So start ducking with your aces. But do not consider yourself graduated until you have successfully ducked with an ace in such a position as to defeat a small slam contract."